TABLE

PREFACE . . . .

Book I - The Halls of Clarence Darrow . 7

    Chapter 1 - Bailiff Jablonski Does
                  His Ballet 7
    Chapter 2 - The Defendants 16
    Chapter 3 - Court Business 23
    Chapter 4 - Opening Statements of
                  Counsel 28
    Chapter 5 - First Witness-Arthur Head 36
    Chapter 6 - The Rape Victim Testifies 48
    Chapter 7 - Cross-examination 72
    Chapter 8 - Birdia Jackson's Extra-
                  marital Affair 75
    Chapter 9 - Examining Physician . . . 84
    Chapter 10 - Detective Lill's Perjury 90
    Chapter 11 - Motion for Directed
                   Verdict 100
    Chapter 12 - Closing Arguments . . . 102
    Chapter 13 - The Verdict 119

Book II - The Investigation 122

    Chapter 1 - A Young Lawyer's First
                  Case 122
    Chapter 2 - Visiting Pontiac Prison . 138
    Chapter 3 - Visiting Skid Row 149
    Chapter 4 - Meeting Other Appointed
                  Attorneys 191
    Chapter 5 - Work in New York City . . 201
    Chapter 6 - Continuing the
                  Investigation 205
    Chapter 7 - Meeting Harden's Family . 213

Chapter 8 - Meeting Mothers of the
           Defendants 220
Chapter 9 - Calkins' First Argument
           in Court 228

Chapter 10 - Giving Sherrod, Meeks,
            Brown Polygraph Tests . 236
Chapter 11 - Harden is Freed 245

BOOK III - A Good Faith Effort 252

Chapter 1 - Helping His Boys Find
           Jobs 252
Chapter 2 - Al Larson of Inland
           Steel Helps 259
Chapter 3 - Meeting His Boys For
           The First Time 262
Chapter 4 - Johnny Sherrod Gets A
           Job   266
Chapter 5 - Johnny Sherrod's
           Wedding 273
Chapter 6 - Errol Meeks Goes to
           College 277
Chapter 7 - Errol Meeks and James
           Harden Go to Church . . 279
Chapter 8 - Fess Wise Accused of
           Stealing $400 285
Chapter 9 - James O'Neil Makes His
           Appearance 289
Chapter 10 - Fess Wise Buys A Car . . 294
Chapter 11 - Errol Meeks Goes Back
            To Prison 302
Chapter 12 - James O'Neil Visits
            Again 312
Chapter 13 - Fess Wise Arrested For
            Armed Robbery 314
Chapter 14 - James O'Neil Sells
            Used Books 319

Chapter 15 - James O'Neil Jailed
            For Life   322
Chapter 16 - A Discouraging Ending   329

CONCLUSION 331
EPILOGUE 332

That lawyer is worthy who lightens the burdens of others.

PREFACE

My name is Richard M. Calkins. I added the middle initial "M" in 1976 after I received a number of checks made out to another lawyer named Richard Calkins of Aurora, Illinois – his father, Dick Calkins, was the creator of the comic book Buck Rogers. Unbeknownst to me, when I added the "M" to eliminate confusion, he added the middle initial "N" and the confusion continued until his untimely demise resolved the confusion.

This is James Harden's story as seen through my eyes. It is a true story, which affirms there is a dark side to the American Dream, which most Americans are unwilling to acknowledge. The story is a snapshot of one short period of time – 1960-1963, which focuses on all that was wrong with the criminal court system in the large cities of America. And it is an exposé of that segment of society which is denied the fruits of the American Dream because of where they live, who they are, and the circumstances with which they were confronted.

I lived on the sunny side of the Dream, which made it even more difficult to understand there was a dark side. I went to the right schools and given every opportunity to enjoy its fruitage. How shocked I was on May 29, 1963, the day I was appointed to represent James Harden on his appeal to the Illinois Supreme Court, when I suddenly realized there was another side to the Dream. James Harden was convicted of a gangland rape of a 32 year old woman in the black ghetto of Chicago and sentenced, with seven other black teenagers, to 20 years in the state penitentiary. In representing James, I spent a thousand hours investigating the case and uncovering the circumstances of his conviction. What I learned, the tactics of the police and even the States Attorney's office to gain a conviction, shocked me. But what was even more disturbing was what I learned about life in the black ghetto of the large city, where gangs roam and shootings are commonplace, which saps the will to live, much less survive.

This book is divided into three parts. The first is based on the actual transcript of the trial, which sent Harden and seven other blacks to the penitentiary for 20 years for allegedly gang raping a woman 26 times. The courtroom was the venue of the great Clarence Darrow, 26th and California, Chicago, Illinois. The trial pitted the Public Defender's Office, with its 12 lawyers and 3 investigators against the States Attorney's Office with its 100 or so lawyers and the Chicago Police Department at its disposal to investigate. The criminal system in that court facilitated the complaining witness and police officers knowingly perjuring themselves to gain convictions. It was conducted without the safeguards of what is now called the Miranda Rule, which requires the state to warn a suspect of his right to remain silent and to have the assistance of counsel.

The second part is the investigation I conducted, which began to uncover what actually happened. Needless to say, I was stunned at what I saw and learned. The dark side was darker than anything I could have imagined. I also realize in retrospect that I took many chances traveling in the areas of Chicago where the crime took place - even walking down alleys at night.

The third part describes my efforts to help these young men adjust to civilian life once they were freed from prison. It was then I realized how hopeless my cause was. I was told that if you do not reach a boy by the time he is five, he is lost for good in the abyss of the dark side. This, unfortunately, I found to be true.

I hope you will enjoy reading this book for the whole experience was eye opening and to an extent influenced me in who I am today.

Dick Calkins

GUILTY BEYOND A REASONABLE DOUBT

BOOK I
THE HALLS OF CLARENCE DARROW

Chapter 1

Bailiff Jablonski Does His Ballet

Bailiff Jablonski raised his hand and brought the gavel down with a loud crack. "Everybody rise. This court is now in session, the Honorable Abraham W. Brussell presiding."
The gavel fell a second time with an even louder crack. People began scurrying to their seats in the crowded courtroom causing considerable noise, and the bailiff let his gavel strike a third time. Not getting the response he wanted, he rushed to the back of the courtroom to the spectator's area, and shouted: "Quiet! This is a court of law - sit down there, mister, or I'll throw you out of this courtroom at once."
The bailiff, rotund, with a portly face and big deputy sheriff's badge on his chest, wheeled around and charged a group of spectators who were creating a mild disturbance because there was one more person than seats.
"Out of the courtroom," the bailiff shouted to one black woman. The bailiff's face was flushed with anger as he mustered all the authority of his office. The woman, rather startled, meekly turned to the door and walked out. The bailiff gave a glance in each direction and slowly waddled back to the front of the courtroom to his seat, scowling with satisfaction that he had fulfilled his primary task for the day.
The clerk of the court, sitting at a large desk to the front and left of the judge's bench, rose and in a matter-of-fact monotone voice called out: "The People of the State of Illinois versus Errol Meeks, James Lee Harden, Fess Wise, James O'Neil, Eugene Brown, Johnnie Sherrod, Edward Cole, and Sammy Dillard." Sitting down, he turned slightly and looked up at the judge behind him.
The judge looked around the courtroom and in a deliberate voice asked: "Are we ready to proceed

with this case?"

    Judge Brussell was a man in his early fifties, well-groomed with his black hair combed straight back. He had a sharp and penetrating look which manifested his inner brilliance and legal maturity, developed over some thirty years of private practice and as an assistant state's attorney. He had practiced law with Arthur Goldberg, who later became a United States Supreme Court Justice, and Willard Wirtz, a law professor at Northwestern University School of Law and later Secretary of Labor during the Kennedy administration. As he glanced down at the attorneys sitting in front of his elevated bench, there was an eagerness in his expression which almost, but not quite, betrayed the fact that this was his first trial since his recent election to the bench. He, like all other newly appointed or elected judges, had to serve his novitiate in the criminal court until such time as there was an opening in the civil branch of the court. Most judges abhorred being sent to South California Avenue where the Criminal Court was located, preferring the comforts and prestige of the Mayor Daley Civil Center in the Loop of Chicago.

    The assistant state's attorney, Fred Toler, rose quickly. "The State is ready, your Honor." He immediately sat down and leaned back to say something to his young assistant, Walter Dillon. All eyes then turned to the defense table where a lone attorney, Ivan Kusak, sat slumped in his chair. With effort he slowly rose to respond to the Court's inquiry. He was heavy set, in his sixties, his clothes disheveled and his hair unkempt. He started fumbling with a shirt button which had come undone, but the unsteadiness of his hands prevented him from improving his appearance.

    "Your Honor, Mr. Doherty, the Public Defender, who represents all the defendants but my client, is not here yet. I believe he is before Judge Spier."

    "Mr. Kusak, whom do you represent?"

    "I represent Errol Meeks."

    The judge immediately rose and turned towards the exit. "There is no need to proceed until counsel is here; call me when he arrives."

    "Everybody rise," shouted the bailiff, rushing towards the door to hold it open for the judge.

Kusak sat in his chair, indifferent to the rush of activity around him. It made little difference to him whether this was a rape case for which his client could get life in prison or a traffic violation. He treated them all alike – with professional distain; after all had he not been one of the most successful criminal attorneys in the city, the Clarence Darrow of the late 1940s. It pained him to think that his talents had to be wasted on clients such as this. Why had the public turned on him; why was he forced to defend the muck of society for nickels and dimes?

Fred Toler and Walter Dillon were engaged in animated conversation. Toler, the older of the two, had a sleek, trim appearance, very sharp facial features, and was meticulously dressed with his Order of the Coif pin dangling across his vest. He was articulate, first in his graduating class at Loyola University Law School. He was aggressive, for the stakes were high in the States Attorney's office where success could mean a judgeship or other political office within the ubiquitous Richard Daley machine.

Dillon, on the other hand, was a recent graduate from John Marshall Law School, and was eagerly awaiting his first major trial. He considered it a real privilege to work with Toler. It was absolutely essential that he win his first case; his whole career depended on his getting the right start, and with Fred how could he lose. He was overweight, which he attempted to hide under his tight-fitting vest. His round, jovial face and friendly manner made him well-liked by all with whom he came in contact.

Though this January day was cold, windy, and damp, the courtroom temperature was comfortable except near the windows, where a steady draft attacked all who dared to approach. The room was large and had the same brown, drab, formidable appearance that it had when Clarence Darrow once paced its floor.

At the rear of the large room there were some ten rows of straight back benches for the press and visitors. A low wooden railing with a swinging gate separated the spectators' section from the arena where the great matadors of the criminal court locked in daily battle. The walls were the same paneled brown expanse of nothingness as they had been for forty years. Overhead hung six large globe lamps suspended on chains which gave the courtroom just enough light to create that needed impersonal touch.

Suddenly, from the back of the courtroom a heavy set young man, in his early forties, raced towards the attorneys' table just beyond the swinging gate. His face was flushed and he breathed heavily as he spread some files on the table before him. With his red hair and fair complexion there was no doubt this was James E. Doherty, the Public Defender. "Kusak," he breathlessly blurted, "what case is this? My God! Did I bring the wrong files?"

Kusak turned his head slightly without moving the rest of his body so as not to exert himself, and mumbled: "The gangland rape case - you know that group of bastards who raped the prostitute in Grenshaw Street - the New Braves."

Doherty continued fumbling through his brief case. "It's not here; where the hell did I put that file? How many do I represent?"

"Only seven this time."

Doherty wheeled around and raced out of the courtroom towards the elevator. "Sam, Sam, let me on. I'm in a hurry."

The heavy, steel elevator door, which was half shut, reopened and then crashed shut as Doherty leaped on. With a jerk the elevator descended slowly down from the fifth to the fourth floor, then the third floor, and Doherty jumped out and ran to his office.

"Thanks, Sam."

Seven minutes later Doherty entered the courtroom again, looking through his files as he hurriedly walked. "Everybody rise," shouted the bailiff in his stentorian voice. Judge Brussell briskly walked through the doorway up the steps to his chair and sat down.

"Now, Mr. Doherty, are we ready to proceed?"

"Judge, I have several motions here -- somewhere here. One moment, your Honor." After about fifteen seconds, which seemed like five minutes, Doherty found his notes.

"Judge, the defendants, Harden, Cole, Brown,

Wise, Dillard, O'Neil and Sherrod move for the production of all confessions, admissions and statements made by the defendants to the police. We understand several were made and we feel under the law we are entitled to them. Also, Sherrod, O'Neil, Cole, Harden and Dillard would like a severance from Brown and Wise, who we understand made some incriminating statements."

"I'll join in those motions on behalf of Meeks," said Kusak without rising from his chair.

Fred Toler jumped to his feet. The daily combat between the prosecution and public defender had commenced. "Judge, Doherty knows he is not entitled to admissions or statements. He does this every time. Under the law he is only entitled to confessions before trial. An exculpating admission need not be turned over. I will state for the record that we have admissions from Brown and Wise and they have implicated Coles, Harden, Meeks, O'Neil, and Sherrod."

"Toler may be right Judge, but one of these days we're going to get the law reversed on this point. In my humble opinion the constitution requires that all statements of a defendant must be turned over to counsel. How else can I prepare my case? I don't even know what these defendants said to the police."

"Just a minute, counsel," interrupted Judge Brussell. "Let me see if I understand your argument. We all agree that if a defendant confessed to a crime, that is, he admits to all elements of the offense, the state would be required to turn it over. Are you now saying that the state should also turn over all admissions a defendant has made even those which are exculpatory?"

"Exactly, Judge. What is the difference between an admission and a confession except that the former admits only some of the elements of the crime? Both are damaging and will convict. Unless I am given these statements I will have a serious problem as to whether I can let the defendants testify, for the state can impeach them with these admissions."

Judge Brussell hesitated a moment, looked at Toler with an expression of uncertainty and then said, "Motion denied."

"But Judge, on what basis have you denied the motion? Give me the benefit of your thinking?"

"Motion denied. What was your second motion?"

Doherty became red in the face, his usual trademark in the courtroom when his efforts were frustrated. In a slow, deliberate voice that was not intended to conceal his frustration he said, "Sherrod, O'Neil, Cole and -" Doherty fumbled through his papers again, - "I believe Harden and Dillard would like a separate trial from Wise and Brown."

"I'll join in that motion for Meeks," slurred Kusak.

Doherty glanced back at Kusak as the alcohol on Kusak's breath reached him. Doherty's face was rigid trying not to show his utter contempt for Kusak. Doherty knew from long experience that before the trial was over he would have a heavy cross to bear before the judge and jury, for Kusak's inebriated condition was certain to be felt. Kusak was always sober enough to collect his fee before trial, but not quite sober enough to conduct a worthy defense. Yet the court and bar tolerated his presence because there were few lawyers who could take these cases and make a living. Kusak's formula was volume, that left a minimum of time and no legal effort for each.

Judge Brussell turned towards Toler, "Any comments on this motion?"

"Your Honor, there is no basis for a severance here. The defendants making the motion were named in the statements of Wise and Brown, and because they were present when they were named, the admissions can be used against them also. For this reason there can be no prejudice in trying them all together."

"I agree with you," responded the judge. "If a defendant is accused of committing a crime by another in his presence and he remains silent when he would be expected to deny the charges, his silence constitutes an admission."

"Thank you, Judge," said Toler smiling, recognizing the penchant of a new judge to look to the assistant state's attorney for guidance, particularly when he is an ex-assistant state's attorney himself.

"But, your Honor, how can I determine the

validity of what the prosecution states when I am denied the right to even examine the statements?" said Doherty.

Judge Brussell hesitated a moment, and then responded, "You'll have a chance to examine them during the trial before they are offered in evidence. Motion for severance denied. Call in the defendants."

"Judge, you can't do that," said Kusak struggling to his feet. "In People vs. Jackson, the Illinois Supreme Court stated that the state has the burden of proving that the defendant's silence was voluntary and not the result of coercive influence." Kusak looked around, almost surprised at the clarity of his statement.

"Mr. Kusak, I have already ruled."

"But you're wrong, Judge. You can't do that - it won't stand up on appeal."

"Sit down, Mr. Kusak," commanded the judge, accenting each word with forced restraint. Suddenly the Judge rose and announced, "We will adjourn until two o'clock this afternoon."

"I still say you are wrong," shouted Kusak, as the judge turned to leave the bench. Kusak looked around to see if Doherty approved his efforts. He knew Doherty was good and just one word of approval would help him recapture a fleeting moment of his past. When a trial lawyer's confidence begins to crack, his demise can come quickly and completely. And when he is also aging, even the smallest crumb of praise alleviates momentarily the frightening specter of failure.

Chapter 2

The Defendants

At two o'clock in the afternoon of January 4, 1961, Bailiff Jablonski once again began his courtroom ballet, rushing from side to side, shouting, "Everyone take your seats. This court is ready to reconvene." Then he turned to a deputy sheriff and in an officious voice that all could hear, he said, "Bring in the prisoners." The deputy sheriff turned and rushed to a rear door to the left of the judge's bench shouting, "Bring in the prisoners, bring in the prisoners."

As the first defendant emerged, muffled voices spread throughout the spectator section of the courtroom. A thin looking black woman sitting in the next to last row, shouted, in a husky cigarette voice, "Jimmy, Jimmy!" Bailiff Jablonski pounced on her in a second.

James O'Neil emerged first with guards on either side of him. He was seventeen years old, slender, about five feet, eleven inches tall. As he walked into the courtroom he held his head erect, trying to maintain a confident almost contemptuous look on his black face; however, the rapid shifting of his eyes from one side of the courtroom to the other betrayed the utter panic he felt at that moment.

Johnny Sherrod emerged second. He was a very handsome twenty year old with a gentle looking face, which was marred by a slight scar across his left cheek. His eyes hurriedly searched the spectator area for his mother. Spotting her, an expression of relief came across his face.

Johnny's closest friends, Errol Meeks and James Harden, came next. They were quite different in appearance from Johnny. Errol had a heavy muscular build and sported a mustache. His deep, clear, penetrating eyes indicated above average intelligence. James was slightly taller and considerably thinner and walked with his head and shoulders bent forward. His eyes were expressionless and glued to the floor as he walked in. They were nineteen and twenty.

There was a slight pause until the next boy,

Fess Wise, emerged. He was seventeen years old and much smaller than the other boys. His suit, which was two sizes too large for him, drooped from his shoulders, his sleeves extending beyond his fingertips. His mother, who anxiously watched him from the rear as he entered the courtroom, had insisted that he look presentable at the trial. His face was drawn and his eyes filled with tears, which he tried to conceal from the other boys.

Eugene Brown and Sammy Dillard emerged together. Eugene was also small in stature, about nineteen years old, while Sammy, who was eighteen years old, was tall and slender with very fair skin. Edward Cole followed immediately, and although dark, he had Caucasian features. A gang war scar ran across the left side of his face. Of the group he had the hardest and most recalcitrant look of all. He seemed to accept the fact that he could get life in prison, but this was one of the risks of the game he played.

The boys were led to the defense table where Kusak and Doherty sat. This was on the left side of the courtroom, as you faced the judge, closest to the jury box. As they began to sit down, it was apparent one chair was missing. "Get another chair," shouted the bailiff in a disgusted voice. One of the guards rushed out and immediately returned with a chair.

Behind the prisoners stood five burly guards with their arms folded, paying very close attention to every move made by the eight. As the boys waited for the trial to commence, most were looking to the rear of the courtroom for their mothers and friends.

"Everybody rise. This court now resumes session, the Honorable Abraham W. Brussell, presiding," shouted Jablonski. All the boys rose, except O'Neil who was seated in the first chair and did not observe the others. A guard lunged at him and jerked him to his feet.

Judge Brussell walked up to his bench with great dignity. The clerk read: "The People of the State of Illinois versus Errol Meeks, James Lee Harden, Fess Wise, James O'Neil, Eugene Brown, Johnnie Sherrod, Edward Cole and Sammy Dillard."

Just as the judge was about to begin, Kusak rose to his feet. "I wish to make a motion - ," he faltered for a second, "a motion to exclude the witnesses."

"Gentlemen," said the judge, "it is my practice to exclude all witnesses except two of the arresting officers whom I will permit to remain in the courtroom."

The Public Defender, Doherty, then rose. "In that case will you instruct the officers not to talk to any witnesses during the course of the trial?"

"I don't think I have that power, Mr. Doherty. Let us proceed with the selection of the jury."

Doherty turned from the judge; a resigned look spread across his face. He was reacting not to the judge's ruling, but the realization that this new judge was prosecution oriented. He felt it in his bones; he could smell it; there was no doubt about it. He was not surprised nor angered, for this was a way of life in the criminal courts, and a public defender had to learn to live with it. The emotion he felt was one of frustration that kept building with each case.

Anger is an emotion which can be released quickly and safely like hot steam escaping through pores in the earth. But frustration is like molten lava which is dense and requires great pressure to force it bursting through the cone of a volcano. It is the wise man who can in one way or another periodically open the vents to release the anger within rather than let it turn to molten frustration, which can be released only with devastating consequences. In Doherty, there was no easy outlet for his emotions. He had to wrestle with them daily because of his concern of what was happening in the courts.

Doherty looked over at the boys seated on the opposite side of the table. Their eyes were flashing as they glanced back and forth, first to the rear of the courtroom, then to the twenty-five prospective jurors who had just entered the courtroom and were waiting to be called to serve on the jury.

The poor bastards. Those boys have no idea what is happening and where they are going, thought Doherty. They are like little children even though they try to act tough. They have no idea what life is, and after this trial they never will find out.

Doherty began to wonder why he ever took this

job five years ago. Twelve lawyers in his Public Defender's office and they were expected to prepare and defend 2,000 ignorant, deprived, fatherless 'boys' a year, charged with everything from murder and rape to indecent exposure. It's been a year now since I have had a case properly investigated before I tried it, Doherty thought. Doherty's cases were all alike: no investigation, no defense; just reliance on courtroom skills to save one, maybe two boys. What kind of a system is this? We need fifty lawyers, not twelve, and twenty investigators, not three. But why should taxpayers foot a heavier bill to defend "criminals" and have them freed "on technical-ities," thought Doherty, sarcastically smiling to himself.

Doherty looked over at Toler and Dillon. They were whispering to each other, planning their strategy for the kill. How could they lose?

"Ladies and gentlemen," said Judge Brussell, addressing a group of prospective jurors standing just inside the railing at the spectator section, "twelve from among your numbers, and two alternates, will be selected to serve on the jury in this case. Before we begin, do any of you know any of the defendants in this trial or any of the lawyers you see before you?"

There was a moment of silence as the judge looked intently at the group. One elderly black man slowly raised his hand as though he was afraid he might be seen. "Yes sir," said the judge in a loud voice. The man spoke, but no one could hear him. "I can't hear you," said the judge. "Please come forward, my good man," said the judge motioning with a sweep of his hand.

The man approached the judge's bench slowly and with obvious depredation. "Mister Judge, I knows the Meeks boy," he said, pulling together all the courage he possessed.

"Thank you," said Judge Brussell, in a kind voice. "We appreciate your candor and forthrightness. You are dismissed and may return to the second floor."

Looking back at the remaining jurors, the judge asked: "Anyone else who feels he cannot serve on this jury?" There was no further response.

The clerk called the first four prospective

jurors and directed them to the jury box. In an understanding voice, Judge Brussell asked: "Do you know of anything that would prevent you from rendering an impartial verdict in this case?" None of the jurors reacted to the question. "Do each of you have an open mind about this case?" The jurors all moved their heads in the affirmative. "Will you consider these boys," the judge gestured with his left hand towards the defendants, "innocent until proven guilty?" Again, the jurors motioned with their heads in the affirmative. "You understand that you will be sequestered for the length of the trial; that is, you will not be allowed to go home until the trial is concluded." No one responded; however, several showed they were not pleased with the arrangement.

The judge continued his line of general questions for some ten minutes and then gave the attorneys for each side the opportunity to question them. Three were ultimately dismissed and one seated on the jury. This process continued slowly and deliberately from Wednesday afternoon until the following Tuesday morning.

Doherty was skilled at this game. He knew how to avoid the Germans, Swedes and Dutch, who could not relate to the ghetto nor feel compassion for the less advantaged. Doherty looked for Italians, Blacks, even Poles because they could relate. In his questioning Doherty was friendly and warm, closely observing the jurors to whom he was speaking. Somehow he could sense how they might lean. But he knew, like all lawyers, that no one can guess what twelve men and women will do once locked together in the jury room. It is one of the great miracles of the system, for you might fool or romance one or two, but somehow the twelve, working together, reach the right verdict most of the time; the twelve as a group cannot be misled very often. Doherty knew this, but he also knew what to look for in individual jurors.

The eight boys became quite restless during this laborious jury selection process, neither interested nor understanding. They were relieved when the selection was completed. By 11:00 a.m. Tuesday morning, a panel of twelve jurors (8 men and 4 women, all Caucasians) and two alternates had been selected and directed to report back at two o'clock that afternoon for opening arguments.

"This court now stands recessed until two o'clock." Jablonski's gavel fell with a loud crack.

Chapter 3

Court Business

"Everybody rise. This court is now in session."

Judge Brussell seated himself behind his bench. "Call in the jury."

The bailiff rushed for the rear door to the judge's right and disappeared. A moment later the jurors walked into the courtroom and stood facing the judge, not sure what to do.

"Will you please take the same seats you had at the close of this morning's session," said the judge in a benign voice. "You may be seated." The jurors took their seats and all looked at the judge, waiting for the next move.

"Call in the defendants." Again the bailiff rushed out and the defendants began emerging through the door. None of the boys dared look at the jurors as they entered and walked toward their seats. Even O'Neil kept his head bent low as he walked in. The tops of the heads of the boys with short hair glowed from perspiration.

Before the judge could commence the trial, Kusak walked towards the judge's bench. His face was taut and his eyes intense. His movements were decisive and aggressive. No longer did he stumble as though lost in a besotted morass. It was as though the scent of battle had permeated his inner being. His thoughts were no longer heavy and laboriously developed, but flowed freely with buoyancy and crispness.

"Your Honor, I have one additional matter that must be discussed outside the presence of the jury.

The judge looked at the jury, which was just settling down in their wooden swivel chairs. He looked down at Kusak as if to discern some delaying tactic on the latter's part, but noting the intensity of Kusak's expression, the judge suddenly rose and exited towards his chamber door. "Come into my chambers, gentlemen," he said with some impatience.

"Everybody rise," shouted the bailiff in a startled voice, having been caught by surprise by the judge's sudden exit.

Assistant state's attorneys Toler and Dillon entered the chambers first, followed by Kusak and Doherty.

The judge's chambers were spacious and carpeted with a soft red woolen carpet. On the wall hung pictures of Abraham Lincoln, Clarence Darrow and Justice Brandeis of the United States Supreme Court. The judge's desk, which was covered with books and legal periodicals, was centered towards the back of the room. Behind the judge's chair was an American flag hanging from a short standard. Along two walls were row upon row of bookcases filled with case books from the Illinois courts and the United State Supreme Court.

The judge walked briskly to the chair at his desk and sat down. Just then the bailiff burst through the door, and walked quickly to a station to the right of the judge, where he stood in silence facing the attorneys.

"Now, what is the problem, Mr. Kusak?" inquired the judge with a heavy voice.

Before the judge could finish, Kusak burst forth with a salvo of words.

"Wait, wait, Mr. Kusak. Please wait for the court reporter. She will be here in a moment," said the judge.

Kusak looked around and then whispered to Doherty, "James, I'm going to give them hell, you wait and see."

Doherty looked on with an air of indifference as though conditioned to any surprise or tactic Kusak might try to pull.

At this moment the court reporter entered and Kusak started again.

"Mr. Kusak, give Miss Hinkle time to sit down and set up her machine." Miss Hinkle, a heavy set middle-aged woman with bleached blond hair, adjusted her stenotype machine, and then looked at the judge.

"Now, Mr. Kusak, you may begin."

"I repeat again," said Kusak, his face flushed, irritated by the delay, "that I have asked the State to produce various police reports made by investigating officers and statements taken from the witnesses and the defendants themselves. The documents have been subpoenaed and the State has ignored the subpoena duces tecum. The State has no discretion in this matter and must turn the requested documents over and – "

"The position of the State, your Honor," said Dillon cutting Kusak off, "is that these documents need not be turned over until after a state witness has testified and the defense has made a proper foundation. Only then is the State required to make a disclosure of these documents and then only those documents which are statements of the witnesses themselves."

"Gentlemen, I am prepared to make a ruling on this." The judge was looking at an Illinois Supreme Court report. "According to People v. Wolf, if – ."

"Your Honor, before you rule," interrupted Kusak.

"Kusak, you don't know how I am going to rule. Why don't you just sit down there and listen quietly for a moment." He looked intently at Kusak, and then continued, "I am ruling that the defendants have a right to inspect the documents in the possession of – "

"Including the detective reports, inter-departmental reports," blurted out Kusak.

The judge's face became red and his poise was visibly shaken. "I withdraw my ruling. Strike everything I said about what I am going to rule. Strike that out. Strike all that out. Defense counsel will have the witness statements, of which there are three, only after each witness has testified. All other documents in the possession of the state need not be disclosed. That is it, gentlemen. Any further discussion of the matter and I will hold you in contempt of court, and I mean what I say."

Doherty just sat quietly with his head in his hands. When the judge stopped, Doherty got up and walked out.

Kusak took one step towards the judge as though he was going to speak, but the judge just stared at him. He turned around and walked out, silence being the better part of valor.

Five minutes later Judge Brussell returned to the bench.

"Good afternoon, ladies and gentlemen," said the judge in a calm, quiet voice. "The court has been engaged in certain administra-tive duties which occur during the course of court business. Because the Court has other matters to attend to at this time, we are going to adjourn for the day. I want you all back here promptly at ten o'clock tomorrow morning.

"Before you leave, I want to admonish you concerning several matters which I will continually repeat during this trial. You are not to talk to anyone concerning this case or what occurs in the courthouse. In the early days of trials by a jury, the jurors were locked up overnight in separate cells to assure that they talked to no one or read newspapers concerning the trial. Today we provide comfortable facilities for you to use while the case is in progress, and we place you on your Honor to abide by the Court's rule. Once the trial is over, you may talk to anyone you wish about it.

"One final admonition. You are to wait until the close of all the evidence in the case and after arguments of counsel and instructions of the Court before you even talk about this case among yourselves. I repeat, do not talk about this case to anyone, not even a fellow juror. You don't want to have me lock you all up in separate cells, would you?" said the judge with a smile on his face.

The jurors, who had been listening intently to the judge, all smiled, some turning to each other. Several sat back in their chairs and all relaxed a bit. The judge was obviously in complete command of the trial and created an aura of great dignity and poise as he looked down from the bench.

Chapter 4

Opening Statements of Counsel

The next day the Court heard some thirty motions of attorneys involved in other cases. The jury waited in the jury room, anxiously anticipating the commencement of the trial. All but one had never served on a jury before, their only courtroom exposure being the courtroom of Perry Mason. After thirty minutes passed, their anxiety turned to impatience. Several sat chain smoking, while one man, fat and squat, munched on a large black cigar, which he repeatedly lit, leaving a heavy musty odor hanging about his person.

"Someone open that window," shouted a woman, consumed by the smoke.

"Can't," responded a man near the window. "It's five degrees outside."

At 11:00 a.m., Wednesday, the Judge took a recess after completing his motions. Five minutes later the jury was called into the courtroom. They stood at their seats, looking at each other for a signal, not knowing whether to sit or remain standing.

Judge Brussell entered and the court came to order. "Ladies and gentlemen," said the judge, smiling at the jurors, "I trust you had a restful evening?" The jurors smiled and affirmatively acknowledged the judge's question. "And I trust you abided by my admonition that you not talk about the case with anyone, including your husbands or wives or even other members of the jury?" Again, the jurors nodded in the affirmative.

"Last night, of course, was a dry run," continued the judge, "For you had little to talk about. From this moment on, the trial actually commences and you must, and I emphasize the word must, not talk to anyone about the case. By taking your oath yesterday you accepted this responsibility, a very grave one indeed, for the liberty of eight young men will ultimately lie in your hands. The whole jury system is founded on this oath and the pledge that you will not reach your verdict until you have heard all the evidence in the case, the closing arguments of counsel, and your instructions which I will give you at the end of the trial. I have great faith in the jury system. I feel it works because intelligent men and women like yourselves are able to abide by the court's admonitions. The bedrock of our entire criminal system is grounded on you, the individual citizen of this great land of ours."

"Gentlemen, are we ready to proceed?" asked the judge, turning to the defense table and then to Toler and Dillon. Doherty glanced quickly at Kusak to see if he was going to present another motion. Kusak remained motionless.

Doherty then rose. "Ready, your Honor."

"Ready for the prosecution," stated Toler.

The judge looked at Kusak, hesitated a moment, and then asked, "Are you ready, Mr. Kusak?"

Without rising, Kusak answered in a slow, thick-tongued voice, "Ready."

Judge Brussell again turned to the jury. "Ladies and gentlemen," he said in a formal voice, "the first thing this morning will be what we call opening statements by the parties for the respective sides. They consist of statements by the attorneys of what they believe their evidence will prove or what theories they are going to present. The statements are not to be considered as evidence, but as statements of counsel."

The jurors looked intently at the judge. An air of restrained excitement swept through their midst as they anticipated the commence-ment of the trial. For a week and a half, from the day they first reported for jury duty, they had waited to perform their designated function.

Judge Brussell turned to the prosecution's table. "You may proceed."

Walter Dillon rose and walked around the table away from the judge and towards the jury box where a lectern had been placed about fifteen feet from the jurors. He assembled his notes and cleared his throat with a nervous staccato "hmmm, hmmm." As was his custom, he wore a close fitting vest under his suit coat that he hoped would give him the appearance of a Harvard man or Philadelphia lawyer. In a courtroom where the provincial and bucolic elegance of Clarence Darrow still hung heavy, such an image even if successful, seemed out of place. It would have seemed far more natural for him to have unbuttoned his coat and perhaps loosened his collar.

His eyes watered slightly, but not enough to betray the nervousness he felt at that critical moment in his first trial.

"If it please the Court, counsel, members of the jury," said Dillon gasping for air. After a slight pause, he continued, "On behalf of the People of the State of Illinois," his voice broke and his nervousness was apparent. "At this time," he began again, "I have the opportunity to make an opening statement and after I have completed it, counsel for the defendants in this case have an opportunity to make their opening remarks."

Dillon took another deep breath, but he was under control now and he knew he could get through the opening argument successfully. Doherty and Kusak never looked at him. Doherty was looking at some notes, and Kusak was looking across the courtroom absorbed in other thoughts.

"What we say at this time is not to be considered as evidence, but merely what we intend to prove, and if we don't prove what we say at this time, it should be disregarded. First, we will prove one Arthur Head and a friend, Birdia Jackson, were sitting in Mr. Head's car, which was parked at a gasoline station at Roosevelt and Central Park. They were talking, when suddenly several of the defendants came up on either side of the car and yanked them out. They hit and kicked Mr. Head, and then they carried Mrs. Jackson down the alley."

Dillon hesitated a moment before he continued. Toler had explained that a slight hesitation just before you get to the dramatic part of your argument increases the impact of your statement. Dillon was almost taken back by the intensity of the jury's attention – no one had ever listened to him that closely before, not even his bride of three months, who was sitting in the rear of the courtroom.

"At this time and place, Mrs. Jackson," – and again he hesitated as though it was hard to put in words the terrible ordeal she suffered – "was attacked and raped by each of these defendants, one after the other." Dillon stopped to let the impact of the crime sink in.

Toler moved slightly in his chair, for Dillon

was getting too dramatic in opening argument, too many pauses. He cleared his throat with the hope that Dillon would catch the signal, and Dillon did. He quickly picked up his story. "Then they took Mrs. Jackson through a gangway, crossed Grenada Street, and into the alley where all the defendants raped her again. Ladies and gentlemen, this woman was raped twenty-six times. We will show that the defendants Cole, Sherrod, Meeks, Brown and O'Neil have confessed to these crimes."

Now, Dillon seemed to be rushing his argument, but he completed it, picked up his papers and returned to his seat. As he sat down, he looked at Toler, who was studying a document and never looked up. Dillon was hoping that Toler would give even a glance of approval.

Doherty, who had his back to Dillon as the latter spoke, slowly rose and turned to face the jury without moving from the table. In a slow and deliberate, but quiet voice, he said, "May it please the court, gentlemen of the prosecution, ladies and gentlemen of the jury. Our theory, the defense in this case, is that if a rape occurred, or if a robbery took place, it was not committed by these boys. Some of them have alibis. Some of them don't."

As Doherty said this, he looked over at the boys huddled around the table. Doherty continued, "But they all deny emphatically both of these crimes." Doherty turned and sat down with a suddenness that caught the jurors by surprise. Doherty folded his arms and stared across the room, waiting for Kusak to make his argument. The jurors looked at him a moment longer and then looked at Kusak. Kusak rose slowly, standing in a slouched position with both hands in his coat pockets. For a moment he said nothing. Then raising his head and looking towards the judge, in a stentorian voice said: "May it please your Honor."

Judge Brussell responded, "Mr. Kusak."

Kusak hesitated and then turned slowly towards the jury, still slouched forward, pushing his hands further into his coat pockets.

"Ladies and gentlemen of the jury." With the word "jury" he looked up at the jurors, glancing from one end of the jury box to the other. "Like my esteemed counsel for the state, my statement is limited at this time simply to stating what we intend to show. I intend to show that if there was a rape committed, it was not committed by my client Errol Meeks."

Kusak walked out from behind his chair and started strolling up and down in front of the jury box. "I intend to show that in fact under the indictment for robbery, there was no robbery committed, there was no money taken from anybody, and I intend to show you by the weakness of the State's case that my client is not guilty of robbery."

Kusak seemed to be getting wound up. His voice already loud, was becoming louder. He clasped his hands behind his back as he walked back and forth. "I intend to show that this lady, who claims that she was raped as many times as she says she was, happened to be in the alley with a man who is married, and that she was also married but they were not married to each other. I intend to show," pointing a finger in the air, "either by cross-examination or by direct evidence that the lady involved in this case had some marital trouble, that she was followed by her husband, and was caught in the act."

Kusak stammered, and then continued emphasizing each word. "This woman was caught in the act. She had no reasonable explanation either before the Court of Domestic Relations or Divorce Court to explain reasonably and honestly what she was doing in the alley with a MAN MARRIED TO SOMEBODY ELSE," shouted Kusak, "with a man who was accused by her husband as a correspondent, which means a man who is trying to break up the family."

Doherty clasped his bent head in his hands and stared at a piece of paper lying on the table before him. A strained expression came to his face as he grit his teeth. His Irish face became flushed. The boys were looking with rapt attention at Kusak, agreeing with every word spoken.

Kusak stopped. Then in a low voice he said, "I intend to show you on cross-examination and other evidence that after she got caught," his voice now building in intensity, "she hollered 'rape', she claimed that she was raped, that when she first made the complaint, that complaint was disregarded, that her husband raised the issue, not for the purpose of enforcing any criminal law, but in his proceedings against his wife, so she hollered 'rape' again," shouted Kusak with arms flailing the air.

Toler rose suddenly. "If the Court, please, I object to counsel's remarks. This is argumentative."

The jury lurched forward with this sudden interruption, it being the first objection made in the trial. All jurors looked at the judge wondering what would happen next.

The judge leaned forward, looking at Kusak. "Mr. Kusak, confine your remarks, please, to what you intend to prove without the other adjectives and qualifying remarks which are inadmissible. Sustained!"

Without the slightest break in his argument, Kusak continued: "I intend to show by the evidence, I will produce evidence that this woman named some people and she identified others in a show-up, but she could not name nor could she identify my client, Errol Meeks." Kusak turned to Meeks and said, "Stand up, boy."

Meeks, who was sitting between Harden and Sherrod slowly stood up. He kept his head bent as though he didn't dare look at the jurors and then he quickly sat down. "I intend to show you that this boy," - Errol looked at least seven years older than his twenty years - "offered to take a lie detector test."

"Objection," shouted Toler, obviously upset at the mention of a polygraph test, which was totally inadmissible.

"Sustained," said Judge Brussell.

"I intend to show," continued Kusak, "that this woman could not positively identify my boy until she had seen him on several occasions." Kusak's voice was now more restrained. "I shall show that Errol Meeks is a young man of good reputation in his neighborhood, not only among colored folk, but people who look like you and me."

"Objection, if the Court please," said Toler instantly. "Sustained as to the particular phrase used."

Kusak stopped. He walked back to his seat, turned again to the jury.

"All I request of you, if I may, is your consideration, logical and honest consideration of the issues in this case, irrespective of the defendant's color and just to uphold his rights under the laws of Illinois and the United States. . . ." Kusak's voice trailed off, and he sat down.

Chapter 5

First Witness – Arthur Head

A short recess was called for lunch after which Judge Brussell returned to the bench. After examining some papers, he looked over at the jury and noticed that they were still standing. "You may be seated," he said, smiling. He then looked at assistant state's attorney, Toler. Lifting his hand upward in a gesture for the State to proceed, he said, "Mr. Toler."

Toler rose. "The State will call Arthur Head as a witness, your Honor." The bailiff exited the door to the witness room. A moment later a thin-looking, almost emaciated black man emerged. He was about thirty-five years of age, six feet one inch tall. He walked hunched over as though his stomach pained him. He was dressed in a light brown suit, immaculately pressed, with an orange handkerchief protruding from the breast pocket and a matching tie neatly clasped to his light blue shirt. A six inch scar ran across the side of his face from his right eyebrow down to the middle of his cheek. His eyes were sunken and there were dark shadows around them caused either by the lack of sleep or the use of drugs. His hair was slicked straight back and reflected the lights overhead.

Head walked right past the witness stand, and most likely would have continued walking through the courtroom and out the door if bailiff Jablonski had not stopped him and directed him back to the witness chair. Finding the chair, he immediately sat down, still looking at the floor as though he were consciously avoiding all visual contact with any other person in the courtroom.

Just as Head seated himself the clerk asked him to rise and raise his right hand. "Do you solemnly swear to tell the truth, the whole truth, and nothing but the truth so help you God?" There was a lengthy pause after which, in a barely audible voice, Head responded, "I do."

"Mr. Head, I want you to speak up so everyone in this courtroom can hear you," said the judge.

Fred Toler then walked slowly, very deliberately, to the lectern where he spread his notes and then looked at Head. "State your name, please."

"Arthur Head."

"Spell your last name."

"H - E - A - D."

"Where do you reside, sir?"

"1575 West Monroe."

"I didn't hear you."

"1575 West Monroe, here in Chicago." Head was obviously nervous which resulted in his dropping his voice in the middle of each sentence.

Toler cleared his throat. "And where did you live on October 1, 1960?"

"1575 West Monroe."

"Are you married?"

"I was."

"Who did you live with on October 1, 1960?"

"Dorine Talbot."

"Are you employed, sir?"

"Yes."

"By whom?"

"Spartus Corporation."

"Can you spell that?"

"Not offhand, I can't."

Toler then moved away from the lectern and asked: "Calling your attention to September 30, 1960 at ten-thirty p.m., will you tell the ladies and gentlemen of the jury where you were at that time and place?"

"I was on the corner of Roosevelt and Central Park in a tavern."

"Do you know the name of the tavern?"

"I don't."

He explained that he was with Birdia Jackson, and a friend of hers named Joe, and his girlfriend named Emma.

He related that they stayed at the tavern until eleven o'clock. Then they went to the Casablanca Tavern over on 13th Street. They remained there until two-fifteen a.m., and then came back to the corner of Roosevelt and Central Park where Head's car was parked at a gas station. He found that one of his tires was flat so they tried to fix it. His jack would not fit the car so Joe and Emma decided to go and find another one.

"Birdia and I got into the front seat of my

car, waiting for them, talking, waiting for them to come back. We was just talking and waiting - I was sitting in the driver's seat and Birdia was sitting next to me on my right, I believe. We was seated there about thirty minutes, the best I can remember, when a bunch of young mens snatched me out of the car backwards. One of them had me around the neck. Snatched me out of the car backwards."

Head lifted his arms and put them around his neck and leaned back slightly to demonstrate what he was saying. His voice was stronger now and he looked up occasionally at Toler, consciously avoiding the stares of the jurors, who were listening with rapt attention. "The mens started to fight and I started trying to fight back, and I tripped one and he fell, and I was on top of him and three or four more was beating me."

Toler in a strong, overbearing voice asked, "You say you tripped one and fell down on top of him?"

"Yes."

"Do you see in court the one you tripped and went on top of?" The courtroom was dead silent. The defendants were all looking down - afraid to look at the witness for fear that they would be identified.

Head looked quickly at the eight and said, "I do. There."

"Will you point him out for the ladies and gentlemen of the jury?"

Head got up and walked to the defense table and pointed across it. "This one right here."

Toler took a step towards Head, looked at the judge and then at Doherty, and said, "For the record, the defendant, Fess Wise."

The jury looked at Fess Wise, whose head was bent so low that it looked as though his neck was broken. His already sad face was now even more mournful than usual, and he mustered all the control he could to avoid breaking out in tears, which would have shamed him to no end in front of the other boys. But the hopelessness of his plight seemed overwhelming at that moment.

"What occurred then?" asked Toler.

"Then two or three more snatched me off of him backwards and started kicking, stomping me on the chest, face and head, and I tried to duck my head

32

because they was kicking me over and over, beating me up."

Toler straightened up as though to highlight the importance of his next question. "Do you see any of those people in the courtroom that were kicking and stomping you, while you were on the ground?" Toler tried to emphasize the words "kicking" and "stomping" but his emphasis was almost too obvious, even to the jury.

"Yes, I can, one of them."

"Walk over and point him out."

Head got up again, with effort, and walked down to the defense table and pointed to another boy. "This one here."

"For the record, indicating Johnnie Sherrod," said Toler.

Johnnie, sitting next to Meeks, broke out in a sweat. He did not look up, but he felt the cold looks of members of the jury peering at him, en masse. At that moment Johnnie felt as though he was swirling around and around, downward into an abyss of darkness, in which he was nothing, nobody, not a thing. Intuitively he knew the end was at hand. He raised his head and glanced at Doherty, his only hope.

"What occurred then, sir?"

"They beat me unconscious and I don't know anything else." Head's voice trailed off as though he was feeling the pain again as he sat there. Several on the jury grimaced in apparent empathy.

"And then what happened?" asked Toler.

Head looked up at Toler now standing at the opposite end of the courtroom. "The next thing I knew was when a police officer had me up against the car. I first noticed Birdia's jacket lying on the hood of the car and her shoes on the ground. Me and Officer Meyer then went to Birdia's house which was just around the corner. When we failed to locate her we began searching for her down the alley walking and looking for her."

Toler again hesitated, and then asked, "At that time, sir, did you have occasion to notice yourself?"

Doherty stood up, almost startling the jury, "Objection."

"Overruled," said the judge. "You may

continue."

"My face was all swelled up, blood all over me, coat tore, pants busted, my hat gone, my wallet, couple pair of pants and two shirts I had in the car, gone."

"What did you do after that, sir, if anything?"

"The officer drove me to the Fillmore police station and after about twenty minutes, two more officers entered with Birdia Jackson."

Toler looked at the jury and then walked several steps towards Head. "Will you tell the ladies and gentlemen of the jury what you noticed, if anything, about Birdia Jackson at the time you saw her in the police station?"

"She came in the police station – " Head hesitated, "blouse was tore open, her clothes were dirty and lip busted. She had no shoes and no stockings."

Toler began walking back to his chair. He then asked in a matter of fact way, "And everything you testified to occurred in the City of Chicago, County of Cook and State of Illinois?"

"Right."

"No further questions."

Toler sat down and made some notes. Dillon whispered to him. Doherty began to rise, but Kusak jumped out of his chair and stepped in front of him.

"Mr. Head, I would like to ask you a few questions, if I may."

Doherty sat down, more dismayed than before, for prior to trial it had been agreed that he would cross-examine each witness first. Now he had no idea what would happen with Kusak beginning the cross-examination on such a crucial witness.

"Are you married?" Kusak asked, "and do you know the name of your wife?"

"Objection," said Dillon, rising from his seat. "One question should suffice."

"Sustained. Ask a single question, Mr. Kusak," said the judge.

Kusak asked, "When were you married?"

"In 1951, but we were separated a year and a half later."

"To whom were you married?"

"Juanita."

"Were you divorced?"

Head looked a bit confused. "No, I wasn't."

"So you were married on October 1, 1960?"

"Yes, I was."

"How many children do you have?"

"One."

Kuask paused and then in a deliberate voice asked, "On October 1, 1960, did you live or reside with your wife?"

"I did not."

"Where did you live?"

"1575 W. Monroe."

"Where did Birdia live? Do you know?" asked Kusak, taking a step closer to the witness stand.

"She lived at 3550 W. Granada."

"Did she live with her husband?"

Dillon rose from his seat. "I object, if the Court please."

Kusak shouted back. "He brought it out."

Judge Brussell leaned forward and with his hand outstretched toward Kusak, said, "No comment, Mr. Kusak. That objection is overruled."

Kusak turned back to the witness. "And she lived with her husband?"

"She did not."

Doherty looked at Kusak. It was very evident what he was attempting to do. It was the very thing the two had argued about just before trial and which Doherty thought he had convinced Kusak not to do. The son-of-a-bitch, Doherty thought, the case is bad enough without trying to depict an illicit love affair. Who the hell cares in this day and age?

The longer Kusak droned on the more frustrated Doherty became. He felt intense heat engulfing his body, and his face became flushed. He continued sitting with his back to the jury so they could not see his pained expression. When will that drunk stop? It was evident the judge was becoming irritated.

"Did you meet his lady at the tavern by appointment or accidentally?"

"We was supposed to go out."

"You had a date with her?"

"Right."

Kusak continued laboriously, retracing the same events previously brought out on direct examination. The jury began looking at the large clock at the rear of the courtroom. Several moved restlessly in their chairs. Judge Brussell was leaning back, his eyes fixed on the ceiling.

Toler finally got up. "Objection, if the Court please. I don't see the relevancy of any of this questioning."

"Sustained."

It was clear that the judge was irritated by Kusak's questioning. However, Kusak continued on for another forty-five minutes. He was determined to have his day in court. He asked questions about the kind of car Joe was driving, personal questions about Joe's girlfriend, none of which were relevant. The jury was quite obviously displeased, but he seemed totally oblivious to the fact that a jury was present. Even the eight boys seemed to lose interest as they sat there, leaning back in their chairs, looking around the courtroom.

Finally, Kusak began his finale. "Now I want to point out my client to you, Errol Meeks. Will you get up, Mr. Meeks."

Meeks looked embarrassed as he slowly rose in his seat. He looked at Johnnie Sherrod and then James Harden, but neither would look at him. He was embarrassed by his attorney's performance and he was concerned about what Johnny would think. In the ghettos of Chicago, a black teenager's friends are more important than his parents. What they say or think is a far weightier matter than any thought or opinion expressed by a parent. He spends the greater part of his days and nights with his buddies, and as long as they are together there is nothing in the world they fear, the police, the Blackstones, the West Side Disciples, nothing. The New Braves were not a big gang, but with Johnnie as their leader they had never been beaten in a fight.

Kusak pointed to Errol. "Is this the man who robbed you on October 1, 1960?"

"I can't identify him," said Head.

"In other words, you do not accuse him that he took any property away from you, did he?"

"I can't answer that just 'yes' or 'no.'"

"Who did you see when you were dragged out of the car and robbed and assaulted?"

"First, Fess Wise and then Johnny Sherrod."

"Objection, your Honor," shouted Doherty.

Kusak quickly said, "I have no more questions at this time."

"Ladies and gentlemen of the jury, we will take a ten minute recess," said the judge. "Come into chambers, gentlemen."

Once inside, Doherty moved for a mistrial. "Your Honor, Fess Wise and Johnnie Sherrod have now been identified both on direct examination and cross-examination. I believe an atmosphere has been created around them by virtue of this second identification, which the State could never do, which has created a prejudice against them. It will foreclose them from receiving a fair and impartial trial in violation of their rights guaranteed by the Fourteenth Amendment to the Federal Constitution."

Judge Brussell looked over to Toler. "Does the State have anything to say?"

"The State opposes the motion, your Honor," said Toler.

Toler did not press the issue hard. From the judge's expression it was clear that a mistrial would not be granted. Both he and the Court knew the only way the criminal docket can be kept manageable was to try as many defendants as possible at the same time. The lack of judges, state's attorneys and money permitted no other course.

"Mr. Doherty," said the judge, "I appreciate your high sense of obligation to these two defendants. But with multiple defendants there is bound to occur some duplication of testimony. I cannot deny Mr. Kusak the right to cross-examine this witness in the best interest of his client. This is the way our system works. Motion denied."

The lawyers and judge returned to the courtroom. Doherty rose and turned slowly and deliberately towards the jury. Then he turned further until he faced the rear of the courtroom. He took two steps in that direction and then turned 180 degrees. The jury watched intently, not knowing whether something dramatic was going to occur.

Doherty's mind was working rapidly. Like most trial lawyers his mind was razor sharp, his reflexes instant. He was keyed up at this moment like a highly trained professional athlete or astronaut. There, in seconds, flashed the entire case before him; the weaknesses of his case which were many; the strengths, none. Kusak had probably destroyed any chance of gaining the jury's sympathy. Johnnie Sherrod and Fess Wise had been clearly and convincingly identified. There was little chance to save them at this point, at least on the robbery charge. The best he probably could do would be to concentrate on the other five and use Sherrod and Wise as the sacrificial lambs.

A Public Defender's lot is a difficult one. It is an appointed position without glamour, totally misunderstood by the general public, slighted by the legal profession, and scorned by the State's Attorney's office. A young person joining the Public Defender's Office looks for no emoluments of a judgeship or political office as one does when joining the State's Attorney's office. Any record he can make stands in poor stead in the public eye.

Doherty looked up at his "boys": James O'Neil, Johnny Sherrod, James Harden, Eugene Brown, Fess Wise, Eddie Cole, Sammy Dillard, and yes, Errol Meeks. For twelve years he had been defending such boys, but for what? If he won a case, which was infrequent, the boy was back for a second lick within months or a year. Had he stayed too long: was he afraid to go into private practice because he knew too well how to lose? If you lose too often and too gracefully in life, you're in trouble unless you have the security of a government job. Then it's not a question of just winning, but to assure that "justice is done." Ha! Justice! thought Doherty, and he turned and looked at Head. He asked several questions which affirmed that five of his defendants could not be identified.

The state next called Officer Alex Meyer, who reiterated most of what Arthur Head had stated. There was no cross-examination. The judge then continued the trial to the next day.

Chapter 6

The Rape Victim Testifies

The following day a heavy snow storm hit Chicago, which slowed traffic considerably. The judge, caught in traffic, did not arrive until 10:20 a.m. Before calling the jury, Judge Brussell had a number of other matters to attend to; a stream of lawyers entered and left his chambers. On several occasions he would take his place on the bench and a defendant would be called in to plead. Frequently, after a conference, the defendant would plead guilty and receive an agreed upon sentence.

It was not until 11:35 a.m., Thursday, that Judge Brussell called the bailiff and told him that he was ready to proceed. Jablonski waddled through his little ritual and the defendants were hurried to the defense table and the jury called.

"Ladies and gentlemen," said Judge Brussell, "did you have a pleasant evening? I am now going to ask you as a group whether you spoke to anyone about the case?"

The jurors all shook their heads in the negative. After a moment one juror, sitting on the far left side of the front row, rose. Judge Brussell looked at him. "Mr. O'Malley."

Juror O'Malley, a red faced Irishman, rather heavy set with greying hair said, "If I am not out of order, your Honor, I want to compliment the Court for our dinner last night and for our breakfast this morning, and for the clean beds we had to sleep in and then I would like to make a couple of requests of the Court."

"What is it Mr. O'Malley?"

O'Malley looked at the other jurors and then in a forced voice, "Well, the request is we would like a television set." He hesitated a second and then continued, "We would also like to have the bailiff or someone else go out and get us some items we have written on a piece of paper for our quarters, to give us a little more than what we have."

Judge Brussell hesitated a moment and then said, "Is that all, Mr. O'Malley?"

"Yes, sir."

"Thank you, Mr. O'Malley."

"You're entirely welcome, your Honor."

Judge Brussell turned to counsel for both sides. "May the record show that Juror O'Malley has made a request to this Court in the presence of the jury and counsel for both sides. If counsel for both sides will stipulate I will instruct the bailiff to make inquiry as to whether the jurors can be supplied with a television set and, of course, attempt to honor their request for these reasonable items."

"The State so stipulates," said Toler, rising half way from his seat.

"No objection, your Honor," added Doherty. Kusak, without looking up, mumbled, "No objection."

Judge Brussell then looked at Toler, "Your next witness, please."

Toler rose and took a few steps towards the judge's bench. "If the court please, we call Birdia Jackson."

The jurors immediately sat up and looked toward the rear door where witnesses entered the courtroom. Their interest was apparent for this was the "rape" victim. Most of the jurors had never seen a woman who had been raped and were not quite sure what they expected to see.

The bailiff rushed through the door shouting, "Birdia Jackson, Birdia Jackson." There was a momentary lull and then the door opened. First, the bailiff appeared and then a thin, light skinned black woman entered. Her face was drawn tight across her cheek bones which protruded slightly. Her dress hung loosely, as though she had lost considerable weight from the time of its purchase. Her head was bent as she entered and it was not until she looked up to find her way to the witness chair that one noticed moisture in her eyes, a moisture created by nervousness and fear. The clerk asked her to raise her right hand and swore her in.

Dillon then rose from his chair with his notes in hand and walked over to the lectern. In a soft and sympathetic voice, said, "Birdia, will you speak up so I can hear you back here. Will you do that?"

Birdia answered, "Yes."

"State your full name, please."

"Birdia Jackson."

"Spell your name, please. "

"Birdia, B-I-R-D-I-A J-A-C-K-S-O-N."

"And where do you live?" Dillon was looking at his notes as he asked the questions, still not feeling enough confidence to leave the lectern and move around as he questioned the witness.

"3550 W. Granada."

"In the City of Chicago?" asked Dillon.

"Yes, it is."

In reply to Dillon's carefully prepared questions, put to her in monotone voice, Birdia Jackson testified that she lived with her cousin and her cousin's husband, and that she had separated from her husband. She further testified that she had worked at Ben Koehler and Company since January of 1959 as a machine operator.

"Calling your attention to the 30th day of September, 1960, did you have an occasion to go out that evening?" Dillon was more relaxed now, having run through the opening questions without objection. As he asked this last question he walked a few feet to the side of the lectern, keeping his fingers glued to the next question in his notes.

As Birdia answered the question in the affirmative, Dillon quickly returned to his starting position behind the lectern, having completed his first venture of a few steps to the side.

So far Birdia was proving to be a good witness. She was responding to each question just as they had been rehearsed the night before when she had spent several hours at the State's Attorney's office, preparing her testimony. She explained how she and her cousin left the house at 10 p.m. and walked to the corner of Central Park and Roosevelt, Harry's Place, a tavern.

She talked to her friends and had a beer. She then testified that she left Harry's Place with Arthur Head, Joe and Emma and drove to the Casablanca in Joe's car. They had another beer and stayed there until two a.m. or so. They then returned to the corner of Central Park and Roosevelt Avenue, "the four of us, Arthur Head, Joe Turner, Emma Darling and myself."

"We then drove to the service station a quarter of a block down Central Park, where Arthur's car was parked. Arthur's car had a flat so he and

Joe tried to fix it, but Joe's jack wouldn't fit his bumper. Joe said he would go and get another jack."

"And then what did you do, if anything?" asked Dillon.

"Well, I sat in Arthur's car. Arthur also sat in the car, and we sat there for thirty minutes. I was on the right side, in the front seat, and Arthur was sitting on the driver's side in the front."

Dillon hesitated a moment and then turning to the witness asked in a loud clear voice, "Now Mrs. Jackson, will you tell the jury what, if anything unusual occurred while you were in the car?"

Anxiety flashed momentarily into Birdia's eyes. She looked at the defendants and then back at Dillon and said, "Well, we was attacked."

"Objection," shouted Doherty.

"Sustained," said the judge.

"Tell the Court and jury what happened, Birdia."

Birdia Jackson turned to the judge as though she was going to speak. She then sat back in the witness chair and looked down uncertain just how to begin. Spectators sitting in the crowded benches in the rear of the courtroom leaned forward, trying to catch her words. Some of the spectators present were "courthouse jockeys," who spent their days traveling from courtroom to courtroom, trying to find a juicy murder or rape case. As soon as such a trial commenced, the word spread like wildfire throughout the building and all the jockeys converged on that courtroom. Such was the present trial. The jockey set was composed mostly of older, retired men. A case like the present one required an early appearance at the courtroom in order to get a front row seat.

"I was sitting there," continued Birdia Jackson, "with my head laying over like this on Arthur's shoulder." She leaned to the left and tilted her head, demonstrating the position she was describing.

"Slut," said one fat woman in a stage whisper which caught Jablonski's ear. He rushed quickly to the rear of the courtroom and gave everyone a menacing look. Unable to detect the offender, he stood for a while at the rear door and watched them.

Jackson continued: "Suddenly someone was

pulling Arthur from the car and I looked around and saw him being dragged to the ground by four mens. Then I was jerked backward and out of the car and one of the mens said 'Give me what you got.'"

"I gave them my purse and they opened it and poured out all my things on the front seat. Then one of them mens said, 'What you got in your bra?', and I said 'nothing.' He then said 'show me.' I began to open my bra, but he couldn't wait and just jerked it loose, tore my bra strap and there was nothing there."

There was a slight pause and then Dillon asked, "Do you see that person in the courtroom today, the man with whom you had that conversation at that time and place?"

Birdia Jackson looked quickly at the defendants and without hesitation answered, "I do."

"Will you please step down and identify that person, please?"

Birdia stood up and slowly left the witness stand and walked to the defense table. Every eye in the courtroom was glued on her, every eye except those of the eight defendants. None of them dared look at her as she circled the table. Walking behind them, Jackson was visibly shaking by the need of having to leave the shelter of the witness stand. Her eyes reflected the fear she felt as she pointed and said in a weak voice, "This one."

Her hand pointed to the smallest member of the group, Fess Wise. Wise again lowered his head so low that it was almost below the level of the table.

Doherty grabbed his pad of paper and noted in capital letters: WISE IDENTIFIED ON BOTH SIDES OF THE CAR AT SAME TIME!! IMPOSSIBLE!!

Dillon then stepped forward with new found confidence and said, "Let the record show that the witness has identified the defendant, Fess Wise." Dillon then walked back to his notes and asked, "And after you had this conversation, then what happened, if anything?"

Jackson was still returning to the witness stand and after sitting down, just sat there, having obviously missed the question. Judge Brussell leaned over and asked, "Did you hear the question, Mrs. Jackson?"

Birdia looked startled. "No, sir." The judge

then turned to the court reporter and asked to have the question read.

"I looked around," continued Birdia, "and a number of boys had Arthur on the ground. One boy stood over him and stomped him in the face several times. He struggled and then went limp and I pleaded with them, 'Please don't kill him.' A man standing next to me said 'shut up', and hit me twice across the side of the face."

Dillon hesitated a moment, as instructed by Fred Toler, and then said in a stentorian voice, which was too obviously of the Perry Mason mold, "And do you see that man in the courtroom here today?"

"That is objected to," said Kusak, who looked this day as though he had been resurrected from the dead, or better said, alcoholic obscurity.

"Overruled," said the judge, not even looking at Kusak, who was still attempting to rise from his chair.

"I do," responded the witness, and without any prompting began her trek to the rear of the defense table. Again her outstretched accusatory hand fell on another defendant and that defendant lost his anonymity before the jury.

"Let the record show that the witness has identified the defendant, James O'Neil," said Dillon.

Dillon, without referring to his notes, asked, "And then what happened after that?"

Again the question was asked before Birdia had returned to the stand, but she quickly answered as she was sitting down.

"Then Fess Wise said, 'Let's take her, man.'"
"And then what happened, if anything?"
"And then they did."
"What do you mean, they did?"
"They just –" Birdia looked at the judge and then the jury as though she couldn't answer the question. "Well – you see at this time I was sitting out of the car like this." Birdia moved forward to the front edge of the chair, elbows resting on her knees and her chin cupped in her hands. "And then they just took me."

Kusak could restrain himself no longer. He jumped up, pounding his fist on the table. "Object

44

to the description of 'they,' who did it? The question before your Honor and the jury is who did it, not they." Kusak sat down abruptly, not certain of exactly what he had said. Somehow he had lost the train of thought.

Doherty just looked up at Kusak in disbelief at his insistence that the defendants be identified. What in the hell is he trying to do to me? Doherty wondered if this could possibly be a deliberate act.

Dillon in a quiet and deeply compassionate voice asked, "Who took you, Birdia?"

Birdia's eyes filled with tears. She tried to speak, but could not. "Those - those - " and she could go no further. She brought her hands to her face and wept with a muffled sound.

The occupants of the courtroom sat in stunned silence. The jurors stared aghast at the witness, never having experienced such a display except on television. The judge was in immediate control of the situation and ordered a forty-five minute break for lunch. Dillon, in full view of the jurors, rushed towards Birdia and solicitously helped her from the stand, escorting her out the rear door to the witness room. Dillon's mentor, Fred Toler, stood with arms folded, watching his protégé perform. A thin smile appeared momentarily across his face.

A lawyer, before a jury, is an actor. The greatest of them, Clarence Darrow, Jerry Spence, Bennett Williams, F. Lee Bailey, Percy Foreman, Fred Lane, were also great dramatists; they made the trial come alive with the jury playing a part in the unfolding drama. Being on stage, the trial lawyer gives thought even to the clothes he will wear depending upon the jury he must face. Before a trial is an hour old, the good lawyer will have his hand on the jury's pulse, surging aggressively ahead when the jury is receptive, quickly retreating when he has tread too far, or shouting when the jury needs to be alerted, speaking compassionately when it is reacting sympathetically. He will even risk antagonizing the judge and take judicial abuse if he feels there is an advantage to playing the role of underdog.

After lunch, the Court reconvened and Birdia Jackson resumed the witness stand. She seemed to have regained her composure. Dillon turned to the judge and, in a deeply respectful voice, requested permission to continue.

"Mrs. Jackson," addressing his witness in a low and compassionate voice, "you testified that someone took you. Could you kindly tell us what you meant when you said 'they took me'?"

Birdia lowered her head and took a deep breath and then looked up. Her face was drained. With effort she answered, "The mens," she faltered, recovered herself, and continued, "them mens sitting at that table," pointing at the defendants.

Kusak leaped to his feet shouting "Objection."

Doherty cringed at the timing of this objection. It was wrong because, in the eyes of the jury, it would be construed to be a boorish act, aimed at humiliating this "poor woman."

"Fess Wise and James O'Neil and – " continued Birdia.

Kusak still standing, again shouted "Objection."

Judge Brussell responded, "She hasn't finished her answer, counsel," emphasizing the word "counsel." The judge looked at the witness and in a kind voice said "Mrs. Jackson, will you please continue, if you can."

"Thank you, your Honor," responded Birdia in a humble voice. "James O'Neil was there and Eugene Brown. And James Harden was also there."

"Are these persons in the courtroom?"

"Yes. They are sitting there, there, there and there."

"Let the record show that the witness has identified Fess Wise, James O'Neil, Eugene Brown, and James Harden," said Dillon. "What occurred then, if anything?"

"The mens carried me. O'Neil, Fess –"

"Objection," roared Kusak, "unless she says who. There are eight defendants. My client is not guilty."

Toler leaped from his chair and shouted, "I most strongly object to the remarks of counsel."

Judge Brussell, visibly restraining himself said, "Overruled."

"Was anybody else present at that time and place?"

"There was a boy coming along behind, a man,

or what have you."

"Did you see him?"

"It was Brown."

Dillon hesitated a moment as though the last answer was not the answer he had written in his notes. He looked at Toler, who sat expressionless - Dillon was on his own. Dillon finally said, "Will you repeat the last question, Mr. Court Reporter?"

Doherty shot out of his chair. His face was beet red. He could take it no longer - the eruption had occurred. "Object," he shouted in an emotional and angry voice. "The last question has been answered and he is bound by the answer. This is a state witness."

Toler then leaped from his chair and rushed to the front of the judge's bench. "That is incorrect. I object to the remarks of counsel."

Doherty looked at Toler with fire in his eyes as though ready to continue the trial by medieval combat. The jury and Dillon gazed at the two combatants in disbelief. The judge immediately rose. "Will you come into chambers, please gentlemen?"

Returning to the courtroom, Doherty said, "I withdraw my objection, your Honor. I misunderstood the evidence, your Honor, and I withdraw the objection." Doherty appeared contrite, but his demeanor suggested he was acting in a spirit of cooperation, rather than surrender.

Judge Brussell in a firm voice said, "Thank you, Mr. Doherty. You may proceed, please."

Dillon quickly returned to the lectern and shuffled through his notes. There was a long pause while he looked at several pages. Then with a panicky expression he looked over at Toler, who sat expressionless. Dillon looked at the witness. "What occurred next, if anything?" Always a safe question to ask when in doubt.

Birdia Jackson glanced nervously at Toler, the judge and back to Dillon. "I - I - could you repeat the question, please?"

"Where is this alley located in regards to the gas station?" Dillon overcame his initial panic and passed the first real test of a trial attorney - learning to adjust to the exigencies of an unexpected situation.

"The alley was located next to the gas

station, directly north of it."

"After you reached the alley, what happened, if anything?"

"Well, they was running with me down the alley. They took me three-quarters of the way down the alley and into a backyard. They took me under the stairwell of one of the buildings. This was in the rear of 3553 Grenshaw. Then they dropped me, Fess Wise, O'Neil and Harden."

Suddenly from the defense table James O'Neil jumped to his feet, his eyes flashing. "You know you are lying, woman." Two guards were on him instantly and slammed him down in his chair with a loud crash.

Looking at the defendants, the judge said, "Everybody is instructed that other than the witnesses and the attorneys, no comments are permitted in order to avoid distracting the orderly process of the trial."

Birdia Jackson was then permitted to continue with her testimony. "The mens dropped me and then one of them pulled off my girdle and stockings."

Kusak jumped up. "Objection unless she says who, not one of them. There are eight of them."

The judge stared at Kusak for a brief second, and then in a restrained voice said, "Mr. Kusak, I believe it is well established that we do have eight, and the Court is trying to get the testimony, as I am sure counsel for both sides are." As the judge spoke he turned slowly and deliberately to look at the witness. "Give us their names, please. You may proceed now."

Birdia looked at the judge and in a halting voice responded, "I can't answer that question, which one."

Kusak, who was still standing, broke in immediately. "I move the question and the answer be stricken if she cannot identify –"

Dillon interrupted Kusak, "If the Court please, I would like to be heard."

Doherty then rose from his seat, but before another word was spoken Judge Brussell stood up. "I think this is a good time for a break. I have a number of motions that must be heard. Let's reconvene in thirty minutes." The judge quickly exited to his chambers.

Birdia exited to the witness room and then left by a side door into the hallway towards the elevators. She was met by some of the mothers of the defendants, Mrs. Robinson (Fess Wise's mother), Mrs. Meeks, Mrs. Sherrod, and Mrs. Barton (James O'Neil's mother). The mothers stared at Birdia with intense hatred as she approached. Mrs. Barton stepped out blocking her path and Mrs. Meeks knocked Birdia with her shoulder. "Whore," said Mrs. Robinson. "Which detective are you sleeping with this week?" whispered Mrs. Meeks as she bumped her.

Birdia Jackson was visibly frightened as she attempted to get past the women for this was not the first time this sort of incident had occurred. The mothers had gone so far as to "visit" her at her apartment and call her at all hours of the night.

At that moment Detective Lill, a heavy set black officer wearing civilian attire, exited from the courtroom and the women immediately dispersed. Lill approached Birdia and put his arm around her, squeezing her shoulder slightly with his hand, and walked towards the elevator with her.

At 3:30 p.m. the trial reconvened. As Birdia resumed her place on the witness stand, Dillon said "You are still under oath. Do you understand that?"

"Yes, I do."

"Birdia, you testified earlier that you were thrown down and your girdle and stockings were taken off. Now will you tell the jury what was said at that time and place in your presence."

Birdia hesitated momentarily and then in a strong voice answered, "Harden said I could lay on his coat."

"What happened after that, Mrs. Jackson?"

"The coat was put down and they pushed me down."

"Objection," said Kusak.

The judge turned towards the witness. "Can you tell us who pushed you down?"

"I don't know who pushed me, Judge."

"Objection," said Kusak.

"Mr. Kusak, the jury will be fully instructed with regard to the question of considering the evidence against each defendant separately. You may note your objection and it may stand as a continuing objection. Proceed, Mr. Dillon."

"And then what happened? Strike that; I withdraw the question. Was anything more said at that time and place?" said Dillon.

"Yes, it was."

"If you can identify the person speaking will you please do so."

"They was swearing and wanted to know who should go first."

"And was anything else said at that time and place?"

Kusak rose again. "I hate to object to that your Honor, to interrupt the witness, but this is a serious case."

Judge Brussell immediately rose. "Come into chambers. Don't continue your remarks, Mr. Kusak."

When the attorneys entered the judge's chambers, Judge Brussell was looking out the rear window. Suddenly he whirled around. "Kusak, I am telling you this for the last time. You stop making that same objection or I am going to hold you in contempt. I can't take any more of your obstinacy. You are not, and I repeat 'not' with all my strength, going to disrupt this trial. You're trying to break me as you did the judge in the Franklin case, and so help me God you're not – not going to succeed."

The judge's face was flushed. The veins on the side of his neck looked as though they were about to burst. For the first time he had lost his composure. He had the power to discipline Kusak, but any prejudicial conduct on his part in the presence of the jury could poison the trial and create reversible error. This was the very thing Kusak was working towards.

Suddenly Doherty, who was standing quietly at the side of the room realized what Kusak had been doing. With a sardonic smile he saw the humor in what was unfolding before him. That old drunk has resorted to the only tool he has left in his depleted arsenal. Antagonize the judge into reversible error so that there would have to be a new trial. I didn't think he had it in him. Doherty for the first time began to enjoy the twisted drama taking place. He knew it would not work, for it took a master like a Belli or Kuntzler to pull it off, but it was an interesting attempt.

"Mr. Kusak," continued the judge, shaking his finger, "for the last time you have a continuing objection. If I am not mistaken, nothing has been said about your client."

"Your Honor," broke in Doherty, "this is the problem with this whole trial. How can the jury keep eight defendants straight and the evidence against each? This Court should call a mistrial and hold three or four separate trials, as I suggested in the beginning."

"Mr. Doherty," said the judge, emphasizing both words, "let's resume the trial."

"Your Honor," persisted Kusak, "my function here is to protect the rights of my client before you and that jury. I cannot do it unless I am allowed to exercise my rights to object. There is no such thing as a standing objection."

"I am sorry, Mr. Kusak. I am the court and you will have to accept my ruling. If I am wrong, I will be reversed."

"You are," responded Kusak arrogantly. "But I don't want to try the case before the United States Supreme Court. I want to win it here."

The attorneys emerged from the judge's chambers and returned to their places. A few minutes elapsed before the judge returned to the bench.

As soon as the judge resumed his position, Doherty rose. "May I address the Court on behalf of Edward Cole, Sammy Dillard, and Johnnie Sherrod. I object to any conversation outside their presence and I ask the Court to instruct the jury that this cannot be considered as against these defendants there being no showing that they were there."

Kusak rose while Doherty was still speaking and blurted out, upon the completion of Doherty's last word, "I have the same motion on behalf of the defendant Meeks."

Judge Brussell turned to the jury and in a calm voice stated, "With regard to this objection, ladies and gentlemen, you are instructed now, and you will be further instructed in writing, if the occasion arises, that insofar as any conversation is concerned that is outside the presence of any of the named defendants, that conversation is not to be in any way considered admissible in evidence against them."

"You now may proceed, Mr. Toler - I mean Mr. Dillon."

Several of the jurors looked at each other with a puzzled expression. Doherty and Kusak sat down. Doherty knew full well that the jury couldn't keep the conversations straight much less the identity of the eight defendants. Kusak, on the other hand, wasn't particularly concerned what the jury thought. He had mapped out his course of action, as Doherty had earlier surmised. Disrupt the trial, creating reversible error for his client.

"Birdia, will you tell the Court and jury what was said at that time and place, if anything?"

"I was down. The boys were getting ready to have their intercourse."

Doherty and Kusak both leaped to their feet as though pulled up by puppeteer strings. "Move to strike that," blurted Doherty.

"That may be stricken, the last part."

Dillon continued as though uninter-rupted. "And then what was said at that time and place, if anything?"

"Fess Wise was at my head and said, 'If this, this -'" Birdia hesitated and looked at the judge in desperation, seeking guidance as to whether she should say a foul word. "Wise said, 'If she hollers I will stomp her brains out.' Cole said he would cut my throat."

Doherty looked up with a startled expression. "May we have that answer read back, please?"

The court reporter picked up the tape he had been using in his stenotype machine and reread the answer. Doherty then rose. "Objection. There is absolutely no showing that Cole was there."

"Overruled."

"Exception," responded Doherty in a disgusted voice. Doherty was beginning to feel that the judge was too one-sided in favor of the prosecution. It was evident that the naming of Cole caught Dillon by surprise. He was not supposed to be identified by the witness until later in her testimony. Dillon looked over at Toler who gave a long hard stare, as though trying to communicate with him by ESP. Dillon then turned towards the witness. "Can you identify Cole?"

"Yes, I can." Without being asked, Birdia

Jackson got up and stepped down from the witness stand, walked around the table, and touched Cole on the shoulder. "Here."

"Let the record show the witness has identified the defendant, Edward Cole," said Dillon. "And what happened, Mrs. Jackson?" he continued.

Birdia walked back to the witness chair and sat down. "Well, they - Harden proceeded to have his intercourse. There was - they were saying 'Hurry up! Hurry up!' You know, they were rushing him."

"Objection."

"Sustained."

Birdia then continued her testimony. "After Harden had his intercourse, Fess Wise had his next. At this moment some more boys was coming down the alley, and Cole says to the boys, 'Over here, man,' and he used a swear word referring to me."

Dillon said, "What were those words, Birdia?"

"He said, 'Over here, man. We got the bitch under here. Do you want some trim?' Fess Wise was having his intercourse and this mans pulled him up."

"Who was this man, Mrs. Jackson?" asked Dillon in a compassionate tone.

"Errol Meeks, and he is sitting right there next to Harden," she blurted, pointing at Meeks.

Kusak leaped to his feet. "I object most strenuously, your Honor."

"On what grounds, Mr. Kusak?" asked the judge.

"On the grounds - on the grounds," Kusak obviously didn't know what to say. His client had at last been identified and there was nothing he could do about it.

"Overruled."

Kusak sat down and folded his arms. It's one thing to make a display before the jury to antagonize the Court, but is another to look like an ass. A lawyer's vanity is a delicate mechanism which he jealously guards by preparing for the unanticipated. Thus, few things pierce it. However, when a blatant error is committed, which even the most inexperienced of jurors can recognize, it penetrates to the very core of this intricately balanced instrument.

"Let the record show that the witness has identified the defendant, Errol Meeks," interjected Dillon, "What happened next, Birdia?"

"Meeks had his intercourse. I noticed he had an inch long beard."

"After Meeks had his intercourse, I mean had intercourse with you, what, if anything, happened, Mrs. Jackson?"

"They were rushing him. Then the next had intercourse with me," continued Birdia. "That was O'Neil. And then the mens all had intercourse again."

"And what were you doing at that time and place, if anything?"

Birdia hesitated a moment. A flash of anger streaked across her drawn face. "My hair was being pulled and my wrist was being twisted. I was cautioned not to breathe loud," continued the witness, "or I would be killed."

Dillon heard the answer the first time. It was the jury he feared who had not heard the answer because of Kusak's objection and he merely used a common trial tactic, taught to him by Toler, to assure himself that the answer registered with each juror. "Would you please repeat your answer. I did not hear you."

"I would be killed," repeated Birdia.

Birdia continued, "Harden said, 'We should let her go man, now. She had enough now. I have sisters, too.' Harden asked me did I live in the neighborhood, and I told him 'yes.' He then said 'We are going to let you go home,' and I said, 'Okay.' Then they brought me out from the alley, only I can't give you the names of who brought me out because it was dark and I had been through a terrible ordeal."

"I move to strike that," said Doherty in a matter of fact voice.

"Yes," said the Court, "that may be stricken and the jury is instructed to disregard the last statement of the witness."

Birdia then continued, although her voice was fading and the jury had difficulty hearing her. It was clear to everyone that she was having trouble again controlling her emotions.

The judge leaned forward, and in a very compassionate voice said, "Mrs. Jackson, can you talk just a little bit louder so that the ladies and gentlemen of the jury can hear you?"

Birdia looked up slowly at the judge, drying her eyes with a handkerchief. "Yes, your Honor, I will try."

"Mrs. Jackson," continued Dillon, "you testified that they picked you up - strike that. How did they pick you up?"

"By my feets and underneath my arms. I was shaking and cold and Harden put his coat around me."

Dillon then asked, "Do you see anybody in the courtroom here today that you saw at that time and place?"

"Fess Wise, James O'Neil, James Harden, Eugene Brown, Errol Meeks, Johnnie Sherrod and Edward Cole."

"Do you see Johnnie Sherrod in this courtroom today?" asked Dillon.

Birdia Jackson rose, without prompting, and took her usual path to the east side of the defense table, placed her hand on the shoulder of Johnnie Sherrod.

"For the record," Dillon continued, "The witness identified the defendant, Johnnie Sherrod." Dillon then looked at Birdia, who was already returning to the witness stand. "What, if anything, occurred after that?"

Birdia sat down. "After we crossed Granada Street, we entered into the basement at 3526 Granada."

"When you say we, whom do you mean?"

"Fess Wise, James O'Neil, James Harden, Errol Meeks, Johnnie Sherrod, Eugene Brown, and Edward Cole."

"After you reached that location, what if anything, happened?"

"Fess Wise said, 'We can't put her down there' and he told the other mens to go back because they was mooching on our bitch. Then they picked me up again, Fess Wise, James Harden and James O'Neil and proceeded between two buildings, across the alley to the rear of 3533 Fillmore. Then they threw me down in the dirt and they had their intercourse all over again."

"Birdia, who had intercourse with you?"

"A man had intercourse with me only I can't tell you who it was because I closed my eyes, scared to death."

"And did anything else unusual occur while you were there at that time and place?"

"Yes," said Birdia. "While Johnnie Sherrod was having his intercourse, Fess Wise tried to take my rings. James Harden said they were mine and that I should keep them. He should let me keep them. They were mine. I put my arms around Johnnie Sherrod's neck and took off my rings and put them in my mouth."

"And was anything else said at that time and place?"

"There was a light coming down the alley and they started yelling, 'You better run, m. . ., f. . . . You get ten years for rape.'"

"Who ran?" asked Dillon.

"All the mens ran before the cops came back to where I was except the one that was having his intercourse and he. . . ."

"Object," broke in Kusak.

"Overruled," snapped the judge.

"Birdia," continued Dillon, "who was having intercourse with you when the police arrived?"

"I don't know who it was." Birdia stopped and looked at Dillon, and then continued, "After the police arrived and all the mens ran, I got up and walked toward the police. When I recognized them I told them: 'It was so many of them and they had sexual intercourse with me!'"

"Now, Birdia, can you tell the Court and jury what you mean by sexual intercourse?"

"Well, I mean they all took their private out and put it in my private. Is that what you mean?"

"What were the names of the police officers that picked you up?"

"Officers Newton and Fogarty, two white officers."

Judge Brussell then rose from the bench. "We will break for the day. Please be back at 10:00 a.m. tomorrow." The defendants were herded out of the courtroom like convicted felons. Fess Wise, who appeared rather frail, lagged behind and one of the officers jabbed him in the back with his closed fist. The defendants were led to the "bull pen" which is nothing more than a room having a concrete floor, surrounded by bars, with an open toilet to one side.

Once the officers locked the gate, the boys began shouting epitaphs – "That whore! That bitch – I'll fix her."

Chapter 7

Cross-examination

The next day the trial continued.
"You may proceed, Mr. Dillon," said the judge.
Mrs. Jackson testified how she drove around in a police car with several officers. She saw James Harden and Errol Meeks standing in front of a pool hall. Later she identified Errol Meeks, James Harden, Johnnie Sherrod and Eugene Brown in a line-up at police head-quarters. Also present were Officers Lill, Lester, Smith, Oreland, Manker and Brady.
"Now, Birdia, all this testimony you have given today occurred in the City of Chicago, County of Cook and State of Illinois, is that right?"
"Yes."
"Birdia, how old are you?"
"I am 31."
Dillon then turned to Doherty, and in a mellifluous voice said, "Your witness, counsel."
Dillon picked up his notes and walked back to the counsel's table next to Toler. He looked at his notes as he sat down, without really seeing them for his only thought was the all absorbing question of how well he had done. He hoped Toler would say something for he didn't feel it was his place to ask.
Toler stared at Doherty, who was slowly rising from his chair. Doherty walked deliberately towards the lectern and dropped some papers on it, and continued walking towards the rear of the courtroom. Then he slowly turned around.
"Mrs. Jackson," he began in a loud voice which could be heard even in the hallway, "you testified that Officers Newton and Fogarty took you to the Fillmore Station, didn't they?"
"Yes."
"And you told your story to the desk clerk, is that right?"
"Yes."
"And were you taken to the hospital by a policeman?"
"No, I was not." Birdia lowered her head as though she was going to weep again.

"Now, while you were at the Fillmore Station was there anyone writing down anything you said?"

"Ah - no." Birdia knew instinctively what Doherty was trying to do and it made her angry.

"And you were taken to Cook County Hospital by your cousin and not a police officer?"

"Yes, that is right."

"At Cook County Hospital you were not treated for any injuries, were you? Yes or no."

"Objection," said Toler.

"Sustained."

Judge Brussell looked at the clock, which indicated that it was 11:15 a.m. "I think we will break until 2:00 o'clock this afternoon. I have a number of other matters which must be attended to. Again I must admonish the jurors not to speak about the case to anyone not even the other jurors."

Quickly the judge rose and left the bench. The jurors were then led out by a woman bailiff who took them to their quarters at the top floor of the building. The defendants were herded out the back door to the lockup. As they left, they tried desperately to wave to their families seated at the rear of the courtroom.

Inside the prison, before entering through the main security gate, each boy was frisked for weapons, including pens and any other metal objects, and gum, cigarettes, etc. One by one they passed through a heavy iron gate which was electronically controlled. The boys were then taken to their respective tiers. Security guards were lined up everywhere carefully surveying each prisoner that passed. Finally each was locked in a cell with two or three other prisoners, who were also awaiting trial. This is where the innocent and the guilty are kept, if they do not have friends or family to make bail.

Chapter 8

Birdia Jackson's Extramarital Affair

At exactly two o'clock p.m., Judge Brussell entered the courtroom and sat down in his chair. He turned to Doherty and indicated he could continue with his cross-examination.

"Mrs. Jackson, you spoke of a lineup. How many people were in that lineup?"

"Seven people."

"Did you identify Sherrod, Meeks, Wise, Harden and Brown at that time?"

"I most certainly did," answered Birdia in an indignant tone.

"Your Honor, I would like to confer with the court for a moment."

"Certainly. We will take a ten minute recess. Come with me, gentlemen." The judge then left the bench and entered his chambers. Once inside, Doherty started talking but the judge stopped him with "Mr. Doherty, please wait for the court reporter." A moment later the reporter entered. Doherty started to walk back and forth, collecting his thoughts. He stopped and stepped towards the judge.

"I would like to make an offer of proof on behalf of the defendants to the effect that if I were permitted to ask certain questions relating to after October 1 and prior to October 7, that Mrs. Jackson made a statement to representatives of the West Side Booster, wherein she said that, and I quote: 'The face' referring to Arthur Head's face 'was badly bruised but the police did not make a move to take him to the hospital. When I told them what had happened to me they did not seem concerned.'

"The report continues, speaking of Birdia Jackson, 'The young woman further reported that the police did not enter their complaint in the book, that in fact nothing had been done when her cousin, Willie McCombs, came by the station an hour later and took her to the hospital.'

"Further, I would like to be permitted to ask this witness whether or not she talked to Moses Turner, a Democratic precinct captain, 24th Ward, who lives at 3422 W. Granada, near where she lived, that this precinct captain talked to the captain of the Fillmore District, on Tuesday, October 4. According to this precinct captain, Turner, the captain promised to look into the matter and determine who the negligent officers were.

"Turner reported that the commanding officer stated that if Mrs. Jackson and her companion were not satisfied with their treatment, they could file an official complaint. That's what I propose to offer by way of proof, your Honor, if I were permitted to ask the questions."

Judge Brussell reflected a moment and said, "Of this witness?"

"Yes. In my cross-examination she said in response to my question, did any police officer at that station tell you that they did not believe you, she said, 'No.' Now she has said to the newspaper reporter that they did not seem concerned. I think there is a foundation here for the question to be asked by virtue of that."

Dillon looked at Toler who nodded to him to respond. "Your Honor, I would like to make a statement for the record, and it is this, that the statement counsel proposes to impeach this witness with is not impeaching and not material to the issue, not germane to the issue and irrelevant, and has nothing to do with the issues in this case."

The judge waited to see if there were any further comments. "Are you ready for my ruling?"

"Surely," responded Doherty.

The judge smoothed his hair as he began to speak. "We have had a discussion out of the presence of the jury with regard to the admissibility or non-admissibility of certain evidence. The Court, taking the offer of proof as stated by counsel, finds that such proof must under the rules of evidence be rejected. Accordingly, the offer of proof is denied."

Without comment, Doherty turned and walked out disappointed, rather than angry. He was not sure where to go now in his cross-examination. He simply had not had time to prepare too extensive a cross-examination and no time to gather evidence which might have been used for purposes of impeachment.

As Judge Brussell resumed court, Doherty quickly glanced at his notes, and then walked to the end of the table, behind the boys and faced the witness. "Mrs. Jackson, on October 11, 1960, do you recall that you appeared before his Honor, Judge Saul Epstein, at 11th and State?"

"I appeared before him but I don't recall the date."

"And on that day you raised your hand," continued Doherty, raising his own hand, "and swore upon oath that you were going to testify and tell the truth in that court?"

"I don't think so," responded Birdia as though she was not sure of the question.

"Well, you remember seeing me there Mrs. Jackson? Do you recall?"

"Well, to be quite frank I don't know whether I remember you or not."

"You don't recall?" asked Doherty, taken somewhat aback by her reply. Recovering, he asked, "Mrs. Jackson, was this question asked of you on that day and did you make this answer: 'Did you know any of these boys before this incident?' and your answer: 'No, I didn't.'"

Toler immediately rose, "Objection, if the Court please."

"Sustained."

In a more emphatic tone that showed suppressed anger, Doherty asked again, "Were you asked this question: 'Who was first in line?' And did you make this answer: 'He wasn't first in line. This night I was frightened in the dark. I don't know who was having intercourse, but they was having it one after another.' Did you recall the question and did you give that answer?"

Birdia squirmed in her chair, showing signs of uncertainty. Finally she answered, "I recall the question."

"Do you recall your answer?" asked Doherty in a penetrating voice.

"I can't say that I do," answered the witness.

Doherty turned and picked up his notes. "Now, was this question asked of you and did you make this answer: 'who is the second person?' Answer: 'I don't know.' Do you recall that question and do you recall giving that answer, Mrs. Jackson?"

"I don't know," snapped Birdia.

"By the way, Mrs. Jackson, on October 7, at

the line-up at 11th and State Street, did you talk to any police officers before you looked at the boys?"

"Yes, I did."

"Who?"

"Beatty, William Brady, Bill Manker, Orelind, Lill and Lester."

"In other words, you talked to all these officers before you viewed the lineup?"

"My answer is yes."

"Thank you." Doherty walked back to counsel's table. He turned and asked, "Did Officer Lill go by you yesterday when we went into chambers and whisper something to you?"

"Whisper something to me?" Birdia was surprised by the question and needed a moment to collect her thoughts.

"Yes, ma'am."

"If he did, I didn't hear it." Doherty walked away from the witness. He knew the witness was lying. She had been lying about a number of things, but this time he was certain the jurors caught it. "Well, did he whisper to you?"

"I wasn't looking at him whether he whispered or not."

"No further questions." Doherty abruptly sat down, catching everyone by surprise.

The judge looked at Kusak who remained seated. "Mr. Kusak, any questions?" Kusak did not respond, apparently not hearing the judge. After a minute that seemed an hour, Doherty nudged Kusak and he looked around as though he did not fully comprehend where he was. His hair was uncombed and his eyes were red.

Kusak slowly rose, staggering forward slightly. A heavy dull odor, like the smell of a bar in the early morning hours, poured forth from him. Kusak's condition was apparent to all. The judge glared at Kusak uncertain as to what he should do. The last thing he wanted was to create a mistrial. To hold Kusak in contempt of court would do just that. Yet to let him proceed might be highly prejudicial to the defendants.

"You are a married lady, are you not?" Kusak asked with obvious histrionics.

Birdia leaned forward slightly. "I didn't hear

that question."

"You are married?" Kusak tried to enunciate each word, but his tongue was thick.

"Sorry. Can't understand him."

Kusak turned slightly red. With a loud impatient voice he asked again, "Are you married?"

"Yes, I am."

"To who?"

Toler rose from his seat, anticipating the line of questioning Kusak was attempting to pursue. "Objection."

"Overruled," said the court.

Birdia now a seasoned witness, immediately answered, "James Jackson."

Kusak then proceeded to ask Jackson about her married life and once again tried to establish she was having an affair with Arthur Head.

Doherty threw down his pencil in disgust. He had spoken to Kusak after his opening argument and asked him to back off this attack on Jackson's affair with Head. It was not strong enough to succeed, not in this day and age. He thought Kusak had agreed, but that was several days ago and by now he had forgotten. Doherty leaned back telling himself that he did not really care what happened.

The boys sat entranced at Kusak's efforts. At last the jury would see this woman for what she was - a slut.

"You made a statement here in front of the court and jury that you were raped. Is that true?" asked Kusak.

Doherty's snapped back as he turned facing Kusak in disbelief. What is he asking, he thought to himself.

"Yes," Birdia replied.

"And how many men raped you?"

Doherty started to jump to his feet, but checked himself. How could Kusak ask such a question? This is the very testimony the State wanted to bring out but couldn't because it is inadmissible. And now Kusak is asking the same question. Doherty looked at Toler who was just as puzzled as Doherty, but he feared some trap that Kusak was leading the witness into.

"Eight or more."

"Did you know them before?"

"I did not."

"And your oath to the ever-living God you cannot say that Meeks is a man who had intercourse with you can you? Answer 'yes' or 'no.'"

Kusak's face was flushed. His voice was tense and emotional.

"I didn't get your question," responded Birdia in a calm, strong voice.

"Did Error Meeks rape you?"

"Yes, Errol Meeks did rape me."

"Did he use any violence?"

Mrs. Jackson hesitated and then asked "Did he use any violence? Is that the question?" When Kusak answered in the affirmative, she said, "Well, if you don't call pulling your hair and punching you in the side – "

"Objection," shouted Doherty.

Toler jumped up. "Let the witness answer the question."

Kusak leaned forward. "I asked the witness a simple question – one she should be able to answer."

"Gentlemen, gentlemen, enough of these comments. The jury is instructed that the comments of counsel and answers of witnesses to which objections are sustained, are, of course, not evidence. Rephrase the question, Mr. Kusak."

"What did Meeks do to you?" asked Kusak.

"He was yanking at my hair and punching me in my side, yelling, 'Roll, bitch, roll.'"

Kusak looked around in bewilderment and asked: "What did he do?"

Doherty rose, "I object to this entire line of questioning."

Toler rose again, "I submit the question has been answered, if the Court please."

Doherty leaned toward Kusak. "Drop it. Drop it, you're killing our case," he whispered.

Kusak faced the witness squarely and in a loud voice that could have been heard in the courtroom across the hall: "Did you have sexual intercourse with Mr. Head?"

Birdia looked up with anger in her eyes. "No," she shouted back.

"Objection," said Dillon.

"Sustained. The jury is instructed to disregard the question and answer."

65

Kusak turned, and said, "That's all," and sat down.

Judge Brussell looked at the large clock on the wall which showed a time of 6:10 p.m. Then he looked at his own watch. Turning to Dillon he asked, "Do you have any redirect, Mr. Dillon?" Dillon responded that he did, about one hour's worth.

Judge Brussell then looked at the jurors. "We will recess until Monday morning at 10:00 a.m." And after completing his litany he left the bench.

Doherty never rose when the judge left the courtroom. He just sat there with his head bent and stared at the pad of paper before him. The jury rose and departed and still he did not move. The heaviness that had pervaded his very being continued to increase in intensity. It was a dull, almost morbid feeling that gnawed at him. He couldn't control it; it was as though someone, something was pulling a black curtain across his mind. Doherty tried to analyze the cause of this distressing condition. It wasn't just losing this case – he was used that. Doherty thought longer. It became clear to him. It was the utter futility of defending these poor bastards, day in and day out. They had no chance as long as lawyers like himself couldn't prepare. They were victims of a system spawned by indifference. That's it, Doherty thought. It's the system that's getting to me, but what can I do? Who am I? I am not a crusader, not with a wife and three children.

Doherty stood up and walked out of the courtroom. Another period of depression had passed – only this attack had been far more serious than any of those previously experienced.

Chapter 9

Examining Physician

When Court resumed at 10:00 on Monday morning, Dillon addressed the court. "Your Honor, I have just a few questions on redirect."

"You may proceed, Mr. Dillon."

Dillon turned to the court reporter. "Will you mark this for identification as People's Exhibit 5?"

The court reporter took what appeared to be a photograph and stamped the back, and initialed it "People's Ex. 5, for identification."

Walking towards the witness, Dillon asked, "I show you People's Exhibit 5 for identification. Will you examine it please?"

Birdia took the photograph and studied it for a moment and then said "Yes."

Doherty rose and said, "Your Honor, this is improper redirect examination."

The judge cut him short, saying, "I have nothing before me yet."

Dillon took the photograph from Birdia, asking, "Does People's Exhibit 5 for identification, truly and correctly and accurately portray Errol Meeks?"

"Yes."

"Does it correctly portray him as you saw him on October 1, 1960, in the City of Chicago?"

"Yes."

"No further questions, your Honor." Dillon sat down and then quickly stood up. "At this time the State would like to offer in evidence People's Exhibit No. 5 for identification into evidence as People's Exhibit 5."

Kusak stood up and said "Objection."

"Overruled," said the judge.

Toler rose from his chair, "The State has no more questions of this witness."

"Neither does the defense," responded Doherty.

"No further questions," added Kusak.

Judge Brussell turned to Birdia. "You may step down. You are excused now."

Birdia rose slowly. Relief was evident as she left the courtroom. It was clear that she had undergone an ordeal, one that she now wished to forget.

"Call you next witness," instructed the judge.

Dillon stood. "Dr. Rahjid."

The jurors leaned forward to see Dr. Rahjid as he entered the courtroom from the rear door. The jurors had rightly assumed that this was an attending physician. Dillon gathered his notes and again walked to the lectern. Dr. Rahjid was directed by the bailiff to the witness stand. The doctor was a young man in his late twenties, with jet black hair. He was dark-complexioned and wore glasses which gave him a studious appearance. Before the doctor sat down he was sworn in by the clerk. Dillon then asked, "Will you state your name, please."

"Mayank Rahjid," he responded in a pronounced foreign accent. It was clear from his appearance and accent that he was East Indian or Pakistani. He spelled his name, without being requested to do so, as though it was requested. Dr. Rahjid spoke loudly and slowly in an effort to make himself understood. He appeared confident. He testified that he was an intern at the Cook County Hospital, had attended undergraduate school at Trinidad University in the Caribbean and medical school on the Island of Grenada.

"How long have you been an intern at Cook County?" asked Dillon.

"Since June 30 of last year."

Dillon looked up from his notes, looked down again and asked, "Now, calling your attention, Doctor, to October 1, 1960, were you an intern at Cook County Hospital?"

"Yes, I was."

"And on that day did you have occasion to examine a woman by the name of Birdia Jackson?"

"I did."

"Now, will you tell the Court and jury what the examination consisted of, and what the findings were?"

Dr. Rahjid took a piece of paper from his pocket and studied it. Doherty began to object for it was error to permit a witness to look at any notes unless it was first determined that the witness needed to refresh his recollection. Doherty changed his mind because the State was going to get this evidence in and an objection would only delay the ultimate outcome.

"Well, the examination consisted of a general physical examination, vaginal examination and microscopic examination of vaginal contents," began the doctor, in his decided accent. He seemed quite self-assured and his monotone voice suggested indifference to the content of the matter about which he was speaking.

"In general the findings were low back pain, no physical injury obvious." The doctor fumbled with his notes and after turning a page, continued, "The microscopic examination, the contents consisted of, oh, I had in my report, I described a semen-like material. Now I would have to describe this as jelly-like, gray material. There was a large quantity of it, I should say. In the microscopic examination there was multiple spermatozoa found without difficulty, and also some black particles which I put in the report, which appeared to be particles of dirt found in the introitus and vaginal walls. No obvious injury to the vagina."

Dillon raised his hand to stop the doctor. "Now, doctor, based on your physical examination, do you have an opinion based upon a reasonable degree of medical knowledge whether or not the conditions that you just described to the jury could have been caused by sexual relations with a male?"

"Objection," said Kusak, "I - "

"Overruled."

"Do you have an opinion, doctor?"

"I have an opinion, yes."

"And what is that opinion, doctor?"

"My opinion is that that these conditions could have been caused by recent sexual intercourse with a male."

Without consulting his notes, Dillon asked, "And what is the basis of that opinion?"

The doctor raised his head slightly, and pushed his glasses up on the ridge of his nose. "The findings within the vagina of spermatozoa and the semen-like material are almost definite evidence of recent sexual intercourse."

"Doctor, could you tell us how such spermatozoa you found?"

"I cannot say the amount I was able to find because this is a microscopic examination and a quantitative amount was not found."

Dillon looked up in surprise. He did not anticipate this answer and realized too late that the question was a poor one and the answer damaging.

Dillon turned around and walked back to his table. "That is all. Your witness, counsel."

Doherty stood up and with pretentious movements walked to the back of the courtroom. "Doctor, are you licensed to practice medicine in Illinois?"

"I am not."

"As a matter of fact, doctor, you are not licensed anywhere in this country, are you?"

"No."

Doherty walked back to the table and picked up a document and walked towards the witness. "Doctor, I hand you a Cook County Hospital medical report and ask whether you prepared this."

Doctor Rahjid looked at the report and responded, "Yes, I prepared the doctor's history sheets and order sheets. The remainder was prepared by clerks in the hospital."

Doherty turned and walked slowly away from the witness, without turning, he asked, "Is it not true that in your findings, you state in this report, quote 'No physical injury obvious.' Is that right?"

Doctor Rahjid hesitated a moment, as though he was examining the report, and then answered, "Yes, I wrote those words in the report."

"No further questions, your Honor."

Doherty was well satisfied with his cross-examination. He felt he had gained as much mileage as possible and had quit at the right time, which is an art in itself. As Kusak began to stand up to begin his cross-examination, Doherty whispered, "Don't ask anything further. We made some points with him."

Kusak ignored the comment and looked at the doctor. After hesitating a moment, he asked, "Doctor, you examined the vagina and you obtained spermatozoa, did you not?"

"That is correct, sir."

"And what amount did you obtain?" continued Kusak.

"I cannot say, sir."

"In other words, you wouldn't know whether

spermatozoa came from one person or more than one, do you?"

"Objection," said Toler.

"Overruled."

Doctor Rahjid looked at the judge who motioned for him to answer. "That would be impossible for me to say, sir."

"I didn't get that answer," said Kusak. It was quite evident that he merely wanted the witness to repeat the answer, which he did.

"Doctor, did you see any bruises when you examined her?"

"No, sir."

"No further questions," Kusak sat down. Doherty looked at him with surprise. His last series of questions had been good and he stopped at the right time.

The judge then adjourned the trial until 2:00 p.m.

Kusak got up and walked into the hallway where he spotted his client's mother and grandmother standing together. "Mrs. Meeks, where is the money you promised? I will not continue unless I have it before the recess ends. You know what I told you."

Chapter 10

Detective Lill's Perjury

At 2:12 p.m. the trial continued. "Call your next witness, please, Mr. Toler."

Officer Lill, a heavy set black detective with a round face, was called to the witness stand. He was a member of the elite society that ruled, bullied and badgered the blacks of the West Side. He owed his status to his ability to obtain convictions. As a plain clothes detective he had two years to prove himself and this was measured only by convictions, not arrests. Failure to succeed meant that he would be returned to patrolman status and his police blues. Great pressure was placed on Lill and his fellow detectives to make certain that criminals, like the eight in front of him, were expeditiously dealt with by the courts. To this end, Lill had befriended Birdia Jackson to assure her presence at the trial, there always being the possibility that a complaining witness would disappear or simply refuse to testify because of threats made by the defendants' friends or mothers.

Officer Lill knew each defendant intimately. He knew their records, their haunts, their friends, their likes and dislikes. In breaking open the case, Lill had applied a proven technique. Find the weakest link, break it, and drag in the entire gang. This then was Lill's hour.

After the witness was sworn in, Toler began the questioning by asking routine questions, qualifying the witness. Officer Lill testified that he had been with the police department's sex unit for a year and a half. Lill spoke clearly and precisely. He seemed composed and confident of himself as he answered the questions asked. As an experienced witness he listened carefully to each question and hesitated a moment before answering to be certain he fully understood the question.

Toler asked, "Did you have occasion to see any of the defendants on October 8?"

"Yes, I did. On October 8, at ten o'clock there was a line-up at the 11th and State Street station."

"Prior to that line-up did you have occasion

to see any of the defendants on the 8th?"

"Yes, I did. I saw Eugene Brown."

"Did you see anybody else?"

Lill's eyes suddenly expressed some uncertainty. His eyes shifted between Toler and Doherty. "Let me think. There are so many of them. If I say – "

"Objection," shouted Doherty and Kusak in unison.

"That last remark may be stricken," said the Court.

Lill looked at the judge. "I am sorry. We had seven men in the line-up."

Doherty was watching the witness intently, for instinctively he knew that Lill was not being candid. His whole demeanor indicated that something was wrong. Doherty had to find the crack, for like a defect in plate glass, if pressed it will shatter into a million pieces.

"In that line-up were Wise, Brown, Sherrod, Meeks and Harden," continued Lill.

Toler asked: "Who also was present in the line-up?"

"In addition to the five I already mentioned there were two other colored men between the ages of eighteen and twenty-five. I don't know their names. Also present was the complaining witness, Birdia Jackson."

"And did she identify the five you already named?" asked Toler.

"Yes."

Toler hesitated momentarily and then asked, "Now prior to ten o'clock on October 8 did you have an occasion to see any of the other defendants?"

"I did. I saw O'Neil, Cole, and Brown."

"Now with reference to O'Neil, Cole and Brown did you have a conversation with those defendants? Will you tell the Court what you said to them and what they said in response?"

Lill straightened up in the chair and continued, "I told Brown to tell O'Neil what had happened to the complainant, Birdia Johnson."

Toler looked up instantly, "Jackson."

"Jackson," said Lill, correcting himself. "On the 1st of October, 1960, Brown told O'Neil – should I use the exact language?"

73

"Yes."

"Brown told O'Neil, he said, 'I screwed her and you were there, too.'"

"And what did O'Neil say, if anything?"

"O'Neil said, 'Yes, I screwed her and you did too.'"

"To whom did he say this?"

"He said this to Cole, and Cole denied it."

At this instant, O'Neil leaped out of his chair. He shouted, "That's a lie." Like a bolt of lightning a hand struck O'Neil on the shoulder and shoved him back into his chair.

Doherty sat there in stunned silence. He could not take his eyes off O'Neil. Then there was almost an explosion in Doherty's brain. That's it, he thought. The pieces fit together.

There was no way in the world O'Neil would admit to raping Birdia Jackson. This kid was tough and arrogant and the police could never intimidate him. Lill had perjured himself when he said O'Neil admitted to raping Jackson when confronted by Brown. And if Lill lied it has to be because Jackson could not identify these boys. Doherty's mind was racing at a fast pace now as he pieced the case together.

As Jackson said at the preliminary hearing, she was frightened and it was dark and she didn't know who was raping her. My God, thought Doherty, it was Lill who got Jackson to finger these boys at the trial - she has memorized their faces and names.

Doherty sat back in his chair. What was he going to do? How could he prove the whole trial was a frame-up? He was convinced of it now.

"May I have a recess of ten minutes, your Honor?"

During the recess, Doherty pulled his thoughts together. First, there was no question the rapes took place and Head was beaten at the car and possibly robbed. However, the police did not take the matter seriously and would not even register Jackson's and Head's complaints at the police station.

Second, Birdia Jackson complained to the newspapers, which ran stories about the rape, which put pressure on the police department, 25th District, to apprehend the criminals. This must have gone to the top because they brought in all the resources of the Sex Bureau to resolve the matter and make arrests.

Third, Lill was the moving force in prosecuting the case. He could not get Head to identify the boys at the car except for Wise and Sherrod. Birdia was the key to getting convictions. She really could not identify the boys because it was dark and she was scared. She so testified at the preliminary hearing, and even during the trial itself. At one point she identified Cole which caught Dillon by surprise as he questioned her. She even identified Wise as being on the right side of the car when Head had identified him on the left side - he couldn't have been in two places at the same time.

Fourth, Lill resorted to the only tactic he could. Break the weakest suspect, Eugene Brown, get him to confess and name the other boys. However, he went too far and testified himself that Brown identified O'Neil who orally confessed. This never happened - O'Neil was too tough. Nothing could frighten him.

Fifth, the reason Lill and his fellow detectives indulged in outright perjury was because of the heat that was generated on the 25th District, probably from Mayor Daley's office itself.

Sixth, Detective Lill was the key.

Doherty faced the witness. How could he break his story, he thought? He felt a sense of urgency - not that which arises from confusion or fear, but that intellectual drive created by the knowledge that something should be done, something extremely important, but Doherty could not think what.

"Was Brown under arrest?" asked Doherty.

"Yes. He had been arrested about an hour and a half prior to this at the Fillmore station. Later we left Fillmore and took him to the House of Correction where these other people were."

"How many hours after arrest did you hold him at Fillmore?"

"One or two hours," said Lill.

"Did you, after you arrested him, take him before a Police Magistrate, a Justice of the Peace or a judge sitting in any court of Cook County?"

"Objection."

"Well, did you have a warrant when you

arrested him?" asked Doherty, raising his voice.

"Sustained."

Doherty's anger was increasing. His Irish was up and he was ready to do battle. "Will this Court glance at Section 660?"

"Mr. Doherty," said the judge firmly, trying to keep his control, "Will you proceed with your questioning?"

"And when you got him in the police station you were asking him questions. Is that right?"

"We did ask him questions."

"And he denied having anything at all to do with this, isn't that correct?"

Lill looked at Toler and then back to Dohety. "No, he did not. Right from the very beginning he said he was implicated in this."

Doherty was floored. He had walked right into that trap by asking the wrong question. Now he was flustered. "As a matter of fact, you beat him, did you not?"

"I did not," said Lill emphatically.

Doherty shot back immediately. "And Lester pushed him up against the wall, did he not?"

"I did not see this. No."

"And Cole was there in the House of Correction, wasn't he?"

"Yes."

"And he denied having anything to do with this, didn't he?"

"Yes, he did deny it."

"How long did you question Brown?"

"Fifteen, twenty, thirty minutes or so," responded Lill.

"Was a written statement taken from him at this time?"

"No. Not at this time."

"Now, when you were questioning him did he have a legal representative present?"

"Objection," shouted Toler, incensed at the question.

"Sustained," said the judge dispassionately.

Without a break in tempo and with a rising crescendo Doherty shouted, "And all this time you and Lester were beating him, weren't you?"

"No, no," responded Lill with his eyes flashing with anxiety. "We didn't touch him except to put handcuffs on him."

"You didn't even allow this nineteen year old boy to call his parents when you booked him, did you?"

"Objection," shouted Toler.

"Sustained," said the judge in a firm voice.

"And you didn't allow him to even call a lawyer, did you?" continued Doherty.

"Objection, your Honor. If you please . . . "

"Sustained," said the judge in a very firm voice.

There was a silence and then Doherty spun around facing the judge. "What are you trying to do?" he shouted. "I have an absolute right to interrogate this witness concerning the manner he treated this witness, to determine whether he protected his constitu-tional rights. I must be heard and I will be heard."

Judge Brussell sat in stunned silence at this outbreak. Once again he had to weigh the possible prejudice which would be created by holding Doherty in contempt of court against permitting him to disrupt the trial. After several moments the judge requested the attorneys to approach the bench. "Mr. Doherty," he said in a whisper which the jury could not hear, "I can't allow another outbreak like this. You may succeed in getting a mistrial, but I promise you, you will end up in jail for thirty days. This case is not worth such a sacrifice. That's all. Continue your cross-examination. You know my ruling to your previous question."

Doherty paused a few moments and then in a quieter voice said, "No further questions."

Kusak then asked a few questions. Toler and Dillon called three more police officers, which affirmed what had already been established.

Toler rose and looking at Doherty said, "Is there a stipulation as to the ages of the defendants?"

"Surely," said Doherty.

Toler then turned to the judge. "Stipulated by the People of the State of Illinois through the State's Attorney's counsel and for the defense that Fess Wise is of the age of seventeen, James Lee Harden is twenty, James O'Neil is seventeen, Eugene Brown is nineteen, Edward Cole is twenty, Sammy

Dillard is seventeen, Sherrod is twenty and Meeks is twenty."

Toler whispered to Dillon and then said, "The people rest in chief, your Honor."

Judge Brussell looked at the clock and said, "This is a good breaking point."

Doherty sat in his chair as the courtroom cleared. Judge Brussell had just announced that the trial would continue the next day at 9:30 a.m.

Suddenly, Doherty looked up. Why hadn't the State tendered the boy's written confessions in their case in chief? The only confessions they submitted were oral statements of Brown and O'Neil. If Brown and Fess Wise had signed written confessions or admissions as Toler stated at the beginning of the trial, they should have been offered.

Doherty pondered this piece of strategy which the State was employing. Is it possible that Toler withheld them in order to crucify my witnesses on cross-examination, or could it be because the statements are not as strong as originally suggested?

The more he thought about it the more disturbed he became because the Court had not ordered these statements turned over to him prior to trial. How can I put any of the defendants on with such uncertainties?

Slowly Doherty recognized the untenable position in which he had been placed. If only two or three testify it would be a sure admission of guilt by those boys who remained silent. And if all testified, those who had confessed would be impeached with their confessions. He was satisfied that he could not offer any defense. He left the courtroom and returned to his office.

At the same time, Kusak was in the hallway confronting Mrs. Meeks. Mrs. Meeks, a slender, light-skinned black woman with intense dark eyes that expressed a lifetime of anger, frustration and disgust, turned around. Anger flashed from her eyes. She quickly opened her purse. "Here is $50.00 and that's the rent money for next week."

"Mrs. Meeks, I told you $150.00 by yesterday or I would withdraw and that means your boy will go to jail for at least twenty years."

Kusak was playing a game he had played many times before. In dealing with "Negros" he knew that if he didn't get his fee before trial he would never get the full amount. His fee was $1000 and so far he had received $200 including the $50 collected today. The most he expected to get was another $50. Once the trial was over, regardless of outcome, he would not receive one penny more.

Mrs. Meeks knew that $1000 was exorbitant for the services of Kusak. She also knew that once the trial commenced, Kusak could not withdraw. Therefore she gave just enough, $200, to get him started, promising the rest in weekly installments, which she never intended to pay. Perhaps another $50 halfway through the trial just to keep Kusak honest. In the end both got just what they bargained for.

Kusak then left for the day.

Chapter 11

Motion For Directed Verdict

"The court will come to order," bellowed Jablonski. Judge Brussell looked at Doherty without speaking as though he expected the latter to take the initiative. The brief silence became pronounced as there was no movement in the courtroom. Finally the judge asked if there were any motions before calling the jury back into the courtroom.

"Yes, your Honor," said Doherty. He rose slowly and walked to the judge's bench with Toler moving beside him. "At this time I would like to move for a directed verdict." Kusak joined in the motion.

The motion was argued and the judge retired to his chambers to consider it.

When the judge returned to the bench, he said "With regard to the motions made by the various defendants, I am overruling each and all of the motions except those made on behalf of Dillard, who has at no time been mentioned during the trial. In his case I will instruct the jury to sign two verdicts, one on the robbery indictment and one on the rape indictment, instructing them to find the defendant Dillard not guilty. Those are my rulings, gentlemen."

Doherty showed little emotion. He had expected this result, having gone through it many times. Kusak did not even hear the judge as he swayed slightly back and forth.

There was a brief pause. Then the judge asked, looking at Doherty, "May I ask this question of defense counsel, and if you want to consider it before you answer that is fine. Do you have any idea how long your case will take in the presentation? The only reason I am asking," continued the judge almost apologetically, "is in regard to the time for the jury and ourselves, both today and the rest of the week."

Judge Brussell stopped. He looked first at Doherty, then Kusak and then back to Doherty. The latter did not move. Finally he looked at Kusak who appeared disinterested and unconcerned.

Doherty said, "Your Honor," he hesitated and

then continued in a thoughtful tone, "the defense rests."

Judge Brussell straightened up quickly – a momentary look of surprise flashing. Quickly he regained his composure. Toler turned to Dillon and smiled.

"And you, Mr. Kusak, do you join with Mr. Doherty?"

"Yes, your Honor," said Kusak with some hesitancy.

"In that case I will call in the jury and dismiss them. I will meet with you gentlemen at 2:00 this afternoon to begin working on jury instructions."

Chapter 12

Closing Arguments

Tuesday afternoon, Judge Brussell, Doherty, Kusak, Toler and Dillon worked on the jury instructions. A considerable amount of arguing and jousting took place, such as normally does at such sessions. This continued to the following morning. At 1:30 in the afternoon Judge Brussell stated for the record the instructions granted and denied on each side. "Call in the defendants, please, and then the jury," instructed the judge.

When all were in place, Judge Brussell turned in his chair, looking directly at the jury. "Good afternoon, ladies and gentlemen. You may resume now, please," gesturing to Doherty.

Doherty hesitated a moment which was perhaps the wrong thing for him to do as the jury's attention was centered on him when he rose.

"May it please your Honor," said Doherty, reading from a slip of paper, "defense rests on behalf of James Harden, Fess Wise, James O'Neil, Johnnie Sherrod, Eugene Brown and Edward Cole."

Kusak immediately rose, "I rest on behalf of the defendant Errol Meeks."

The jury sat expressionless. They had anticipated that a defense would be offered for they had been told in the beginning of the case by defense counsel that evidence would be offered showing conclusively the innocence of the defendants. One or two of the jurors exchanged glances. The jurors then looked at the judge waiting further direction.

Doherty sat down, knowing full well that the jury was reacting negatively to his last statement. He had no choice - he had to take this route - it was not his decision because there was no decision to be made.

Judge Brussell again turned to the jury. "Ladies and gentlemen of the jury, it will now be the privilege or opportunity of the attorneys for the State and the attorneys for the defense to address the jury. The State has what we call the right to open and close the arguments. Mr. Doherty and Mr. Kusak have a right to address you after the

State has completed its opening address."

Dillon rose and addressed the jury. He went through the facts as established by the testimony of witnesses: how Birdia and Arthur had a date and were sitting in Arthur's car waiting for Joe and Emma to return with a jack to fix Arthur's flat tire. He described how Arthur was beaten and Birdia taken down the alley and raped. How she was then taken to another location and raped again. He named the defendants Birdia identified.

Dillon concluded his remarks referring to the police lineup, where Birdia was able to identify Wise, Sherrod, Meeks, Harden, and Brown and the confessions made by Brown and O'Neil, also implicating Cole.

Dillon then turned to the jury, hesitated, and said in a solemn voice, "Why should they try to make Birdia Jackson into something that no one cares about, and therefore we should forget about her and the fact that she was raped? But she is a human being and in no way hurt these defendants.

"Did it have to be Birdia Jackson that night in question or could it have been somebody else? It could have been somebody else's loved one, his wife, his sister, a friend, could be your neighbor. Did it have to be Birdia Jackson or was it she happened to be the one there at that time and place and they struck?"

Dillon walked away from the lectern and in a low voice said, "Ladies and gentlemen of the jury, the defendants in this case are entitled to a fair American trial, but so are the People of the State of Illinois. The People are entitled to a fair trial. The People in this community are entitled to a fair trial, and I am sure, members of the jury, from this testimony you have heard here today you will not let this happen again, by these defendants or anybody else like them in the community, and you will give them a warning. All people in this community are entitled to your protection - all the people here, no matter where they live, on the North side, the South side or anywhere else in this community.

"These defendants are guilty. They are all guilty. They are guilty of the crime of rape and guilty of the crime of robbery." Dillon was shouting now and the jury was listening. He stopped suddenly, and in a quiet voice said, "Thank you very much." Then he slowly turned and walked to his seat. All jurors watched him as he sat down. Toler smiled.

Kusak rose quickly and walked to the lectern. His clothes were disheveled, hair uncombed, but the briskness of his steps showed a certain alertness and aggressiveness which he had demonstrated periodically throughout the trial.

He stood at the lectern a moment and, with a degree of poise, looked at the jurors, the judge and then Toler and Dillon. With a deferential voice, he began, "Your Honor, ladies and gentlemen of the jury, counsel for the State and my associate, I represent a human being who by virtue of this proceeding is subject to losing his liberty. All of us have a function to perform. I speak for him because from the evidence in this case I do not believe that he is guilty."

"Objection, your Honor," said Toler, without looking up.

"Sustained," responded the judge automatically.

Kusak continued as though there had been no interruption.

"I speak for him because I would like to point out to you certain items in the evidence that do not prove his guilt beyond a reasonable doubt as the law requires. There are two charges. One is for rape involving not a girl, not a child, but a fully matured woman, who is legally married and who is a mother of some children. She was in company of a man who was also married, also the father of children at the time the occurrence was alleged to have occurred."

Kusak hesitated a second having become twisted by his own sentence. "We begin with the same idea, as the State's Attorney has suggested to you when he qualified you before you became jurors in this case. He asked you whether or not you would be prejudiced by reason of the fact that the two of them were together, even though they were not married to each other, but each one was married to somebody else, about 2:00 or 3:00 o'clock in the morning, near an alley."

Kusak thought he was waxing eloquently, his

finest moment. The words flowed easily, increasing in intensity where emphasis was needed. "We are not asking you for sympathy. What we are afraid of is prejudice, because prejudice is a much stronger feeling than sympathy. We do represent seven remaining boys, and I am addressing you who resemble my skin, the color of my skin, but we all know what is going on today, that little children born three or four generations ago cannot go to schools, cannot go to universities and cannot exercise their rights as citizens and it is a great issue. It is not only a Caucasian issue but an issue of Mohammedism and Judaism and it is unfair to condemn or suspect anybody simply because the Almighty God created him in a little different color, but still if you consider it, they are the same creations of the same God, if you believe in God, or if you believe in the Divinity, that of the human soul and human heart."

Kusak was suddenly getting confused and he started talking faster. He realized that he had gotten into an argument that was upsetting the jurors but he did not know how to stop. Doherty closed his eyes. Kusak continued: "These defendants are the descendants of people who came from Africa in chains. They didn't come here voluntarily. They were chained and brought here. But there were two great Americans, one was Abraham Lincoln who liberated them and he paid for it with his life. And the other was another great American, Franklin Delano Roosevelt, who had advanced them."

Noticing judge's expression, Kusak hesitated a moment and then changed directions. "About the facts in this case, I say to you with all my sincerity and honestly as I can that this indictment charging Errol Meeks, my client, with the crimes of rape is not supported by the evidence of any kind beyond a reasonable doubt. The court will instruct you according to the law, and I believe the law, that rape is the carnal knowledge of a woman against her will and with force.

How did she testify against my client that he was guilty of any those acts? Robbery is the felonious and unlawful taking away of money and goods from the person of another. You can see the indictments if you wish, but there is nothing in the indictment wherein Mr. Arthur Head is a complaining witness."

"Objection, if the Court please," said Toler hurriedly.

"Sustained," responded the judge instantly.

Kusak turned on the judge. His whole being seemed to be enveloped in emotion. With great firmness he shouted, emphasizing each word, "There is no proof that anyone took a dime from him."

"Objection," shouted Toler, rising quickly and moving toward the judge.

"Sustained," answered the judge with angry firmness.

Kusak took a step towards the judge. "Show me, show me. This is the indictment – "

Judge Brussell turned to the jury. "The jury will be instructed as to the law pertaining to robbery. Proceed Mr. Kusak," said the judge, emphasizing the word "proceed."

"Liberty is a precious thing. Some people have died for it, some have lived for it. People with courage have lived for it and they still do. You would rather die than to be confined behind bars. So much the more when you are not guilty, and it is our contention that they are not guilty, and if you have any doubt about it, it will be a reasonable doubt, because there is no direct proof. There is no proof of any force."

Without looking up Toler said, "Objection. If the court please."

"Overruled."

Kusak said, "No proof of any larceny. There is proof that two people illegally got together, and they got caught."

"Objection," said Toler, rising from his chair.

"Sustained."

Oblivious to the objection, Kusak added, "And they put the blame on somebody else. My client was looked upon and he was viewed by the woman that claimed he raped her."

"Meeks, get up." Meeks looked around, confused, not knowing what to do. He raised his bulk slightly as though responding, but not really rising out of his chair. "And she said that he is not the man. And after three days they arrested him, and those are the facts. Those are the facts and nobody can dispute them. He was not seen running away from either side of the car. Above all, exercise the divinity of your soul, the godliness in you and don't condemn an innocent man."

Kusak sat down slowly. Doherty looked at him, not certain that he had finally finished. Never had he heard such an argument and he had heard many, from the less competent to the incompetent. But this argument fell into a new classification, as yet unnamed. Kusak thought he had done a pretty good job, and as he wiped his forehead with his handkerchief, he felt he had earned his fee several times over.

Doherty rose deliberately from his chair and looked at each juror before beginning. Then in a gracious manner he turned to the judge and the prosecution. "May it please the Court, gentlemen of the defense and prosecution, ladies and gentlemen of the jury. On behalf of the Public Defender's Office I would like to thank each and every one of you for the sacrifices you made in being petit jurors. You have been confined away from your normal pursuits of happiness and while this is a sacrifice, I think that you are all going to look back on this when it is done, when it is over with and you are going to find that this experience is its own reward.

"I think that somewhere in the remarks of His Honor Judge Brussell in the very beginning, he said that if you are in fact selected to serve as jurors in this case you will never in your lifetime perform a more important civic duty. If I remember correctly, those were his words."

Doherty was speaking with a restrained voice. It was compassionate yet firm. "Most of you for the first time in your life hold the liberty and destiny of fellow citizens in your hands. But there is something else that is placed in your hands together with this liberty, and that is the law, the law as it is going to be read to you soon by His Honor Judge Brussell. That law is going to be stated and is going to be handed to you, placed in your hands. One of the basic premises of that law is the presumption of innocence. You know when you were a child in grammar school you learned and you memorized those words. In the United States anyone accused of a crime is presumed innocent until proven guilty beyond all reasonable doubt.

"How many boys are before you? There are six of these boys that I represent. Wise, Harden, O'Neil, Brown, Cole and Sherrod. Now, you have heard the law; the law is sacred. The laws that we live by here began when our ancestors shed their blood in the Revolutionary War and it has remained the way it is because the cream of American youth have shed their blood to preserve our way of life. On Heartbreak Ridge above the 36th Parallel, they died so that we could live as we live here, with dignity for the individual so that these boys here could come before an American tribunal and place their fate, their destiny, in the hands of twelve of their neighbors without any trepidation in their hearts whatsoever. And thank God that it is that way, and thank God too, that there is nothing more powerful in these Untied States than a petit jury."

"Turning to the evidence, in the alley where this woman was raped, if she was raped and mind you, I have no desire to dirty this woman up. I don't quarrel with her, if she was in fact making love with a man that wasn't her husband."

"Objection," shouted Toler.

"Sustained," shot back the judge instantly.

Doherty continued, "I don't quarrel with that at all. We know that they had a flat tire yet she lived only a block away. Oh, God, I should be so lucky that every time I get a flat tire I wind up in a gas station. How preposterous do we get? Doesn't it stultify the human nature to have you believe that they wait for a jack to come when they are less than a block from home? How long would it take you or me to walk a block, no matter how loaded you were? But they say they were just talking, not fornicating. That is an objectionable word. They were there to talk.

"What do you have to begin with? You have Arthur Head who comes here, mind you, and charges robbery, yes, robbery. Arthur Head says he was robbed, and what does he do? He identifies two people. That is all. Two people. Who are they? Well, you know who they are. Twelve memories are better than one.

"He said, 'I tripped over one. I had him down. I had one of them down.' Who was it? Fess Wise.

Keep that in mind because when Birdia comes on, she said somebody ripped my brassiere off. And who was it? Fess Wise. Now, I ask you, how can a man be in two places at once?"

Doherty stopped a moment, looked around and then signaled the bailiff for a drink of water, which was immediately provided.

"The indictments were returned on October 25, 1960. Remember she went to the 25th District Station and told them what happened to her, and lo and behold, they don't even send her to a hospital. Isn't this in the evidence? She had to sit at the police station for an hour and a half. She had to wait for cousin Willie to come and drive her to Cook County Hospital. Why, because they didn't believe her. Later she raised hell with the 25th District so that they had to call in the whole Sex Unit. I am not calling these men dishonest. You can smile all you want, sir." Doherty became slightly irritated when he saw a juror smile. "I am not calling them dishonest. But I am saying this to you that they know the opprobrium attached to the districts, so they put 52 men on the case. Get 'em! Get 'em! Can you hear behind the closed doors down there at 11th and State? I don't give a damn how you get 'em. Get 'em!"

"Objection," said Toler.
"Sustained."

Doherty continued, referring to the preliminary hearing where Jackson was unable to identify who was having intercourse with her. He stated: "Now she said that while back in this alley having intercourse that she sees some boys come through the alley. Now this phenomenon is not explained. How one can see from a supine position while having sexual intercourse down a dark alley, and ascertain that there are people coming down there, but this is the evidence on which they want you to take the liberty away from these boys. They have the temerity to tell you to take the liberty of these boys.

"You told me, and I believed you then and I believe you now. I won't guess anybody into the penitentiary. I won't do it.

"There is one part of the law that I forgot to talk about, and when I sit down I am going to think of ten thousand things I forgot to say, but that is the way it is always, but you know this, you know for a fact, there are no confessions in this case."

"Objection, if the Court, please," said Toler.

"Sustained."

"Do you see any here today?" continued Doherty.

"Objection."

"Sustained, Mr. Doherty," said the judge in a deliberate voice.

"There are no admissions," continued Doherty, to which Toler again objected, only this time Judge Brussell overruled the objection.

"There are no admissions on the part of Harden, Wise and Cole.

"Now, of course, there is always something that you forget to do, like I say. If I had a chance to answer the assistant state's attorney, who gets the last word, I would probably be able to answer him. They are honorable men, decent men and Fred Toler is a decent person. I don't think he would say anything to sandbag us, but if they happen to bring up something that hasn't been covered by Mr. Kusak or myself, then it is up to you people, and twelve minds are better than one no matter whose mind it may be.

"So, you answer them, and apply the Golden Rule lesson to the voice of conscience and write a verdict that squares with your conscience and with Almighty God and we can't ask for anything more than that. That is it. Thank you."

As Doherty turned to sit down, he was drained. He knew, however, that his speech was not good – he had given it too many times. Although he did not want to admit it, this speech could not substitute for the preparation this case totally lacked from the beginning.

Toler rose quickly and walked smartly to the lectern. He was closing in for the kill and all knew it. The only issue was the number of years the defendants would be sentenced. In a quiet professional voice he began, "Your Honor, counsel, ladies and gentlemen of the jury.

"My purpose primarily is not to give you another opening statement. Mr. Dillon covered the subject very well and pointed out the facts of this case, the unrefuted facts, the uncontradicted testimony that came from the witness stand which you are to govern yourselves by in deciding this case, but primarily it is to answer arguments made by defense counsel, as they addressed you also.

"I also wish to thank you for your patience and your consideration, the way you followed this case."

Toler was smooth. He had a good memory which permitted him to walk in front of the jury box without referring to his notes. In a quiet voice he continued: "The theories of the defense in this case appear to be, number one, there was no rape; number two, no rape was proved against these defendants; and number three, wave the flag.

"A fair trial was conducted in this courtroom. Witnesses were produced before you and examined and they were cross-examined. This is the way it has to be done. And then when it is done, justice has to be determined, and that is your function. Our function is to produce the evidence, present it to you and you have to deliberate upon it.

"Ladies and gentlemen, certainly we all appreciate, particularly this jury, one's liberty. No question about it. Liberty that people die for, have fought for, that the courts maintain, is a liberty that is not just there because it is there. It is because it is important.

"These defendants have forfeited their right to live in a free society among
their – "

"Object," said Kusak.
"Sustained."

Toler continued: "The action of these defendants, upon your finding them guilty beyond a reasonable doubt, should put them in the penitentiary. Sure, that takes their liberty away but that is the only way law and order is preserved. When a crime is committed and they are caught and convicted, that is what is done.

"Mr. Head said Fess Wise was one of the individuals that was on his side of the car. They tripped and went down. Birdia Jackson said Fess Wise was on her side of the car.

"Ladies and gentlemen, this may on the surface appear contradictory to that point of time but it also speaks of the truth of these witnesses. It is apparent that both of them are naming the same defendant on both sides of the car, so the simplest thing to do is place somebody else there. They didn't. This is what they honestly thought and certainly you have two identifications of Fess Wise on the scene."

"Objected to as to the defendant Meeks. Never identified him," said Kusak, rising slightly from his chair.

"Thank you, sir. Mr. Kusak, on cross-examination of Birdia Jackson, went into quite a bit of detail as to the identification of Meeks, and what was the complete clincher of Meeks was the goatee one inch long which is shown in People's Exhibit 5, which you have seen."

"Objection. No evidence of any kind," blurted Kusak again.

"Overruled. Proceed, Mr. Toler."

Toler hesitated, and then in an indignant voice stated: "And you heard Birdia Jackson say that Meeks raped her. And you have heard nothing to contradict that.

"On the 8th of October, all the defendants were arrested. This is a fact testified to by police officers, Birdia Jackson and others, that on the 8th of October at 11th and State there was Meeks, there was Fess Wise, there was Harden, there was Sherrod, and there was Brown. Also on the same day, at a different location, the House of Correction, there were the defendants O'Neil and Cole, all on the 8th of October.

"This prior picking up of defendants and releasing all happened prior to that time. There is only one reasonable inference. The police wanted to get them all at one time, and they did it. The Court will instruct you on the law, but if from the evidence you find these defendants guilty of the crime of robbery beyond a reasonable doubt, as the Court will instruct you, you may sign a verdict to that effect, as to each of them that it applies to, and that is all your duty is as to the robbery charge.

"And the indictment charging rape, the evidence proves that each one of these defendants beyond any reasonable doubt, on October 1, raped

Birdia Jackson. In addition to finding that fact it is your duty to set a fit and proper punishment, and in so doing you must realize, as I am sure you do, we are all members of this community, and the whole community looks to the courts to enforce the law.

"The court will instruct you that the penalty for rape is a term of years in the penitentiary, of not less than one year and may extend to life. Now, these defendants are from seventeen to twenty. Keeping that in mind, the State is not asking you to sentence them to 199 years. But the State is asking you to see to it that they are put away and out of society for at least fifty years. This will act as a deterrent to others. It is a fit and proper punishment. Thank you, ladies and gentlemen." Toler turned, walked slowly to his seat and sat down.

Judge Brussell waited until Toler was seated. The jurors then looked at the judge, waiting for his next words. "Ladies and gentlemen of the jury, it is now the Court's responsibility to read to you the instructions pertaining to the law in this case. These instructions will be given to you later on, as they are in writing, but I would like to read them to you now and have you carefully listen and consider them."

The judge then began reading the instructions which had been submitted by the attorneys and which the judge had approved. He explained the crimes of rape and robbery and the elements of each which the State had to prove beyond a reasonable doubt.

After completing the reading of the instructions, Judge Brussell stopped and looked at the attorneys, the defendants and then the jurors. Smiling slightly he said, "Now, ladies and gentlemen of the jury, the Court is going to permit you to grab a bite to eat in the custody of the bailiffs. After that you will return to the jury room and immediately elect a foreman or forelady, after which you will begin deliberations. You will now be handed forms of verdicts that will refer to each defendant individually concerning the crimes charged."

Turning to the bailiff the judge said, "You may now take the jurors out." The jurors rose and exited the courtroom to the jury room. The defendants sat in silence, watching them leave, knowing that their fate had been placed in the hands of twelve citizens.

Doherty sat motionless – emotionally drained as always after a trial. At first he didn't care which way the verdicts went for he was just glad to have a bad case end. Looking at Fess Wise and then Eugene Brown, he thought: "The slobs. They still think they are going to win." He could look no more, so he turned to the windows so he wouldn't have to watch them walk out.

Kusak rose and then turned to the judge who was gathering his notes. "We object to all the instructions given by the State and the defense instructions denied by the Court."

"Your objection is noted, Mr. Kusak. The Court will be adjourned until 7:30 this evening." Judge Brussell then walked out.

Toler started to walk over to Doherty with his hand outstretched, but Doherty turned and quickly exited the courtroom going directly to his office. He was beginning to feel ill and needed a stiff drink to bring him back. The smell of another defeat nauseated him.

Chapter 13

The Verdict

At 7:30 that evening all were in their places, except the jurors. Judge Brussell asked the bailiff if the jury had reached a verdict and the latter responded in the affirmative. He then asked the bailiff to call in the jury.

Slowly the twelve entered the courtroom. They were unusually solemn and quiet as they took their seats. Judge Brussell turned to them and asked: "Have you reached a verdict?"

The foreman rose and said, "Yes, we have your Honor."

"Please hand the verdicts to the bailiff, and he will give them to the clerk." The clerk stood up as they were handed to him, and then turned to the judge, who directed the clerk to read them.

Through the entire process, the seven remaining boys sat motionless, hardly able to breathe. Sammy Dillard had already been separated from the other boys because of the directed verdict in his favor. With great intensity the seven watched the clerk open the first verdict.

"We, the jury, find the defendant, James O'Neil, guilty of rape in the manner and form as charged in the indictment, and fix his punishment at imprisonment in the penitentiary for the term of twenty years. And we further find from the evidence that said defendant, James O'Neil, is now about the age of seventeen years."

As the clerk read, O'Neil buried his face in his hands. Doherty stared in stunned disbelief. "Twenty years, twenty years - Good God! They are only teenagers," he mumbled. Doherty wanted to leave that instant. This was far worse than he had anticipated. Kusak, on the other hand, sat impassively as Meeks was likewise found guilty on both charges and given the same sentence.

The clerk continued reading the verdicts, first finding each boy guilty of robbery and then rape with a sentence of twenty years for each defendant. Fess Wise broke down and cried. Several of the mothers in the rear of the courtroom began to weep, and one shouted: "Oh, God in heaven, it cannot be."

The judge turned to the jurors: "Ladies and gentlemen of the jury, you have performed your duty. We are indebted to you for your service, your conscientious attention, and your devotion to your oaths of office. As I said in the opening remarks, your service as jurors is a service which is of the highest character insofar as our whole system of government is concerned. I say that as the presiding Judge, that you have served under circumstances which were difficult, and yet you have indicated a devotion to duty and responsibility which will be a shining example for others coming after you. I want to thank you, each and every one of you, and wish you well and say that we have all participated in a sacred duty of our citizenship. Thank you very much."

As soon as the jury retired Doherty rose. "Motion for a new trial on behalf of Harden, Sherrod, Cole, O'Neil, Wise and Brown."

"Motion for a new trial on behalf of Meeks," chimed in Kusak.

"Anything else, gentlemen?" inquired Judge Brussell. Hearing no response, he responded, "Denied." With the sound of his gavel, the trial was at an end. All left.

Bailiff Jablonski turned out the lights of the empty courtroom.

BOOK II
THE INVESTIGATION

Chapter 1

A Young Lawyer's First Case

Attorney Richard M. Calkins, fourth from the bottom on the letterhead of the Chicago La Salle Street law firm of Chadwell, Keck, Kayser, Ruggles & McLaren, picked up an envelope mailed from the Clerk of the Illinois Supreme Court. Opening the envelope he pulled out a one page letter, which read:

State of Illinois
Office of
Clerk of the Supreme Court

Mrs. Earle Benjamin Searcy, Clerk
May 29, 1963

In re: People State of Illinois v.
James Lee Harden (Impleaded)
No. 37647

Dear Mr. Calkins:

The Supreme Court today appointed you as counsel to represent plaintiff in error in the above entitled cause. Although your abstract and brief would ordinarily be due thirty days after the record was filed, by order, the Supreme Court has extended the time for filing your abstract and brief until on or before July 23, 1963. Should you find that you will be unable to prepare and file the abstract and brief on or before the due date, we suggest you contact a justice of this Court before such date and obtain an order for an extension of time.
Enclosed under separate cover is a copy of the trial transcript of the above entitled cause. Please acknowledge receipt of the above mentioned motion and transcript

by signing and returning the copy of this letter, which is enclosed.

Very truly yours,

s/Mrs. Earle Benjamin
Clerk of the Supreme Court

Dick put the letter down, and then picked it up and read it a second time as though he had missed something the first time. It still read the same. The receipt of the letter could not have been more unexpected than if it had been a "Greetings" letter from Uncle Sam. Yet, like the latter, its salutation is one of the facts of life every young lawyer in Illinois could anticipate with the hope it would not arrive at the very moment it always does.

"Margaret, is there a package in your office with a transcript in it?" he shouted in a professional voice.

"Yes, Mr. Calkins, it just arrived. I'll bring it right in."

Attorney Dick Calkins sat in silence. He did not know how to react to his court appointment for he had neither the experience nor inclination to help some defendant attempt to escape his just fate for the crime he had committed. Calkins was no crusader nor liberal intellect who could find intellectual stimulus in helping a guilty man go free. Yet, here was the chance to conduct his own case and go to court for the very first time.

His secretary, a frail middle-aged woman, entered his small office and laid a large bound transcript on his desk. Dick stared at it for a moment and then whirled around in his swivel chair and looked out his solitary window to the broad expanse of the twenty-second floor window of the Harris Trust and Savings Bank Building across the alley from him.

Lost in thought for a few minutes, he finally sighed and resolved to get the job done as quickly and efficiently as he could. He had been told by others in the office that all you had to do was write a thirty page brief and argue for twenty minutes before the Illinois Supreme Court in

Springfield, Illinois. The quality of the work was unimportant, so long as you went through the motions to complete your servitude to the State as gracefully as possible. Every young lawyer had to handle such a pro bono case at least once, so perhaps this was as good a case as any to get it over with.

Dick swung his chair back facing his desk, propped his feet up on the desk, and began skimming through the transcript which was a verbatim record of what had occurred at the trial. After reading it for a few minutes he became rather interested for he had never read a real criminal trial transcript before. As a matter of fact he had never seen a trial before, criminal or civil, for his two short years in the practice had been spent primarily in the law library working on motions for the firm's large corporate clients.

As he worked his way through Arthur Head's testimony he began to feel a certain sense of excitement for at last he had his own case which would take him to court. The further he read, however, the more he realized how little he knew about criminal law, and he questioned whether he would be competent to represent a convicted person on his appeal before the Illinois Supreme Court. Yet, he was willing to try. After all this was an opportunity to learn a great deal and get some real courtroom experience.

Dick put the transcript down on his desk having second thoughts about the project. It would take a lot of work if he was going to do a good job. Then he caught himself for he realized he was questioning his own competency to handle such a case. Of course he could to it and if he had any questions there were any number of lawyers he could turn to for help.

After a quick survey of the older lawyers in the office, Dick learned that the normal procedure in preparing a brief of this type, was to examine the trial record carefully for possible reversible errors committed at the trial. Normally, this was just an intellectual exercise, for about ninety to ninety-five percent of the convictions were affirmed on appeal. Yet, he had to find some error in order to show good faith.

Dick was able to spend only a little time reading the transcript the rest of the day. At day's end he placed the large transcript in an oversized brief case and began his evening walk north along Michigan Avenue to Lake Shore Drive until he reached 1550 North Lake Shore Drive. As he entered the revolving door to the large apartment building, the doorman, George Sayre, a part-time evangelist with the best of intentions, greeted him with his usual warm smile, and drawled "Good evening, Mr. Calkins. Looks like you have a little homework there."

"Hello, George. Have a new case I have to work on," responded Dick, pleased that he had been given the opportunity to mention his new lawsuit. "Any mail, Henry?" turning to the young frail-looking clerk at the desk.

"Mrs. Calkins already picked it up. Can I help you with that load?"

"No thank you. I'll make it."

The apartment building, 1550 Lake Shore Drive, not only had an impressive address but it was a magnificent structure, immediately adjacent to Lincoln Park, jutting some fifty stories into the sky. As one proceeded south along Chicago's famous Lake Shore Drive the "1550 Building" was easily identifiable with its flat roof that looks like a helicopter landing pad and its blue textured stone. The lobby was expensively decorated with tasteful paintings and pieces of sculpture, a large gold chandelier hanging from the ceiling and candelabras scattered throughout. Dick turned and headed for the elevator. He could have walked up to his second floor apartment, but it was fun rubbing elbows with the rich. He got on the elevator and a half second later got off and started walking down the corridor to Apartment 2-D the only apartment in the building which really faced nowhere. All the apartments on the north side of the building overlooked the park and Lake Michigan; on the west side, the park; and on the south side, except for Dick's apartment, the lake. From Dick's apartment one could only see the garage roof and the large apartment building next door. It was for this reason that the rent was only $190 per month, which was as much as he could afford when he first moved in as a bachelor a year before.

Now that his young bride was with him the

addition of her teaching salary easily facilitated their keeping the apartment and enjoying a couple of years of gracious living until they had a family.

Dick knocked on the door and Anita opened it, and with a bride's enthusiasm threw her arms around his neck and planted a big kiss on his lips, almost knocking his briefcase from his hands.

"Oh, I see you have some work to do tonight, again," said Anita, feigning disappointment. Her husband of two months had already impressed upon her the need to work long hours to succeed in a Chicago law firm.

With a slight air of importance, Dick responded, "I was appointed by the Supreme Court to represent a Negro who was convicted of rape, and I need to review the transcript of the trial."

"Oh honey, that's wonderful. You mean they specially picked you to represent this man?"

"Not exactly, Anita. Every attorney receives such an appointment sooner or later and this happened to be my time."

Anita took the transcript out of the briefcase and put it on a table. "Well, I know you will do a good job on it anyway."

The apartment had a living room, a bedroom, a kitchen and bathroom. The furniture in the living room was all second hand, but it looked neat and was in good condition. The bedroom furniture was new and was a wedding gift from Dick's parents.

Dinner was not yet ready, so attorney Calkins sat down and began perusing the transcript for the "legal argument" he could make to the Supreme Court. After reading only a short while he noticed for the first time that James Harden and the other defendants were, at the time of their convictions, only "teenagers", ranging in age from seventeen to twenty years. Dick thought for a moment. Twenty years in the State penitentiary is a pretty stiff penalty for a teenage boy. However, this was not a legal argument, for the jury had the power to give them life imprisonment. But it did add the first element of interest to the case, however slight.

After reading awhile, Dick put the transcript down. "Anita, let me ask you a question. If you were on a jury and confessions were made by two of eight defendants charged with rape and the judge told you to consider those confessions against only the defendants who made them, could you do that?"

Anita stuck her head out of the kitchen and looked into the living room where her husband was sitting in his favorite arm chair. "I don't understand your question. You mean, if two of eight boys confessed to a crime, would that influence me in determining whether the others were guilty? That's a hard question to answer."

Dick got up and walked to the kitchen doorway. "Well, if you knew they were all from the same gang, or at least the State gave you that impression, could you still treat them individually?"

"Just a minute, honey, my hands are wet." Anita disappeared for a second and then emerged from the kitchen. "I would certainly try to treat them individually if the judge asked me to, but I think it would be difficult."

A look of enthusiasm spread over Dick's face. "That's the point I am making. It seems to me that if eight defendants are tried together and seven are represented by the same Public Defender, they are receiving no more than gang representation. They are being tried and convicted as members of a gang. Anything any one of them states will be held against all of them. Maybe this is the legal argument I could make."

"Oh, honey. You're so intelligent. I certainly am glad I married you. You ought to tell your theory to Jack when he arrives in a few minutes. I think he will be impressed."

"Jack? Jack who? Are we having guests for dinner?"

"Oh, yes. Did you forget? Maxine's husband is here in Chicago on business and called Monday night. I invited him to dinner."

The dinner invitation to Anita's ex-college roommate's husband whom Calkins had never met, perhaps best epitomized one of the basic differences between a "Yankee" and a "Southerner." Anita was born and raised in Shreveport, Louisiana and came to Wilmette, Illinois to teach. When she came north, she brought not only her charming southern accent but her southern hospitality. As a result, Dick at any time could expect to find at the dinner table a southerner passing through town, no matter how remote an acquaintance he or she might be, particularly if they were from Louisiana or Texas.

Dick, on the other hand, being a true Yankee, begrudgingly gave of his evenings, particularly during the week. He reluctantly invited only the best of friends, and when traveling never imposed on acquaintances for he preferred to read a good book in his hotel room to spending the evening in idle conversation.

After the annoyance of losing an evening had worn off, Dick mused over the realities of marrying southern charm. Here was a young lady who was born and raised in the south, attended Louisiana Tech University, 70 miles from Shreveport, and thoroughly shocked her family when she announced she was moving north to the land of sin, alcohol and Yankees. Her first trek north was financed by a Women's Christian Temperance Union scholarship, which was awarded to young Southern Baptist women by the national headquarters in Evanston, Illinois for a summer of study in Chicago. Her courses consisted of watching fish swim in a bowl of water, and die when placed in a bowl filled with alcohol, thereby demonstrating the dire effects of drinking. Her class outing was a visit to Skid Row on West Madison Street in Chicago on a hot summer afternoon, where she saw things she never knew existed. Like most of the young southern girls in her class she became nauseated and thoroughly frightened of the evils she found in the north. Yet the following fall she moved north permanently to begin her teaching career in the Wilmette school system.

Her commitment to move north also meant that she had to accept Yankee customs such as joining a ski club and traveling eight hours to the Michigan ski slopes each weekend, if she was going to meet eligible young men; and oh, how she hated the cold, but no sacrifice was too great. It was on one such ski trip that she met Dick, an avid skier, who was charmed by her Southern accent and love of the snow and winter sport.

The next day Dick wrote James Harden and informed him of his appointment by the Supreme Court. He asked him to relate some of the circumstances surrounding the "incident" in question, whether he got along with the Public

Defender, Mr. Doherty.

On June 26, 1963, Dick received a letter from his new client, and was quite surprised at how well written it was. He wondered if Harden had written it, or whether it had been prepared by a "jailhouse" lawyer for him. It read:

"Dear Mr. Calkins,

This to acknowledge receipt of your letter, and I am happy to have you as my attorney. I will send my Bill of Exceptions and common law record as soon as I can get them cleared through the prison officials.

Here are the answers to your questions. No, there was no attempt to make me confess, and no difficul-ties existed between me and my attorney, although I do believe my counsel could have represented me better, if he hadn't been burdened with six other defendants.

I had a Public Defender, his name was Mr. James Doherty, his efforts in my behalf were earnest and tireless, but as I mentioned previously, Mr. Doherty also represented six other co-defendants, and so sometimes a point that could be brought out that would be to my advantage would have to be suppressed because it might be detrimental to one of the other defendants that was also a client of Mr. Doherty, for instance, there were two statements made by two of my co-defendants, Eugene Brown and Fess Wise, exonerating me in both crimes. Those statements were never brought into the trial because Mr. Doherty's strategy was if he could confine the case to cross-examining the complain-ing witnesses with satisfactory results, he would not have to put any of his clients on the witness stand. And as long as the defendants did not testify the statements could not be used against any of them.

Now, if my counsel hadn't been defending six other co-defendants he could have questioned Wise and Brown about the statements rather than suppressing them.

The only evidence that was offered against me was the testimony of the complaining witness in the indictment No. 60-3345 (rape). And though no testimony or evidence was offered against me in indictment No. 60-3346 (robbery), I was still found guilty.

Trusting I have supplied sufficient information to help you start processing of my case. Thanking you for your efforts on my behalf and hoping to hear from you in the near future.

Sincerely yours,

James Lee Harden"

After reading the letter, Dick decided to contact the Public Defender, James Doherty, and see if he could get some ideas as to how he should approach this appeal. He tried several times during the day to reach him, but his calls were never returned. Finally, one week later he was able to get Doherty on the phone and make an appointment at the Public Defender's office.

At eleven o'clock, Tuesday morning, he took the Jackson Park CTA train to California Avenue, where he transferred to a bus which took him to 26th and California. This was a trip he was to make many times in the future. At eleven forty-five he arrived at the Criminal Court Building, and Dick was duly impressed with the large square edifice with the large Doric pillars in front. As he walked up the steps he was thrilled with the thought that the great Clarence Darrow had walked up these same steps only a few decades before. Entering the lobby he inquired at the desk the location of the Public Defender's Office, which was on the third floor.

Entering the large steel-caged elevator, he was engulfed with cigar smoke, which obliterated the "No Smoking" sign hanging in the elevator. On the third floor he exited and proceeded north down the corridor until he came to a door which had a small sign above it which read, "Public Defender's Office." He opened the door and walked down a narrow corridor about fifty feet until he came to a receptionist.

"May I help you, please?"

"Yes, I have an appointment to see Mr. Doherty, please."

The receptionist noted the visit in a book and shouted in the direction of the hallway - "Jim Doherty, a visitor is here to see you."

A few seconds later a man in his mid-thirties emerged. He was heavy set, had sandy colored hair and mustache. His complexion was very fair and looked the Irishman he was. "Calkins, what can I do for you? I don't have much time so let's get down to business. Come into my office."

Dick was directed to a small nine by twelve room which was used by three lawyers. There were three desks and two tables piled high with books and records. "Grab that desk chair and sit down. Now, what case are you interested in?"

"People v. Harden."

"I don't recall that case. Let me get the file and take a look." Doherty went to a file cabinet standing in the hallway and took out a file. He glanced at it as he walked back to his chair. "Oh, yes. James Harden. There were eight boys involved in that case. They were all guiltier than hell. Judge Brussell was the judge - a good judge, too. Now, how can I help you?"

Dick hesitated a second and then replied, "I was hoping that perhaps you would help me get started on this appeal. Give me some ideas of what to do."

"Well, frankly, Calkins, this is a pretty hard case to appeal, but I don't want to discourage you. One thing I would do, however, and that is go down and see your boy. It will mean a lot to him, and even if you can't get him out it will help him to know that someone cares enough to visit him. Those poor devils, no one cares about them and they sometimes go for years without having a visitor. Look here. It's time for lunch. How about joining me?"

Dick promptly accepted the invitation and the two went to the parking lot where Doherty's car was parked. "How about Ding Ho's in China Town - I like Chinese food and this is one of my favorite spots."

"Fine with me, Jim."

Once seated in Ding Ho's, Dick asked the

question, "Doesn't twenty years seem like a rather stiff sentence for teenagers"

"My friend, twenty years seems particularly long if you are the one serving the time. But these boys belonged to a teenage gang which had been molesting people in that area and the jury let them have it. However, I agree that twenty years is a healthy sentence. Normally, they give these kids about five years for rape. The thing that makes it so damn bad is that these kids are thrown in with hardened criminals. By the time they get out of prison they are really lost souls and normally wind up right back in prison within six months. No, I agree. It's a hell of a note when they send youngsters like these to the state penitentiary."

There was a moment of silence. Dick asked for the tea and filled his cup. Then he picked up his tiny Chinese cup, blew across its surface to cool it and took a sip. It was still quite hot so he set it down. "Jim, let me ask you a question. Why didn't you let Harden testify?"

Doherty looked up. Although it was rather dark in the restaurant, his face became visibly red. "Look, my friend," and the way he emphasized the words "my friend" indicated he was not pleased with the question. "I had a decision to make and I did what I thought was best for all the boys, including your client."

"Jim, please believe me. I am not criticizing what you did. I am only trying to understand what happened and why." There was another pause and then seeing that Doherty had calmed down a little, Dick continued. "Do you think one lawyer, even yourself, could represent so many boys at the same trial?"

Immediately Doherty flared up again, showing his Irish temper and making it most apparent that he did not want anyone - but no one, to pass judgment on his work.

"Calkins, I am going to give you some of the facts of life. Day in and day out these niggers come trooping into our office and we have to defend them. Last year we represented over 2,000 of them, and we have only fourteen lawyers and three investigators. You figure out how much time we have to spend on each case. When I am assigned to represent a gang of seven boys, I don't have time to ask for separate trials and the office does not have enough lawyers to give each of them an attorney. They are lucky the State is giving them any legal assistance at all. Here's what it comes down to. I talk to these boys and I have to decide in my own way whether I think they are innocent or guilty. If I think they are innocent, I will call for additional help and send out one of our investigators to look for evidence. If I think they are guilty, then I am simply not going to burden my office with running down the bunch of lies they spout out. And in this case those boys were guilty, guilty as sin."

Doherty stopped talking, but his irritation did not subside. It was obvious that the whole question of legal representation for the indigent bothered him immensely, so Dick decided to drop the subject. Doherty then broke the silence.

"One thing you are going to learn. These boys can lie like you have never seen before. They will look you in the face and you will swear they are telling you the truth, but they are lying. I am just warning you in case you do visit Harden. Remember, ninety-five percent of these boys are guilty. Our office only hopes that it can spot and help that five percent."

When lunch was over Doherty got up and Dick followed. They paid the cashier and stepped out on to the sidewalk. Doherty smiled and said, "Look, kid, I hope you don't take me too seriously. Certain things get me a little warm under the collar; it's nothing personal. If I can help you in any way, let me know. There's the station to the Loop."

"Thanks, Jim. I appreciate the time you spent with me. I'll keep you posted on how things work out." They shook hands.

Chapter 2

Visiting Pontiac Prison

The day was bright and sunny, and fairly warm for a June day. Traffic was light this Friday morning so Dick and Anita were able to make good time heading south on the Tri-State. They took the exit which merged into Route 66. After pulling away from the last toll station Dick remarked with obvious indignation, "That's forty-five cents and two toll stations to go about five miles. No wonder people avoid using the Tri-State. I'll be glad when the Southwest Freeway opens."

Anita said nothing and continued looking out the window, obviously enjoying the scenery. Finally she spoke in a reflective voice: "You know, we have a lot to be grateful for and somehow when I take a short trip like this and break away from the confines of a daily routine I appreciate all the things we have even more. I feel sorry for people less fortunate than ourselves, particularly the Negro here in the north, for I am sure that most of them will never know the feeling of contentment I feel right now."

Then she sat quietly and said nothing more, obviously absorbed in her thoughts. Dick continued to drive along the expressway to the prison at Pontiac, Illinois. On both sides of the highway, they passed mile after mile of the richest farmland in the world. Here and there the beautiful landscape was marred by a dirt pile many hundreds of feet high, the vestiges of an exhausted coal mine. This, however, was nothing compared to the vast wasteland left by the strip coal mining operations further south.

The hundred mile trip seemed short. Dick pulled off the expressway on to a side road which took them through the small town of Pontiac to the foot of the prison. The prison loomed in front of them, a fortress of concrete and steel bars. Dick parked the car and the two walked to the gate house. The grounds were perfectly groomed with flower beds exploding with their June harvest. It was a privilege for an inmate to be selected by the guards to serve on the ground keeping crew because it permitted those selected an opportunity to go outside the prison walls on occasion.

Entering the gate house, the first one either had ever seen, Dick and Anita hesitated a moment, looking around. The reception room was not very large, about twenty-five feet long and twenty feet wide. A guard sat behind a desk facing the visitors' entrance. Immediately to his right there was a small room and to the right of that a steel barred door which was electronically controlled, which permitted entry into the prison yard.

"All right, buddy, what do you want?" the guard bellowed at Dick. "Don't just stand there. You're blocking traffic." The guard was rather heavy set, with a "beer belly," and like the other guards, wore brown trousers, shirt and tie with a small identification tag over his pocket. His expression was glum and he appeared irritated.

Dick was somewhat taken back at this reception. He looked around but no one was following. He approached the surly guard and rather hesitantly stated that he wanted to visit a prisoner he was representing.

"Sign right there," said the guard in a somewhat officious manner, after looking at Dick's I.D. "Then go into that little room." Dick signed the book, listed Harden's name and prison number and entered the small room where a second guard asked him to empty his pockets. Then, as though he questioned whether Dick had complied with his instructions, he frisked him. Finding nothing, he said "Are you carrying any gum or ball point pens?"

Dick answered in the negative and the guard put the contents of his pockets into a paper bag and put the prison number of Harden on it. He was also given a slip of paper with Harden's name and number on it.

"Okay. You can go in," said the first guard in a gruff voice. Dick smiled at Anita as he stood there waiting for the steel door to open. There was a buzzing sound of the door unlocking and Dick stepped quickly through. Leaving the gate house and walking towards the administration building, Dick was most surprised at the immaculate condition of the lawn and gardens.

Dick hesitated a second and looked at the

administration building he was approaching. The building was ancient and looked like a medieval fortress, probably built sometime in the late 1800's. It had spiraling turrets rising into the sky. It's façade was a newly painted red which made it stand out even more. To the right of the administration building was a large concrete cell house, some seven or eight stories high, which housed a portion of the inmates. The walls of the cell house were made of solid concrete with window slots near the top only.

    Dick walked up the steps of the administration building. He had to wait a minute before another steel door opened. Finally a guard opened it manually but not until the steel door at the other end of the room, which opened into the prison proper, was closed. On gaining entrance he was given a metal plate with a number on it and instructed to wait in the receiving room until the number shown on the plate was called. Dick, in turn, gave the guard the slip of paper with Harden's name and prison number, which he had received at the guard house.

    As Dick entered the reception room, he noted that the room was about half filled, mostly with Negro mothers waiting to see their boys. Dick sat down on one of the steel chairs (which were set out in rows) and started to read an article. Approximately forty-five minutes later number 28 was called and Dick got up and walked towards the guard he met on his way in. "This way, buddy," motioned the guard pointing toward another steel door. Dick walked past a prisoner-run concession stand where candy and gum were sold. The prisoner standing behind the stand had a docile almost complacent expression on his face, but then so did all the prisoners on this side of the steel door. Working on this side was for the privileged.

    "Go right through there," said the guard, pointing to a steel door which was opening. As Dick walked through, the door clanged shut behind him. The room he entered was fairly large with two long tables spanning the length of the room. Chairs were set on either side of the tables with a glass partition about shoulder high running down the middle to separate the inmates from their visitors. The inmates entered through a door at the rear of the room, which permitted them to sit in chairs on the inside of the tables. A guard sat at an elevated desk where the prisoners entered.

At the time Dick entered the room six prisoners were talking to visitors. Standing next to the guard at the elevated desk was a slender black man, approximately twenty-two years of age. He was light skinned and stood there with a rather passive almost blank expression on his face. "Sit over there," said the guard pointing to empty chairs half way down the table.

As they moved towards the chairs, Dick said "James, my name is Mr. Calkins, and I have been appointed to represent you." James said nothing as they sat down.

Dick felt a certain awkwardness. How do you begin a conversation with a young man who has been in prison for several years? Ask him how things are going - or about the weather?

"Well, James, at last we meet. I have been anxious to talk to you, to learn a little about you and the case. First, tell me how they are treating you here."

James looked up. There was moisture in his eyes. In a soft, almost inaudible voice he replied, "Fine, Mr. Calkins," and then he hesitated. A silence followed as Dick expected him to continue, but he didn't.

Dick then said: "James, I need to know all about the case. First of all, did you rape this woman?"

Harden's eyes dropped. It was clear from his demeanor that he was having difficulty communicating because he was deeply touched by the visit. James raised his hand to his eyes and rubbed them violently and slowly looked up. After a moment, like a victim struggling to reach the water's surface for a breath of air, he took two quick gulps. Then looking directly into Dick's eyes, he said in a barely audible voice, "Mr. Calkins, I did not commit that rape. I was home in bed at the time. Please believe me." As he spoke, his eyes filled with tears but there was no other sign of emotion.

Dick was surprised, not because he didn't expect this answer but because it was so convincingly given. Jim Doherty's admonition notwithstanding, there was something in the way James gave his answer that made it credible. Of course, Dick wanted to believe him, for what greater cause could there be for a young lawyer at the dawn of his career than to free an innocent man from prison. "Are you sure you weren't there, perhaps just in the background while the rape took place?" Dick asked in a low deliberate voice.

James looked down while small beads of perspiration broke out on his forehead. "I did not even know about it until the next day when I heard some boys talking. I went to bed that night at 11:15 and was nowhere near that alley at the time."

"How do you know it was 11:15 that you went to bed?" Dick snapped back as though he didn't believe Harden.

Without any hesitation James replied, "I had been instructed by a doctor to be in bed at 12:00 until my stomach healed."

The blood seemed to rush to Dick's face and he shot back, "A doctor told you to do what?"

"My stomach was healing and I needed lots of rest, and the doctor told me I had to be in bed before midnight every night."

Dick was now looking at James with great intensity, trying to detect the slightest flicker of his eyes or a sideward glance which might indicate that he was lying, signs that Doherty told him to look for when questioning a defendant.

"What ever happened to you?" The urgency of Dick's voice startled James slightly and he straightened up. Dick caught himself, realizing his zealousness was getting the better of him. He, too, straightened up and looked around, trying to smile. "What I mean is how is it you were under the care of a doctor?"

"About five weeks before I was arrested, I was stabbed in the stomach."

Dick leaned forward again, speaking with great intensity. "James, please tell me everything that happened. Who stabbed you?"

"A group of teenagers tried to rob me and they stabbed me with a knife in the stomach when I started to run."

"Well, how badly were you hurt?"

"Pretty bad, I guess."

Dick realized his questions were not getting the answers he wanted, so he tried again. "Were you taken to the hospital?"

"Yes."

"Which one?"

"Mount Sinai Hospital."

"What did they do to you there?"

James thought a minute. "Well, I guess they operated."

"How long were you in the hospital?"

"They let me go after one week, but I had to go home to bed for another week and a half."

Dick hesitated, and then with obvious excitement asked, "How were you physically at the time of the rape?"

"Mr. Calkins, I was still very weak and could not stay up very long because I got such pains in my stomach."

Dick took out his legal size pad of yellow paper. Here was something to go on! He inquired about the names of individuals that were familiar with James' physical condition. James mentioned his girlfriend, Leona Williams, her mother, and after further prodding, the names of several neighbors and other friends. Dick put his pencil down and asked whether James had given this information to the public defender. James, slightly surprised, answered, "No, he never asked me about it although I told him at one time during the trial that my stomach hurt."

With great effort, Dick then learned that James had gone to a party that evening, but left at about 10:30 because he was experiencing severe pain. This was the first party he had gone to since he was stabbed. James explained that at the time of the rape, he could hardly walk up the stairs to his parents' second floor apartment. And yet, Birdia Jackson had identified James as one of the boys who ran down the alley carrying her to the first rape location.

Dick sat there stunned at the revelation. This was a major lead in the case and he was anxious to pursue it. If Harden was suffering from the wound and surgery, he could hardly have been physically capable of committing a rape.

"Times up," said the guard. Dick would have

liked to ask a few more questions, but he had learned so much that he was satisfied. Getting his notes together he stood up to leave. James rose slowly, again with moisture in his eyes. "Thank you for coming," he said, turning and walking towards the guard.

Dick watched James leave the room. He thought to himself that throughout the entire conversation Harden never once got excited or agitated – only in the beginning did he even proclaim his innocence. If only half the evidence James gave him proved true he should never have been convicted.

Dick wanted to believe in the innocence of his client, yet the admonitions of Doherty kept coming back to him, and he surely did not want to act naïve or unprofessional. However, even with no prior experience he sensed that he might have an innocent man on his hands, a thought which was exhilarating and left him a little light headed.

Leaving the prison for the gate house he asked himself how he would have reacted if he had been in the penitentiary for almost three years, as an innocent person. He could just feel how bitter he would have been and how he would have shouted his innocence to anyone listening. But that's the problem: when you are black and poor and you come from West Roosevelt Street in Chicago, no one listens or cares. If you are innocent of this crime, you probably still belong in jail for another crime for which you had not been caught.

Dick's thinking suddenly focused: either Harden was a very convincing liar, which seemed totally out of character with his reticent demeanor, or he was the innocent victim of a totally inept criminal system at 26th and California in Chicago. In any event, he had some leads to develop, and the remote possibility that Harden was innocent was enough to stimulate overwhelming interest in the case.

Dick walked through the final iron gate into the reception room where Anita was waiting. When he saw her he could see she was obviously upset.

"What's wrong, Anita?"

"I'll tell you outside."

After Dick recovered his wallet and other possessions from the guard, he asked him to check the records to determine how many visitors Harden had had over the past few years. The guard responded that Dick was the first visitor Harden had had since he arrived.

    A twenty year old man sentenced to twenty years in the penitentiary and only one visit in nearly three years. Innocent or guilty, this would be difficult for any person to endure. But if innocent, what a grievous injustice society had committed against this lad – to be placed in prison with hardened criminals during the formative period of his life without family or friends. If innocent, how could our criminal system have so utterly failed with one of its younger citizens? Something was wrong. Something had to be wrong. Dick almost hoped that James was guilty, for if freed after four years because of Dick's efforts, he could not complain of his incarceration. But if innocent, how could Dick or anyone else explain to him in meaningful terms what had happened?

    Outside, Anita's face became redder with visible anger. "That man," she blurted, "how could any person be so cruel?"

    "Slow down, honey. Whom are you talking about, what happened?"

    Anita took a few more steps toward the car and made an effort to regain her composure. "That guard, that man at the desk, Officer Hall. Every person that came in to see a prisoner, he was rude to and made them wait. One Negro mother, who had come from California was told that she could not see her boy because this was not his visiting week. She tried to explain that this was the only time she could get off work and had come all this way by bus and had to return in two days. That man made no effort to arrange for her to visit, but sent her away in tears. How could he be so cruel?"

    Dick said nothing for in only a few months of marriage he had learned when to leave his bride alone to work out her own frustrations. He started the car and they began their return trip to Chicago in silence.

Chapter 3

Visiting Skid Row

The car moved west along Madison Street, hitting almost every light along the way. You either time the green lights correctly and make a run of it or you get caught at every red light. First, they passed over the Northwest Expressway, now renamed the Kennedy Expressway, through that infamous jungle of anonymity called "Skid Row," where a man can lose his identity, his senses and his soul. Staggering, stumbling humanity can be found here - lost in a bottle by day and a two-bit cubicle at night if such can be afforded. The area smelled - of what it is hard to say - but it had a sickening stench that one could not forget. Each man looked like the other and they seemed to flow as a mass - back and forth - like waves slowly washing up debris on the shore, then receding only to return a moment later - not going anywhere nor accomplishing anything, but always in constant motion.

"Dave, would you believe that the WCTU brought my bride here directly out of the south to show the evils of alcohol?" Dave Dunsten, a young stock broker about Dick's age, sat behind the wheel of the car. He had graciously consented to accompany Dick on his first investigation into the near west side of Chicago to find evidence for the "big" case. Dave was of medium height, already showing signs of balding. He, too, had just recently married. He had nearly lost his bride on their honeymoon. His bride had had difficulty making up her mind whether or not to accept Dave's proposal and rather than wait indefinitely for her answer, Dave planned a trip to the Amazon jungle to spend two weeks with missionaries. At the last moment Kathie consented and rather than give up all his plans they married and she accompanied him.

On their arrival in the Amazon, the natives, still in a Stone Age culture, ran around nude. When Kathie emerged from the single engine Beechcraft, the natives were beset with curiosity because they could not determine if Kathie was a male or female because of a playboy haircut. At their insistence she had to visually identify her sex. Peace was maintained with the tribe but the tranquility of the bridal bed (a mat) was shattered for the remainder of the stay.

Dave looked out the window to his left and observed a man slumped in a doorway. "Pathetic sight. How could this happen to a human being? I understand that many a successful businessman, who could not bear the pressures of Wall Street or La Salle Street, has given up family and friends to submerge himself in this hole. Everyone should come down here and see it for himself."

"I agree," Dick responded, "but I can't see bringing sweet innocent girls off the farm to a place like this. Can you imagine a bunch of old ladies from Evanston calling themselves the Woman's Christian Temperance Union, holding classes every summer on alcoholism, bringing their cherubs here as the final working session? Why, Anita with her non-drinking, non-smoking Southern Baptist background, never knew such a thing existed. She was nauseated as were most of the girls."

Several blocks later the boys drove into what was obviously a ghetto area. The buildings were dilapidated, some burned out and others boarded up; the area was hardly recognizable as once having been the proud neighborhood of a well-established white middle class that had abandoned the area only a few years before. Garbage lined the curbs; windows in many of the houses were broken; children darted in and out of parked cars, making the way hazardous.

"What's the address we want?" asked Dave.

"3552 West Washington."

"That would be one block over." Dave turned the corner and drove down one block and pulled into a parking space. Dick and Dave got out of the car and went to the address. A middle-aged black woman sat on the steps with her hands folded over her rotund stomach. "Excuse me, please. Does Arthur Head live here?" Dick asked.

"Huh?" grunted the woman.

"Does Arthur Head live in this house?"

"Never heard of him," said the woman in an indignant voice.

Just then a man started up the steps. His eyes were bloodshot and it was clear from his demeanor that he had just visited the local pub on the way home from work. Hesitating slightly, as though to grab a quick breath of air, he blurted "Arthur don't live here no more. Gone six months ago." Dick turned to the man and asked where he might be found. The only response he got was "Don't know."

By this time a small crowd, mostly children, began gathering around. A few adults stuck their heads out of windows. Their expressions clearly indicated their interest was not just idle curiosity. The presence of two white men was not a welcomed sight for it meant one of two things: either they were detectives or bill collectors, and neither was welcome in this area.

The boys headed back to the car, resigned to the fact that they were not likely to find Arthur Head, one of the complaining witnesses. As Dave closed his door and put the key in the ignition there was a sudden screech of brakes. There, only a few feet to the street side of them, was a car with four big black men in it. The blacks just sat there glaring at the two "investigators" as if they were daring them to move one inch, seeking any provocation to attack. The hatred in their dark eyes could only have been the accumulation of wine and the bitterness they felt towards all whites, the source of their shortcomings and frustrations in life.

Dave rolled up his window and locked the doors. The two of them just sat in silence looking straight ahead. Several people on the sidewalk stopped and watched. Finally, after what seemed like five minutes, the car moved slowly by with the blacks still glaring at the boys. Dave started the car and pulled out, driving hurriedly back to the near north side of the city and relative safety.

The next day, around eleven, Dick left the office with two stops on his agenda. One was the Public Defender's Office and the other Mt. Sinai Hospital. At James Doherty's office he was given access to Doherty's file concerning the trial. As he was thumbing through the file, he came across a newspaper article with the headline "SET BAIL FOR RAPE SUSPECTS AT $30,000. ROUND THE CLOCK MANHUNT SNARES SEVEN OUT OF EIGHT." Dick hurriedly read the article which set forth the details of how seven boys had been apprehended on Saturday, October 8,

1960, by police and detectives, an eighth one still being at large. Dick went back and read the article again, examining it for the names of each boy. The names given were Fess Wise, Eugene Brown, Errol Meeks, James O'Neil, Edward Cole, Jimmy Dillard and Henry Tripplet. James Harden's name was not mentioned. Next to the article was a photo showing the arm of a woman pointing to three boys whose heads were bowed low. Under the photo the following appeared:

> "The hand of Mrs. Birdia Jackson points as she dramatically identifies youths who recently raped her. This scene took place in Sex Unit of the Detective Bureau, 1121 South State Street, Saturday afternoon, October 8, where Mrs. Jackson had been taken to make identification after the suspects were apprehended."

Dick stopped momentarily, looking towards the blank wall in front of him. I thought she testified at the trial that she had identified Harden at the same police line-up on this date. This article and photo would indicate the contrary. After getting permission, Dick took the article and put it in his brief case.

He next came across a letter which read:

> "Chicago 8 Ill.
> 911 South Paulina

To my Dearest Mother:

> Mrs. Evelyn Brown how are you find I hope I was glad to get your letter Saturday. We had visitor day Thursday you may can't see me Thursday but if don't see doing that day I no you tryer to come and see me. tell Charles I am save my sugar for him to hoped in the lord from the mornin watch even unto night, let with him in the lord. Because with the lord ther is mercy, and with him plentiful redemption. and he shall redeem Israel from all his iniqites. the policeman talk the lady in the room then she came out

and take the picture and they talk her poin at us and did. the policeman beat me and talk me to singe a piece of papper and I singe it and went they brough me here and a p.d. called me and I told him and he said he would tak cared of that. *and they make me tell on a boy I don now but* lord don like argen I find that out of my they lose of boys in here I dont and never seen before. Mama will you call by suppionsion office and tell him about me and tell I don on everything about policeman pick me up on the streets and alrigh had my name on a yellow sheep of paper and tell him I said I am sorry if I don't write him soon and tell him to try to something for and help me and tell him I wish he could come and see me for I can talk to him and tell him I did not do it and I don't on how they got my name but all I now I am in jail for something I did not do but the lord now all about it he will make away one of those days oh yes he will, out of the depths I have cried to thee, 0 lord, lord, hear my voice Let thin errs be attentive' to the voice of my suppicatuns. if thou, 0 lord, shalt makr iniqites, lord, who shall stand for with him ther is mersiful forgiveness; and by reson of thy law have waited for thee, o lord, my soul hath relied on his word, my soul hath – "

There was this sudden break in the letter. At the top of the back page there were words "my love is God and my family – Love, Love, Love, Eugene."

Dick blinked his eyes. The letter was not only difficult to interpret but it was almost illegible. It seemed to be saying that Brown had identified a boy he did not know because he did not want to argue with the police. Dick wondered if that was Harden. There was also a question of whether Brown had been beaten by the police. Dick added this letter to his file. Dick instinctively and perhaps naively began to feel some compassion for this boy, not only because of his present twenty year predicament, but because of his apparent ignorance of what was happening to him. However, if he were guilty, could it really matter?

At this moment Doherty walked into the office. "How are you, my fine friend? Did you uncover anything of value?" Dick took out the newspaper article and showed it to Doherty. "Did you consider using this at the trial?"

"What for?" was the sharp response.

Dick hesitated a second to determine if Doherty was getting a little red under the collar. He was, so Dick decided to drop the matter.

"Never mind, Jim. Just a thought I had. Thanks for the use of your file. I'll return the things I took just as soon as I am done with them."

Jim Doherty stood there in silence with his hands on his hips, his face red, as Dick exited. As Dick walked down the hall he resolved to be more discreet in questioning Doherty for he seemed to be extremely sensitive to any criticism relative to his handling of the case.

Dick reached his car and began the drive to Mr. Sinai Hospital to check his first big lead. As he proceeded on California Avenue, north, he again was made totally aware of the changing neighborhoods. One could tell the very street where a black area began or stopped. The identical buildings, which in the block before appeared to be neat and clean, painted and well maintained, were neglected and in some instances actually disintegrating. The lawns in front of such buildings were long gone, replaced by garbage and trash. Even the trees in the area seemed to lose their will to live. Passing one of Chicago's "integrated high schools" Dick observed that nearly all the students were black with only an occasional Puerto Rican or white emerging from a building. Most of the students standing around the buildings were smoking. Waste paper and bits of garbage were deposited all over the grounds as students dropped used wrappers and bags wherever they happened to be standing.

Dick's thoughts were interrupted as he pulled into a parking lot one-half block from the hospital. Across from the hospital was a park which was relatively safe during the daylight hours. By night this park and the many others like it, with their lovely trees and flowers, turned into tinder boxes of crime for the unwary, as gangs of youths roamed as though they held the deeds to them. Dick was not critical of these conditions nor was he shocked by them; he simply accepted them as a cancerous condition of the inner city.

Dick entered the waiting room of the hospital which was overrun with blacks waiting for free medical attention. Most of these people existed on some form of relief and each sat in impatient silence. About all a black needed in Chicago to survive was several children and a strong will to withstand long hours of waiting in line. All these people looked alike, absolutely conditioned by the "system" which had sapped every ounce of incentive and ambition they might have once possessed. They sat there with no hope for the future, no thought of the past. Only the present mattered with its long hours of waiting for that ADC check, that free medical examination, that unemployment compensation. There were no uncertainties, no challenges, no anticipations. Life was long, dull and heavy.

Dick finally caught the eye of the receptionist and was directed to the records office. There, a Mrs. Morales solicitously listened to Dick as he explained what he wanted. She obtained a file and began examining it; stopping at a card she said: "I think this is what you are looking for,

> James Harden, age 19;
> Admitted 8/10/60;
> Discharged 8/15/60;
> Diagnosis: abdominal wound
> Penetration in abdominal cavity.
> Surgery was performed 8/10/60, which included an exploratory laparotomy - closure of a peritoneum laceration."

Dick hesitated a second and then asked, "Well, what does that mean in layman's terms, Mrs. Morales?"

She smiled, "This means that a stab wound was repaired by surgery. This card indicates that Harden was admitted to the emergency room because the stab wound had penetrated his abdominal cavity. A Levine tube and Foley catheter were inserted while the patient was in the operation room."

There was a certain eagerness in Dick's face

as Mrs. Morales spoke. He finally asked, "This was a pretty serious thing I take it?"

"On the contrary, Mr. Calkins, this was a very simple and routine operation."

Dick's face showed his disappointment at her response. He immediately asked: "What I mean is would this type of operation leave the patient incapacitated for a period of time?"

"This would depend entirely upon the individual," Mrs. Morales said in a matter of fact voice. "A young healthy man would recover quite quickly - in a matter of weeks."

Without sounding too persistent Dick asked, "Do you think there could have been a complete recovery in six weeks?"

"Mr. Calkins, this depends entirely on the individual. If you will excuse me, I must get about my work."

Dick thanked her, gave her his card, and asked her to write a report which she consented to do. Dick also obtained the names of the attending physician, Dr. Gonzales, who had an office in Elmhurst, which was a suburb west of Chicago. With a certain impetuosity he decided to drive to Dr. Gonzales' office without calling first. It took Dick about a half hour to drive the twenty miles to Elmhurst where Dr. Gonzales practiced. He was not in when Dick arrived so he waited.

"Mr. Calkins, will you come this way?" A nurse in the usual white uniform stood in the doorway trying to catch Dick's attention as he sat deep in thought.

"Oh yes. Thank you. Is the doctor back?"

"Right this way, please. In here, sir. The doctor will be in with you in a moment."

Dr. Gonzales emerged a moment later. He had Latin features and spoke with a decided accent. Dick concluded he was possibly Puerto Rican or Cuban. "Mr. Calkins, may I help you?"

Dick explained the case and gave the doctor the background of what had occurred. The doctor thought for a moment and then said, "I am sorry, Mr. Calkins, but I don't remember this boy at all. You must realize, this was three and a half years ago, and I have hundreds of such knifed patients in the course of a year at that hospital."

Dick shifted his weight as though to emphasize his disappointment. "Let me ask you this then, doctor, do you think that physically a young man could commit a rape after having this type of operation only six weeks before?"

"Mr. Calkins, I have seen these people get off the operating table and have intercourse with a woman. They are an amazing people when it comes to sex."

"But, doctor, do you think that a young man under these circumstances would have a very strong desire?"

"This is difficult to say. It is entirely up to the individual and how quickly the wound heals. It's strictly an individual matter. I am afraid I can't help you any more than this."

"Thank you, Dr. Gonzales. I appreciate your talking to me. I think I can find my way out."

Dick walked slowly accenting each step with the disappointment he felt because of the inability of the doctor to help him. If only he could have remembered Harden and the fact that James was having trouble when the wound was healing. This would have knocked the State's entire case out. I wonder if Harden could have had intercourse? Of course, if he was only there, he would still have been convicted as an accessory. However, Birdia Jackson testified that Harden was one of the four boys who picked her up and ran with her down the alley. If he was having the trouble he described to me, he hardly would have been able to run with her.

As Dick drove back to the city he was determined to find out more concerning Harden's physical incapacity. He wondered if Doherty had been aware of this and if so, why he didn't bring it out at the trial.

The next day Dick arrived early at the office. He went through his mail - the usual letter from the Illinois State Bar Association which he tossed in the waste basket and a letter from Northwestern University School of Law soliciting money for the annual alumni fund. Dick put this in a pile with other pending matters with the full intention of sending a check, but with the subconscious desire to forget about it until after the drive was over. It was not that Dick was niggardly with his money but that there were so many demands upon his limited resources - Dartmouth College, Northwestern law, church, the United Fund, Red Cross, YMCA, Salvation Army, etc.

After several phone calls of no moment, Dick took out the newspaper article which he found in Doherty's file. Perusing it again, he decided to try and contact the editor in chief of the paper, Westside Booster, and see if he knew anything about the line-up which Birdia Jackson attended. Dick looked in the phone book but could find no listing for the Westside Booster. He finally decided to call another black run newspaper called The Defender for possible leads.

"Good morning. I wonder if you could possibly help me. I am trying to make contact with someone from the Westside Booster which I believe is now a defunct newspaper."

"Look here, mister, this is The Defender. I have never heard of the Westside. . . . "

"Booster," said Dick.

"Booster. I am too busy to talk now." The very sound of the voice at the other end annoyed Dick. "Wait a minute, sir," said Dick emphasizing the word "sir," "May I please speak to someone else?"

"Rubbie," said the voice at the other end. "Will you talk to this man?"

A female voice inquired into the nature of Dick's business and he explained what he was looking for. "I am sorry I can't help you." There was a slight pause. "I do recall that Frank Meadows, who works part-time at our south side office, worked with that paper. I don't know if you can get him at this time because he works during the day and works for us in the evening and on weekends."

Dick got the number of the south side office and thanked his informant. He called the new number. Frank Meadows was not in so he left a message for him to call.

As Dick sat at his desk be began to wonder whether he was really getting any place. He found nothing substantial to reopen the case. Suddenly the idea occurred to him to call the State's Attorney's office to see if he could see the entire file in the case. He wasn't sure whether the State's Attorney disclosed such files to defense counsel. Might as well try, Dick thought. Dick called the State's Attorney, Dan Ward, and was referred to the office of his first assistant, Edward J. Egan. After speaking to a clerk, Mr. Egan answered the phone.

"Mr. Egan, my name is Dick Calkins. I was appointed by the Illinois Supreme Court to represent a James Harden. I was wondering if I could see your file on Harden because I am attempting to make an investigation of this case."

Egan hesitated a moment and then answered, "Come on down and I will see what I can do for you. There really isn't much to look at." Dick was elated for he felt if only he could see the police reports he might make some real progress in this matter. "I'll be down this afternoon. Thank you very much, Mr. Egan."

"Not at all, Dick," and there was a click of the phone.

That afternoon the weather was hot and humid, a typical Chicago summer day. Dick entered the Dearborn Street subway and descended into the coolness and darkness of its subterranean passageway. Reaching the platform he plunked a nickel in a gum machine and bought a package of gum. Facing the tracks, he hardly noticed the posters plastered on the walls opposite him for he was deep in thought. He wondered why few young lawyers were interested in entering the practice of criminal law in Chicago. Probably because the fees at best were modest until you built a solid reputation. And then your clients came from the poorest segments of society where collecting a fee was as difficult as defending the client. The only lawyers who really made anything out of such a practice were those who defended white collar crimes, stock manipulation, income tax fraud, or were retained by the crime syndicate. Besides, it was such a hassle to get from your loop office to 26th and California. Of course, you could take a cab, Dick thought, but that was a luxury he could not afford.

Dick's reluctance to become enmeshed in criminal law was twofold: his office was not interested in the practice because of the limited remunerations available; and second, he had already been the target of several oblique remarks in the office concerning his efforts to free a convicted felon. He was really immune to the latter insofar as it applied to the Harden case because he was only carrying out what he considered to be his appointed task. But this criticism did dampen any thoughts he had in developing a criminal law practice generally.

Suddenly, there was a gush of wind and the Douglas "B" train pulled in. He entered the almost empty car and the train took off down the tracks, curving to the west, dipping under the Chicago River and finally emerging into the hot sunshine, running along the median of the Eisenhower Expressway. Several stops were made and then it proceeded up an incline and turned south at a rapid clip for several miles. The area it went through was semi-industrial with a number of houses backing up to the tracks. Dick wondered how people living contiguous to such noise day and night could enjoy a normal life. Yet the appearance of their homes certainly suggested that they took pride in their appearance.

At California Avenue Dick got off and descended the stairs to the street, and waited for a bus. The sun beat down and the humidity seemed to move in with a premeditated intent to strangle any victim foolish enough to venture outside at this hour of the day. Dick removed his coat and found his shirt already dripping wet.

Fifteen minutes later he emerged from the CTA bus and proceeded to the second floor of the criminal court building to the State's Attorney's office.

"Mr. Egan, please."

"Won't you have a seat? I'll tell him you are here. What is your name?" A heavy set rather pleasant woman sat behind a reception desk. Everything in the office reflected efficiency. Clerks were hurrying about while assistant state's attorneys entered and left the office, signing in and out. The State's Attorney's office was the only office in the building that was entirely air conditioned.

A young boy of about seventeen emerged from behind a swinging door and said "Right this way, Mr. Calkins." Dick was led to an inner reception room where he was directed to wait. Finally he was directed into Mr. Egan's office, which was fairly large, nicely carpeted, with a large mahogany desk at one end of the room.

"Sit down, Richard. What can I do to help you?" Behind the desk sat Edward Egan, a handsome Irishman about forty years old. His voice was gentle and his manner dignified.

Dick responded with perceptible enthusiasm. "I would like very much to see the State's Attorney's file of the Harden case on which I am working."

It was perhaps the naïve and direct manner in which he made the request which saved him from being thrown out. It was quite evident to Egan that he was unaware of the fact that such a file is never disclosed to defense counsel except pursuant to court order, which is most difficult to obtain. And then only certain police reports are turned over to defense counsel for purposes of impeaching or discrediting a particular witness.

With little thought Egan called to his clerk and told him to give Calkins the Harden file. The young clerk went to a file cabinet and pulled out a file jacket and handed it to Dick. Dick thanked Mr. Egan and walked out to the reception room where he sat down at a table. At a single glance Dick realized that all he had was a cover file which would do him little good.

After spending about five minutes Dick turned to the clerk who was examining some correspondence at his desk and said, "Excuse me. I have finished examining the cover file. I wonder if I might see the regular file now."

The young man looked non-plused as though he was not sure what he should do. He glanced into Mr. Egan's office and saw that his boss was in conference with two officials from the Attorney General's office in Springfield. The boy got up from his desk, shrugged his shoulders slightly and said, "Follow me, Mr. Calkins," and led Dick out of the office and down a long corridor to the end of the building. They turned right, down another corridor and entered a large file room, the inner sanctum of the State's Attorney's office of Cook County, Illinois.

An elderly man, with snow white hair sat at the entrance of the file room and as the two entered the room said, "Hello, there, Tommy. What can we do for you today?"

"Mr. Johnson, this attorney has been cleared by Mr. Egan to see the file in People v. James Lee Harden, Indictment No. 37647. Do you suppose you could take care of him?"

"No problem, son. Miss Robinson would you please take care of this young attorney?" A medium-sized black woman, about forty-five years old, came over to the entrance. She had a pleasant smile and made a very efficient appearance. Johnson handed her a slip of paper on which he had written the indictment number. "Let this young man see anything he wants. He has been cleared by the front office."

Dick followed the woman and directed to sit at a table near the door. The room was very large with seven long rows of filing cabinets containing pending and recently completed cases being handled by the State's Attorney's office. Along the entire perimeter of the room were metal book cases filled with files which reached from the floor to the ceiling. At another table sat four clerks feverishly looking through files piled high before them.

Miss Robinson disappeared behind the second row of filing cabinets in the middle of the room. Several minutes later she emerged with three large files, which she placed on Dick's table. "Here you are, sir."

"Thank you Miss Robinson." Dick rose from the chair to help her put the files down. Inwardly, he was extremely pleased with himself at having gained the inner sanctum of the State's Attorney's office.

As Miss Robinson walked away, Dick emptied the first file jacket, spreading the documents before him on the table. He picked up each document and slowly read it placing it in a neat pile when he was finished. As he read he became more and more excited. His pace increased because he was concerned about being discovered. The intensity of his search increased so much that his head began to throb slightly and the back of his neck and ears turned red as they often did when he was excited or under stress.

As he read each document he placed it in chronological order in the second pile, and in doing so began to see the case unfold before him. He could not believe what he was reading. It did not seem possible that the assistant state's attorney had such information before him and failed to turn it over to defense counsel. By this time Dick was working at a feverish pace. His head was pounding now as much from excitement and anticipation as it was from the severe strain he was working under. At any moment Mr. Egan could walk in and seal off forever the only tangible evidence establishing Harden's innocence.

Closing time was approaching and a decision had to be made. He knew he couldn't copy these documents by hand - he had to have them Xeroxed but how could he remove them from the file room?

Miss Robinson finally said it was time to close. Dick knew that it would take several days to copy the documents by hand. Suddenly a temptation arose to take the documents to his office. Sweat broke out on his forehead because he knew what he was contemplating violated the confidence and trust Egan placed in him. Yet the documents he read proved Harden's innocence and raised a serious question as to whether any of the defendants should have been convicted.

Dick began to question ethically what he should do. In fact the State had withheld important statements from key witnesses that should have been turned over to defense counsel as a matter of law. Had not the assistant state's attorneys acted unethically?

"Come along now, we must close. You can leave your files on the table. No one will disturb them." Without further thought, Dick placed a number of key documents in his briefcase and left the room. "I will see you tomorrow, Miss Robinson; thank you."

Walking out the door to the bus stop, Dick felt uneasy. He did not like what he had done, and he wondered if any client was worth such compromise. He knew what the answer was, but it was too late to undo what had occurred.

Dick got back to the office as quickly as he could. Everyone had left except for a few of the younger lawyers, who were expected to put in the long hours as part of the baptism of the profession. Dick turned on the Xerox machine and copied the documents in question, which took over an hour. Feeling a certain sense of satisfaction he began to rationalize what he had done; after all, the freedom of an innocent man was at stake.

The next day he returned to the file room and returned the documents he had "borrowed." He remained for about forty-five minutes strictly for show. He then returned to his office and began sorting out his cache. However, he was rudely interrupted when Mr. Keck's secretary called and said the boss wanted him right away. That not only took the rest of the afternoon, but he was given a research project for the evening which had to be ready at 9:00 o'clock the next morning. As he returned to his office with his notes, his secretary, Margaret, was leaving for the evening. Dick was tired and mentally drained. As he cleared the Harden documents from his desk to make room for his research project, he suddenly realized that the Harden case was beginning to absorb all his thinking and was becoming the most important thing in his life. His regular assignments at the office were becoming a source of irritation rather than the challenge they had been in the past.

Dick worked until 8:30 p.m. and decided to go back early the next morning to complete the job. Leaving the Field Building at the Clark Street entrance he began walking north on Clark Street. It was still light out and the early evening air was hot and heavy with thunder clouds hanging limply in the western sky.

The air, although humid, seemed to revive Dick. He told himself, as he walked, that he could not do an effective job in the Harden case if he allowed himself to become emotionally involved. This was neither professional nor healthy, and he knew this. In his brief legal experience he had seen lawyers tear at each other in emotionally charged encounters as though their personal lives were at stake. Many times they succeeded only in looking foolish; other times they tested the patience of the court; rarely did they accomplish their goals. Unquestionably, it was the disciplined lawyer who maintained a professional mien that was heard by the court.

Dick continued north and as he passed over the Chicago River bridge he felt a slight breeze cross his face which felt most refreshing. He was so deep in thought that he missed the beauty of the western sky which turned a dark red before fading into darkness. Dick realized that objectivity in a lawyer comes with experience and maturity, but he knew he had to begin right now. Becoming emotionally obsessed with a case, he was told, not only neutralizes the effectiveness of a lawyer, but it can be very demanding on one's mental health and well-being.

By the time Dick had gotten home he felt he had things sorted out, and he made a determined pledge to be professional.

The next day Dick arrived at the office at 7:00 a.m. and finished the Keck project. At about 9:13 a.m. Frank Meadows called, but Dick was with Mr. Keck. When he returned, the message was on his desk and he dialed the number.

"Mr. Meadows, please."

"I am sorry. There is no one by that name here."

"Margaret," he shouted in an angry voice, "where is Meadows' number?" Margaret rushed in obviously flustered. Mr. Calkins, that is the number he gave me, on the red slip in front of you."

"This is the number I just tried and it's a wrong number." His agitation indicated that he was very tense about the case. He didn't like the prospect of losing Meadows, who was his only contact with the Westside Booster. He dialed the number again; this time a man answered.

"Mr. Meadows?" asked Dick.

"What do you want?" said a very distrustful voice at the other end.

"My name is Dick Calkins and I am trying to locate the editor-in-chief of the now defunct Westside Booster. You see, I am an attorney representing a negro teenager who was wrongfully convicted of a very serious crime, and I think the editor-in-chief can help me." There was a long silence. Then Dick asked again, "Do you think you can help me?"

Again there was silence. Finally the voice at the other end said in a halting voice: "His name is Herman C. Gilbert and he works at the Illinois Public Commission."

"Is that on Canal Street?"

"Yes, it is."

"Thank you ver ...," there was a click at the other end so Dick hung up. Realizing that trying to talk to someone on the phone about such a delicate matter was most difficult, Dick decided to walk over to Canal Street and talk to Gilbert personally. It was only six blocks and taking a cab seemed like an unnecessary expense.

Dick walked through the revolving door of the Public Service Commission building into the typical sterile and impersonal lobby of a public building. An information desk was in the middle of the lobby where all inquirers were treated with equal indifference. Dick thought how easy it is to be reduced to a number when you are dealing with a governmental agency.

After waiting in line impatiently for ten minutes, Dick was waited on and given directions to Gilbert's office. Taking the elevator to the second floor, he proceeded down a long corridor and entered the office at the far end. A young black man was sitting at a desk.

"Mr. Gilbert, please."

"Will you please be seated. May I have your name?"

Dick gave the man his card and sat down. The air conditioned room felt very comfortable after walking over in the heat of the morning. After a lapse of about fifteen minutes a slim black man, in his early forties, walked out. He had a trim moustache and made an above average appearance.

"Mr. Calkins, what can I do for you?"

Dick identified himself and explained his interest in helping James Harden. He then showed Gilbert the article. "Mr. Gilbert, did you work on the paper at this time?"

"Why, yes, I did. I was managing editor of the paper. We were in business for only a year and a half."

"Do you recall anything about this rape story?"

Gilbert looked at the article Dick showed him, read it carefully and then put it on the table. "Yes, I do remember this story. I wrote it." It was a rather sensational case because of the violence of the crime. Yes. Now I remember, there was a great deal of concern about the rape because the police had failed to take any action until a number of days later. As a matter of fact it was because of an earlier article I wrote that the police began investigating the case."

Dick leaned forwarded slightly. "Mr. Gilbert, could you tell me exactly how you got involved in this?"

"Well, let me think. As I recall it, a Moses Walker, a precinct captain, came to me and complained that one of his constituents, this Birdia Jackson, I believe, had been raped by a gang of boys and that her escort had been beaten and robbed."

Gilbert pointed his finger on the name Birdia Jackson under the photograph, along the side of the news article. "She had gone to the police station, but they had refused to do anything about the case so she went to Moses to complain. I then wrote up the first story. We got additional circulation from that issue because of the furor it caused. By the next day the police had three detective squads on the case, working around the clock. By the end of that week they had rounded up these boys."

Gilbert hesitated a moment as he skimmed the article trying to refresh his recollection. "On the evening of October – October, yes October 8th, Detective Lill called and told me to hurry down to the 11th and State Street station if I wanted a good story. I called our photographer, Jud Hollis, and we hurried down. One of my young reporters, Dutton, was already there. As we entered, several boys and detectives were coming out of the line-up room. I walked over to Lill and asked him to give us a picture. He turned to the first three boys coming out of the room and told them to line up against the wall."

Dick interrupted with some urgency and asked, "Did you see any of the other boys?" Gilbert hesitated a moment and said, "Yes, but I don't recall who they were now."

"What happened then?"

"Well, this Jackson asked to be in the picture, which in my opinion was highly unusual for a rape victim. They normally don't even want their name printed. Hollis then took her picture pointing at the three boys. Later we cut her face out of the print we used so that only her arm showed."

Dick then asked, "Why were not more of the boys in the picture?"

"The room was too small to include any others."

"Tell me, Mr. Gilbert, do you recall if James Harden's name was ever mentioned?" Gilbert hesitated again. I'm afraid I can't help you there. I honestly don't remember the names of any of the boys. Actually I am not much good on names and this happened several years ago."

"Well, do you recall how you got the story?"

"Lill gave me the information."

"Well, did you report accurately the names he gave you as being identified by Jackson?"

"Yes, Mr. Calkins. I may not remember names too well but I take pride in the exactness of my work. I know that I copied each boy's name down carefully."

"In other words, if they had given you Harden's name, you would have listed it also?"

"There is no question about it," responded Gilbert with a positive voice.

Dick gave a perceptible sigh of relief. He seemed to have been holding his breath during the entire interview. It was not as good as it could have been, but it was something.

"Mr. Gilbert, would you consent to testify at a hearing that will most likely be held this fall?"

Gilbert hesitated. Dick quietly added: "We have reason to believe that several boys that were convicted of this rape were innocent."

Gilbert still remained silent. Finally, he said in an uncertain and cool voice, "I'll have to think about it. I have no desire whatever to become involved in a case like this. You understand, my job here is important to me and my family."

"Mr. Gilbert," responded Dick in a louder voice, "innocent boys are in prison and you can help them." Dick hesitated and then stopped, lowering his head. Once again he felt a sense of frustration grip him, and it took all the self-discipline he had to control his emotions. Why do these people refuse to help their own, he thought to himself.

"Mr. Gilbert, here is my card. I will contact you later. Perhaps you could sign an affidavit for me."

Gilbert said nothing until Dick moved for the door. "Goodbye, Mr. Calkins."

Dick thanked him for his time and left. As he walked out the door of the building he was hit with oven-like heat. His stomach seemed to swell and his head felt heavy. He began to experience a feeling of nausea. For some reason he had accepted the idea that everyone would immediately join his "crusade" with his enthusiasm. Instead he found apathy, disinterest, absolute unconcern for the welfare of these young men. But what was his crusade? What was the catalyst that seemed to magnify each minor setback into a defeat and each dead end into an abyss? As he reflected, he realized that he was not sure of his own motivation. Was this almost insatiable drive to succeed merely his own ego that hungered for some form of recognition among his fellow lawyers? Was it an altruistic response to an inborn desire to help one in need? Perhaps it was even an intellectual challenge by a criminal system that appeared to be archaic and outmoded in so many ways. Dick just did not know.

For Dick the desire to succeed in law was all important. Right or wrong, he measured his young life not by the good experienced, but by the successes he had achieved. Each success seemed to be a plateau for which he strove, but when once reached was quickly forgotten or taken for granted, a new goal already appearing on the horizon.

The swelling within him subsided. The putrid odor from the Chicago River hit his nostrils as he proceeded slowly back to the Field Building, wondering what his next step would be. He took the elevator to the twenty-second floor, entered the inner office, walking past his secretary without a glance of recognition and slumped down in his chair. He was hot and tired and had little desire to work on the new project he had received from Mr. Keck. As he thought about this project it seemed almost an imposition because of the work he had to do on his criminal case.

He stared at the wall for a moment and then took out the police reports and other documents obtained from the State's Attorney's office. Mechanically he began placing them in chronological order. As he started examining the documents he came alive again, and the more he reviewed them the more stimulated he became. He finally decided to spend exactly one hour on the Harden case, and he would time himself, and then he would get started again in the library on another Keck research project.

After he had placed the police documents in chronological order he squared the corners, placed the pile directly in front of him on his desk and picked up the first one. It was a police report dated October 4, 1960 made by two police officers who had interviewed the rape victim and her boyfriend. It related the facts as they were testified to at the trial. However, when Dick carefully read the last paragraph he leaned forward in his chair. It stated, "Due to the fact that there were so many offenders, victim asserts she could identify only two (2) of them. Description as follows: #1 C/M 16 5'4" 140-150 dark skin, stocky built, short wool jacket. #2 C/M 17-18 5'8" 150 brown skin bush hair, white shirt. No further descriptions."

Dick hurriedly examined the next document, a police report also dated October 4, 1960, taken by two other policemen. It gave essentially the same story as the first except that it had the added statement that as the boys ran when the police approached, one shouted "Come on. You know you get ten years for rape." It concluded with the following identification:

"Q. Can you describe these men that raped you?"

"A. I believe I can recognize two of them. #1 C/M, 16 5'4" 140-150. Dark skin, stocky build wearing a short wool jacket. #2 18 yrs. 5'8" 150. Brown skin, bush hair, wearing a white shirt. No further descriptions."

A third report, dated the following day, indicated that the Sex Unit, a special division of the Chicago Police Department, had been assigned to the case. This raised the number of officers working on the case to six. This last report stated nothing new except that the victims had been interviewed for the third time in two days.

The next report, dated October 7, 1960, raised the number of officers investigating the case to twelve. This report stated that the police had made contact with James Harden, M/C, age 20, of 3417 West Grenshaw, Errol, Meeks, M/C, age 19, 3328 West Grenshaw, and Fess Wise. The last had been positively identified by Birdia Jackson. Harden and Meeks were scheduled to go the station the next day for lie tests. Dick rested a moment. These bits of information were falling into place. It was clear that in the first two reports neither Birdia Jackson nor Arthur Head had identified Harden. Jackson had identified two boys and only two. The taller of these two was 5'8" whereas James was 6'2". James also weighed considerably more than 150 pounds. Second, the October 7th report stated that only Fess Wise had been identified. Yet the police had contacted both Harden and Meeks. The question that had to be answered was whether Birdia Jackson had seen Harden and Meeks as well as Fess Wise prior to October 7, for it was clear that she had failed to make any positive identification of the two.

Dick picked up the next report. This was a statement by Birdia taken at 2:45 on the morning of October 8, which identified Fess Wise only as one of her assailants. This was followed by a statement given by Fess Wise at about the same time. This read: "I was in the pool room at 12th and Central Park Avenue and about 0100 I came out and as I walked across 12th Street and saw a bunch of guys in a gas station and there was some fighting going on, I walked towards the gas station and I saw some of the New Braves beating up a colored man. I told them to 'keep cool, man' and to 'cut it out.' Ed Cole told me to get away from here, I walked down the street and stayed about two houses away. Then I saw them pull a woman out of the car and start to take her down the alley. I walked around the corner to the J B Grill and had something to eat. I stayed there till about 1:30 a.m. Then I walked from Grenshaw to Fillmore and when I got to a gangway, Edward Cole called me and asked me 'do you want some trim' I told him no. I walked back into the rear of the house and saw this girl laying on the ground and someone was f . . . her, I told them I was going on home because I did not want to get in any trouble. I went home and went to bed."

Fess according to the report, identified the

boys that were at the car beating Arthur Head as "Edward Cole, a guy named James who runs around with Cole, and one more named Donald, called Dunk, who used to go about with Cole or Cole went out with Dunk's sister, Cerise (at least I think that is her name)." Fess also identified the following boys as being on the other side of the car where the woman was: "James Harding, Eugene Brown, Earl Meeks, Johnnie Sherrod. They pulled the woman from the car and carried her down the alley. James Harding, Eugene Brown, Earl Meeks and Johnnie Sherrod had her by the arms and legs and carried her. I saw Eugene Brown take her purse and put something in his pockets. I don't know if it was money. I talked to Edward Cole who suggested I join them. Cole was high from drinking." The report continued:

"Q. Do you know how long you get in jail for rape?"

"A. Maybe about ten years."

"Q. Fess, are you being treated well, and you gave this statement of your own free will without any threat or promises, is that correct?"

"A. Yes. I am being treated very well, and I told you all this because it's the truth and no threat or promises was given me."

"Q. After reading this statement and finding it to be the truth and all that you have told me, will you sign it?"

"A. Sure I will because it's the truth."

"Q. Is there anything else that you can add to this statement?"

"A. Well, I know that if these boys find out that I told you all this, they will kill me, so don't tell them about this, that's all I got to tell you."

Is it possible? Is it possible? Dick mumbled. There was no question that Fess had been the one who identified the group, including Harden. Either James lied to me or Fess lied to the police.

Dick thought about this longer and a third possibility arose; could the police have filled in the names as they saw fit. Dick dismissed this for the moment for there was nothing to suggest that the police were doing anything but an effective job.

Dick put the documents aside and reluctantly picked up a note pad and headed for the library to work on the research project he had been assigned. As he walked to the library he was so engrossed in his thoughts that he neither saw nor heard anyone. He kept thinking, "Could Harden have been involved?"

The next day Dick arrived at the office early. He decided to write a letter to each defendant requesting that they send him a resume of what happened on the night in question. Perhaps this would furnish some leads. Just as he was completing a form letter, Margaret walked in with the mail. One letter caught his attention because it was from Bell Savings and Loan Association and signed by an attorney names Robert Ulbricht. A quick perusal of the letter indicated that Ulbricht had been appointed by the Illinois Supreme Court to represent Fess Wise. Ulbricht proposed that the seven lawyers appointed to work on the case meet for lunch to talk the matter over. A date had been set for that coming Friday at 12:00. Dick immediately called Bob and accepted the invitation.

A few minutes later the telephone rang. Dick picked up the receiver and answered. A timid female voice, with Negro inflections, asked, "Is you Mr. Calkins who is working for James?"

"Yes, I am. May I help you?"

"James told me to call you to see . . ." Dick missed the last words because the voice was barely audible.

"To whom am I speaking?" asked Dick.

"My name is Irene."

"Who?"

"Irene."

"Irene, what is your last name?"

"Woodward."

"Now what can I do for you?"

"Well, I knows that James didn't have relations with that lady."

There was a long pause and then Dick asked, "How do you know this?"

There was another long pause. Then a muffled voice answered. "I just knows because I is his girlfriend. He had an operation and could barely walk."

There was a long hesitation and then Dick asked, "Irene, when he walked, did he have any difficulty that you noticed?"

141

In a louder and more responsive voice she answered: "Oh yes. I lives on the second floor and when he came to visit me he had trouble getting up the stairs."

"Was he bent over when he walked up to your apartment?"

"Yes, sir."

"Did he ever hold his hands to his stomach as though he was in pain?"

"Yes, sir. And often he had to stop half way up to rest."

"Irene, was he having any of this trouble at the time he was arrested?"

"Yes, sir," answered Irene with emphasis.

"Irene, I want to see you and any other people who saw James and would be willing to help us. Please give me your telephone number."

Dick was given the number and arrangements were made for Irene to call back in a few days. Suddenly it occurred to Dick to call Harden's parents and those of the other boys to see if he could get any new leads. He got the transcript out and wrote down the addresses given, checking their names in the phone book. He was unable to confirm the telephone number of a single one. All had "unlisted" phones.

"Margaret, please bring me that Harden letter. I want to add one sentence." Dick wrote an additional line requesting the telephone numbers of each boy's parents.

Attorney Calkins then proceeded to work on the long delayed research project and did nothing further on the Harden case until after 5:00 p.m. At 5:10 p.m. he returned to his office and brought out the State's Attorney's file and proceeded to examine it further. He picked up the next report, an October 8th police report signed by seven detectives from the Sex Bureau. The report stated that the officers involved had been given a special assignment to investigate the matter. It further stated that confidential information had been received implicating Fess Wise and James Harding. Fess Wise had been identified by the victim and had been arrested. He was taken to Assistant State's Attorney Patrick Egan's office for further interrogation. He was first interrogated by two teams of officers for four hours and then two hours by Egan. The report then stated that Fess Wise finally admitted knowledge of the crime and said he would implicate the other youths involved. Armed with this information the named detectives arrested Eugene Brown, who was then interrogated for seven hours, and subsequently implicated Henry Triplett, Sammy Dillard, Edward Cole, James O'Neil and Donald Duncan. A subsequent investigation revealed that "Henry Triplett is now in custody at the 23rd District for the rape of a fourteen year old girl." Also arrested with Triplett for the same crime, and held at the Juvenile Home, was Sammy Dillard. Edward Cole and James O'Neil were located at the House of Correction, where they were being held on charges of vandalism at the Manley High School.

The report continued that, "under interrogation Cole denied any knowledge of the crime, but O'Neil admitted his part in the crime and implicated Cole." Dillard denied any knowledge of the crime, but Triplett admitted his presence at the time the crime took place, but denied participating in the rape. He did "place all the aforementioned perpetrators on the scene at the time of the attack." The report concluded by stating that at 2200 (10:00 p.m.), a line-up was held at the Sex Bureau at which time Birdia Jackson positively identified the arrestees.

Calkins thought a moment. This report again establishes that Birdia Jackson had not identified Harden at least up until 10:00 o'clock in the evening of October 8, 1960. He quickly glanced at the line-up report that followed which established that Jackson had identified Harden along with Errol Meeks, Eugene Brown, Fess Wise and Johnnie Sherrod. This was in conflict with the newspaper story which omitted Harden's name as being identified at this line-up.

The next document was the "confession" of Eugene Brown mentioned at the trial. Dick eagerly read it noting that in addition to Brown, there were four other defendants present – "Wise, Harding, Meeks and Sherrod." Eight detectives and officers were present, interrogating Brown. According to Brown, he and Fess had just come out of a pool room at 3:30 in the morning when they noticed a fight taking place at a gas station a half block away. Brown tried to see who was there and saw a man on the ground. Quickly the fight ended and the boys started to leave when Brown saw several boys carrying a woman down the alley. They followed the group and saw James O'Neil and Eddie Cole having intercourse with the woman. Errol Meeks came around and pulled the boys off and had intercourse. A few minutes later someone whispered, "The police are coming" so Eugene left and went home.

Brown saw seven or eight boys in the alley and identified Fess Wise, Meeks, Sammy Dillard, Eddie Cole, James O'Neil and Donald "Dunk" as being some of the group. Brown denied having intercourse but maintained he remained in the background until he went home. He was then asked:

"Q. If you were asked these same questions at some future date, will your answers be the same?"

"A. Yes."

"Q. Why?"

"A. Because it is the truth."

Brown's signature appeared at the bottom of the page. Dick immediately noted the fact that while Harden and Sherrod were present in the room, Brown had not identified either of them.

An October 9th statement taken from Head stated that he could identify only Wise and Sherrod. In a line-up held the same day he identified the same two boys, although several of the other boys were also in the line-up.

On October 10, 1960, the boys were processed and subsequently booked on charges of rape and robbery. An assistant state's attorney, Mr. Donigan, and several officers working on the case, went to Bridewell to confront Cole and O'Neil and according to an October 10th report, Cole admitted being present at the scene of the crime and implicated Wise, Meeks, Sherrod, Brown and Harden.

Dick shuffled through the papers and found the Cole admission. He immediately read it, searching for the names of those identified by Cole. According to Cole he was leaving Lorain's tavern and saw two boys going down the alley. Thinking that they might have a bottle of wine he followed them. When he got down the alley he noticed several youths, Fats, Pooky and Trugo go under a stairwell. The boys kept arguing as to who was next. Cole stood watching and finally left and went home to bed because he was too drunk and getting sick. He identified Brown and Meeks as being there. He was then asked:

"Was James Hasten there?"
"A. Who?"
"Q. James Harden?"
"A. Harden, no sir."
"Q. He wasn't there?"
"A. No, sir."
"Q. How bout Johnny Sherrod?"
"A. No sir. I didn't see him."

Dick put the statement down. He tried to evaluate this statement. It was clear that both Brown and Cole failed to identify Harden, and Cole had specifically stated that Harden had not been present. Dick took several more notes and then started examining the O'Neil statement taken just after the Cole Statement.

At first O'Neil, questioned by assistant state's attorney Donigan, denied any knowledge of the crime. When asked where he had been Friday night, September 30, he responded that he and Cole had gone to a dance. "Then we come back from Roosevelt. Then we left there and went to Independence Boulevard after we left Roosevelt . . . I can't remember what we did, and I don't know exactly what time I got home, but after we left Independence I don't know where we went." O'Neil did not remember what time he arrived at his home. After several such denials of the crime, the court reporter was asked to leave the room. The questioning was resumed when the reporter returned. O'Neil then admitted he saw some fellows in the alley but refused to mention any names.

"Q. Did you see two boys taking a girl into an alley?"
"A. Yes."
"Q. What boys were they?"
"A. I don't want to mention no names."
"Q. What did you see after your took her into the alley?"
"A. I didn't pay too much attention, we, they took her back there. I didn't pay too much attention."

The assistant state's attorney then stated:

"Now, look, you're smart and you're not being very smart here. You're being very foolish. Whatever the officer said to you before or not, you're here to help yourself if you can. Just tell what happened. That is all I want to know."

"Q. Are you afraid of Coles? Are you afraid that Coles is going to beat you up?"

"A. I ain't got nothing to say."

"Q. You're a damn fool, do you know it? You ain't going to get any place that way and Coles ain't going to beat you up. Now, do you just want me to waste my time and let the case go the way it is? Whatever I say that is going to happen to you and you're not giving me much of an out, are you?"

"A. No, sir."

At that point in the interrogation a detective took over and asked O'Neil:

"You were there, but you would rather not talk about it, is that right?"

"A. I was there, but I tried my best to prevent what was happening."

"Q. Did you take part in the robbery?"

"A. No. Before I ever got around there they were out in the street."

"Q. When you got there the man was lying in the street and you tried to prevent it?"

"A. I tried to stop them."

"Q. You tried to stop them?"

"A. Yes."

"Q. But you would rather not talk about it, but you know who was there?"

"A. Yes, sir."

Dick put this confession down, trying to weigh the importance of this document in relation to Harden, but he could not. He thought a little longer and then suddenly, he saw a pattern emerging. The police had pressured the four youngest youths into accusing each other while attempting to exonerate themselves. In other words, the police got each boy to admit that he was at the scene of the crime as a bystander where he saw his cohorts commit the crime, thereby in fact admitting to part of the crime - physical presence. If the rape victim then identified them at trial, their conviction was thus assured.

Dick began to wonder why the State had not

used the confessions at the trial. Then the answer became obvious. Because two of these confessions Brown's and Cole's had exonerated Harden and Sherrod - the first by Brown's failure to name them as participants when they were present at the time he made it, and the second, by Cole's statement that they were not present. They could not be used at the trial if the State wanted to convict these two as well as the other five.

Dick slowly rose from his desk and moved towards the door. "Why didn't Doherty request these statements prior to trial for he could possibly have used them to protect Harden?" Dick reached for the file of papers Doherty had given him. He found the document he was looking for, a motion to produce directed to the State requesting, among other things, all statements made by the defendants. So a request had been made but the State must have refused to produce them, but on what grounds? Dick immediately weighed the possibility that the State had suppressed favorable evidence in violation of Harden's constitutional rights. But what was their theory for not turning over the statements? Dick tried to remember, as he started thumbing through the transcript.

After several minutes he found his answer. The State had relied on the highly technical argument that these statements were exculpatory admissions and not confessions, and only the latter had to be turned over to defense counsel.

That's absurd, thought Dick, as his mind dissected the argument. What possible difference does it make to a jury whether a man, identified by a rape victim, confesses to the rape, or instead says "yes, I was there, but I stood in the shadows and watched my buddies rape her." In either case he is going to be convicted, particularly when each of his cohorts admits he was also present but he too watched the others do it.

Dick, who had been standing while examining the transcript, sat down in his chair. Burying his head in his hands, he shut his eyes while his thoughts darted almost at will from disgust, to anger and then to reason. No, the assistant state's attorneys, Toler and Dillon, acted in bad faith in withholding these statements at trial. There is no other way to rationalize it.

Dick opened his eyes - they were heavy for he was tired. Much had happened in these last few days and there were many things he did not understand about criminal court procedure.

Reaching for the transcript he began scanning it to determine whether Harden was prejudiced by not having access to these statements. As he reread the transcript his face became flushed again and a new anger swelled within him. Now he recalled that Toler had specifically told Doherty and the court that Harden and Sherrod had been implicated by Brown in the rape and that when they were so identified they failed to deny the charges. Based on this admission by silence, Toler stated that the State intended to use the admissions against Harden and Sherrod.

Dick slammed the transcript shut. How could Toler have made such a false statement? Slowly he began to understand why Doherty did not allow Harden to testify. Because of Toler's remarks, Doherty believed that the State, on cross examination, would question Harden about the Brown confession allegedly implicating Harden, bringing out that he, Harden, had remained silent when he was accused by Brown. The jury, hearing this testimony, would have understood that Harden's silence, when accused, was an admission of involvement, for the innocent protest and protest loudly. Doherty, therefore, had no choice but to keep Harden off the stand.

For the first time Calkins began to appreciate the predicament in which Doherty had been placed when preparing his defense. But why had the judge permitted the State to do this when Doherty on several occasions requested the statements.

Almost as quickly as the anger had engulfed Dick, it lifted like fog being burned off by the sun, for a legal theory began unfolding which could very well result in a general reversal of the convictions.

Again Dick rested his tired eyes. Suddenly, he recalled that there had in fact been an oral confession at the trial, concerning which Officer Lill testified. Again thumbing through the transcript he finally stopped at page 512. There it was, the testimony of Defective Lill wherein he stated that he and Officer Lester had taken Brown to the House of Correction where O'Neil and Cole were being held and that in their presence Brown stated that he had raped Birdia Jackson and accused O'Neil of doing the same. According to Lill, O'Neil said that he had, and implicated Cole, who denied committing the rape.

Dick sat in stunned silence. Here was the entire case. Lill utterly perjured himself. The written statements taken from the boys unequivocally established, one, Brown did not implicate himself, and more important, did not identify Harden as being present, as Lill testified; two, O'Neil did not admit he raped Jackson and, more important he did not implicate Cole or anyone else, contrary to Lill's testimony; three, Cole was specifically asked whether Harden was present and he stated he was not.

Dick leaned back in his chair. What made this so serious was Toler and Dillon knew the facts and allowed Lill to testify falsely. Then they fought to prevent the written statement of Brown, Cole and O'Neil being turned over to the defense, because production would have undermined their entire case based on Lill's testimony. They were aiders and abettors to perjury, a felony crime.

This is extremely serious. Dick wondered what he should do. If he reported the matter, it will disclose that he illegally spirited the documents in question from the State's Attorney's office. He, therefore, decided to keep developing the case and later decide what action to take. After all, his goal was free Harden, not indict Lill, Toler and Dillon.

Chapter 4

Meeting Other Appointed Attorneys

Friday arrived and Dick left for his luncheon appointment at Bell Savings at about 11:45. He walked through the door where he was greeted with a warm smile from one of two young receptionists, sitting at a table some twenty feet inside. On the table was a bowl filled with candy. He glanced at it but declined to take any, inquiring instead about Bob Ulbricht's office.

Receiving instructions and another warm smile, he proceeded to the elevator which quickly took him to the second floor. On leaving the elevator he found himself in an immense room, carpeted in a deep red and furnished with endless rows of desks. The only thing that distinguished bank officers from the other employees was the size of their desks and their window locations. As in all banks there was no privacy unless an officer chose to take a client to a conference room located at one end of this large hall.

The second floor receptionist directed Calkins to the desk of Mr. Ulbricht, who was absorbed in a telephone conversation. Upon seeing Dick, he motioned him to a chair adjacent to his desk. As Dick sat, he looked out a nearby window with a view that was slightly better than his own office window. On the desk in front of him was the huge transcript of the case, so he knew that Ulbricht also was working on the appeal.

Bob Ulbricht hung up the receiver and extended his hand: "Comrade, welcome to our elite Open the Prison Doors and Free All the Criminals Club."

"Glad to meet you, Bob," Dick stated in a friendly voice.

"Several of the other boys are already here and have gone on to the dining room. I had a room set aside for our peace conference. Follow me."

Bob rose and without a glance backward led Dick down to the end of the room and out the south exit. Thirty feet down the hallway he entered a dining room decorated in an Old English décor, which created an elegant setting worthy only of the executive set.

"Good afternoon, Mr. Ulbricht. Your meeting is in the King George Room," said an attractive looking woman in her late thirties. Dick took a quick glance and was again impressed with the attractiveness of female bank employees.

"Thank you, Ellen. I believe there are two more yet to come, so will you direct them in when they arrive?"

"Certainly, Mr. Ulbricht."

Dick hesitated a moment, smiled at the hostess and then followed his host into the King George room. "Gentlemen, Mr. Calkins." Dick was introduced to Norman Rothenbaum, Harry Verros and Thomas Burke. Harry Verros was the first to welcome Dick to the meeting and invited him to sit next to him.

"Let's get started. Perhaps the others will come shortly," said Bob. "Where do we begin? Has anyone had a chance to read the transcript?"

Norman Rothenbaum responded first. "I have and I am in the process of finishing my Supreme Court brief. I think there are several good legal points which we can raise and probably get a reversal." Rothenbaum spoke with considerable assurance. Although in his early thirties, he showed the maturity and confidence of an experienced trial lawyer, and Dick was impressed. It was clear from the lack of response from the others, that he was the only one who had really worked on the case, apart from Dick.

Dick spoke up and began explaining what he had been doing and how he had examined the State's Attorney's file. He was suddenly interrupted by Rothenbaum. "Dick, why don't you file a petition under the Illinois Post-Conviction Hearing Act?" This caught Dick off guard for he was not entirely sure what this act was and he hated to show his ignorance to his peers, although he was sure from the facial expressions of the others that they were just as much in the dark.

"Well, Norm, what chance do you think I would have under that act?" Dick spoke in a matter of fact tone, in an effort to conceal the probing nature of his question.

"Well, for one thing, if you raise a constitutional point you are entitled to a hearing which would permit you to offer as much additional evidence as you desire to supplement the record. In this way you could get those police reports in as well as the admissions, including the one by my client, Edward Cole." Dick was aware of the fact that in an appeal a party may not present new evidence to the Supreme Court, and if he wanted to add certain evidence he had to have a new hearing before the trial court.

At that moment Robert Hansen walked into the room. He was small in stature and had a rather pale complexion. He responded to the introductions in a soft voice. As he sat down at the table he receded into the background behind a curtain of silence. He did interject, at one point, that he had little love for his appointment to represent James O'Neil, which he received the year before, but just had not had a chance to really do anything about it. He was already using up his fourth extension of time.

Tom Burke then carried on with the discussion. "Look. I am going to be frank with all of you. I am here today because I hope one or two of you will take me off the hook for I just don't have any time for this case."

"Whom do you represent, Tom?" asked Ulbricht.

"Errol Meeks. Poor slob. He keeps writing me and his mother calls once a week, but I just don't have time to get a brief prepared."

Dick seemed to be missing much of the discussion for he was still pondering the post-conviction hearing suggestion. The more he weighed the idea the more he became enamored with it. The discussion continued through the meal but few concrete suggestions were forthcoming. Most of the lawyers seemed to be hoping to get through their assigned task on Rothenbaum's coattails. The latter was stimulated by this vote of confidence and dominated the conversation. Dick remained rather quiet, listening to the comments being made with a critical ear.

"I plan to have my brief filed in three weeks," said Rothenbaum in a hurried manner. "My principal argument will concern the failure of the State to produce certain witnesses' statements which, under People v. Moses, it was required to do." The others in the party gave a nod, but it was clear that none of them had ever heard of the Moses decision.

"Now, is it clear that if you get a reversal, it will apply to Meeks also?" asked Burke.

"I can't be absolutely certain, but it seems to me that all defendants suffered the same constitutional violations," said Rothenbaum.

At this point, Bob Hansen, almost deferentially, interrupted Rothenbaum. "Do you think there is a good chance for a reversal?"

"Yes, I do," remarked Rothenbaum.

"My, God!" said Hansen in a loud voice. "Do you mean these niggers might get back on the street and rape more innocent women?"

The group was stunned at Hansen's comment for it was clear that he spoke with great feeling. His face was flushed, and the intensity of his words cut off any response from the others. Rothenbaum tried to say something but desisted when Hansen's eyes focused on him. It appeared that almost any comment might spark an explosion.

"Gentlemen, the hour of adjournment is here," said Ulbricht in an obvious effort to end the meeting. Dick rose with the others and took leave of his host. As he proceeded to the elevator, he quickly forgot about Hansen's remarks for his thoughts were pondering the possible results he might obtain when he examined the Illinois Post-Conviction Hearing statute.

Immediately upon his arrival at the office, Dick went to the library and pulled the Illinois Statute books off the shelf. They were in three extremely large red volumes. The last one contained an index. Dick examined the index, found the section number and turned to the statute. A quick reading demonstrated that any defendant who claimed a violation of his constitutional rights was entitled to a hearing on the question, at which evidence could be offered and witnesses heard. Dick walked back towards his office, weighing the constitutional arguments he might raise.

"Mr. Calkins, Mr. Calkins," Margaret came quickly into his office. "Mr. Chadwell has been looking for you for fifteen minutes!"

"Oh, no," said Dick as he dashed out his office to Mr. Chadwell's office. Mr. Chadwell was THE MR. CHADWELL, and head of the firm.

That evening Dick entered the apartment building and walked slowly to the elevator. He failed to respond to Henry's greeting as the elevator door closed. At his apartment, he stopped, hesitated and then knocked. Anita opened the door, her face beaming with enthusiasm ... as it always did. "Hi, honey. How was your day? .. oh, oh, not so good; I can tell."

Dick said nothing but walked in giving his wife a peck on the cheek and proceeded to clean up for dinner. About half way through dinner Anita asked, "What happened? Can't you tell me?"

Dick looked at her, gritting his teeth. Then in a slow and deliberate voice, which permitted the anger and frustration that had been locked up inside him to escape, said "I have been informed that I am spending too much time on the Harden case and neglecting my office work."

There was a moment of silence and Dick took a drink of water.

"Who told you you were spending too much time?"

"Mr. Chadwell."

At the mention of the name, there was a prolonged silence because Anita appreciated the full impact of the obvious criticism of her husband's work.

Finally Anita asked, "What are you going to do?"

"I don't know."

The next day at work there was a message on Dick's desk to call Norman Woodward. Dick dialed the number and waited while the phone rang four times.

Finally a woman's voice, masked in somnolence answered. "Yea."

"This is Mr. Calkins. Is Norman Woodward there?"

"Who?"

"Norman Woodward."

"There's no one by dat name here."

"Don't hang up," said Dick. "I am the lawyer helping James Harden. Norman called and wanted to talk to me."

"Oh!" There was a pause. Then in a loud voice she shouted: "Norman, come here. Some mans wants to talk to you. Something about Jimmy."

There was another long pause and then a voice answered, "Hello. Is this Mr. Calkins?"

"Yes, it is. Did you call me?"

There was a slight pause and then the voice said, "May I come to your office to talk to you about Jimmy Harden?"

"When would you like to come?"

"It don't matter."

Dick looked at his watch which showed 9:15. "Can you come by 11:00 o'clock ... on second thought, come at 4:00 p.m. Are you working?"

"I'm starting a job next Monday so I can come at 4:00 o'clock."

"I'll see you then." Dick hung up the receiver, grabbed a pad of paper and hurried to the library to work on his research project.

At lunch time Dick saw a letter from Harden sitting on his desk and opened it. Other than listing the names and addresses of Harden's sister, brother-in-law and the latter's father, it contained little additional information. James did request that Dick contact Sammy Dillard whose address was given. He had been acquitted at the trial and there was possibility he could help.

Dick thought about the possibility of visiting Dillard that evening, but he did not want to go into the area where he lived, alone.

At about 3:45 Dick was paged over the office intercom. "Mr. Calkins, telephone. Mr. Calkins, telephone." Dick dialed the switchboard. "Yes, Nancy."

"Hon, a Mr. Norman Woodward is here, and I think you had better get him out of the reception room before the boss comes through. Dick hurried out of the library and shot up the stairs to the 23rd floor reception room. "Norman?"

Norman was a young man, very black, unshaven, wearing worn clothes. He got up and slowly shuffled toward Dick who rushed him out the door to the fire exit stairwell, where they walked down to the 22nd floor. Once in Dick's office, Dick breathed a sigh of relief. "Well, Norman, what do you want to discuss?"

"Mr. Calkins, I know that James didn't commit that rape."

"How's that, Norman?"

"Well, on October 10th, on Monday me and Jimmy Struthers were in the bull pen at Boy's Court when they brought James and the other boys in."

"Why were you there, Norman?"

"Me and Jimmy had gotten caught in Marshall High School."

"What happened when James was put in the bull pen?"

Norman took a quick glance around. Then avoiding Dick's direct gaze, he stated: "About 10:00 in the morning, a guard came in the bull pen and took all of us into the courtroom. There was this lady there and the judge asked her to point out the boys that raped her. She pointed at all seven of us, including me and Jimmy. As she pointed she said 'Them's there.' An officer pulled me and Jimmy away and said, 'Not these two. They're waiting for the next case.'"

Dick straightened up. His face lit up suddenly. "You mean she pointed at you as well as James Harden at this hearing?"

"Yes, sir."

"Norman, if this is true, this is very important evidence for us. Are you certain that this lady identified you and Struthers as well as Harden? It would hurt James Harden if we brought you in and the State proved you were lying."

"Oh no, Mr. Calkins. Ah's telling the truth. She identified me and Struthers along with the other boys."

"Norman, this will be most helpful. I will talk to you more about this as we get further along." Dick was excited by this evidence and after directing Norman to the elevator, wrote a short note to Harden explaining Norman's story, and asking if he recalled the incident.

At five forty-five Dick rushed home, and called Dave Dunsten to see if he would go with him to visit Sammy Dillard. Kathie, his wife, informed him that Dave was not home yet. Dick then decided to go alone against the wishes of Anita. Driving to 3840 West Douglas Boulevard, he parked the car and walked up the steps to the door. As he opened the door he was almost overcome by the nauseating smell of urine. In the small lobby, plaster was falling from the walls and ceiling, and there was paper and garbage strewn around. There were no names on the mail boxes and several of the mailbox doors were hanging open. Dick walked up the stairs to the first floor. The stench was even worse. The lights were out and the banister was broken. He knocked on the first door. After a minute the door slowly opened and a man in his fifties, who obviously had been drinking, looked out. Dick's voice faltered slightly as he asked if this was the Dillard's residence. The man looked at him with angry eyes. As he opened his mouth to speak, Dick was almost staggered by the smell of alcohol.

"There." The man pointed to the apartment across the hallway. Dick thanked him and started walking towards the other door, but the man just stood and stared. Dick knocked on the door but there was no response. He knocked again, and still no response.

"They ain't home, mister."

"Thanks," said Dick and he hurriedly left the building and drove home having made a decision to forget about seeing Dillard.

Chapter 5

Work in New York City

Several weeks elapsed and Calkins did nothing more than ruminate over his case. His project for Mr. Keck was nearing completion and he was scheduled for a big trip to New York City with his boss. He was, of course, pleased to be asked to go, but past trips with Mr. Keck had been, to say the least, anything but satisfying. Such trips entailed working laboriously from dawn to late in the evening, with much heavy cocktailing at night with the client. Frequently conferences were held in smoke-filled hotel rooms which left Dick limp and his clothes contaminated with cigar and cigarette smoke.

Dick felt a sense of inadequacy, locked as he was in close quarters with the high-priced legal talent of LaSalle Street, Wall Street and Philadelphia surrounding him. He hesitated to speak for fear of sounding foolish, and he certainly did not want to embarrass Mr. Keck. But the inadequacy he felt was deeper than intellectual uncertainty. He found that at times he was losing interest in the cause he was being paid to fight. Somehow the impersonal corporate client lacked the motivational stimulus to push him on.

At first Dick was overwhelmed with the brilliance of the lawyers attending these New York meetings. Each senior attorney had two or three younger attorneys assisting him, carrying his bags, feeding him documents or handing him notes. The younger attorneys, like Dick, were not expected to speak, but when they did it was clear that they had done the legal research and were equally brilliant. It was also clear that there was at least one lawyer too many who really served no function other than observe, and bill his time. Dick quickly learned that this was a practice of the giant New York and Chicago law firms to pad their billings. Dick was glad that his office did not do this for there was just Mr. Keck and himself.

It was also clear to Dick that as a matter of routine these lawyers thought nothing of fifteen to twenty hour days and work on weekends. It was not that Dick was unwilling to work as hard as the next lawyer, but for what — the corporate client? Dick knew he had much to learn about the real world.

Dick left from O'Hare airport at 7:00 a.m. with Mr. Keck on TWA's flight 706. The flight was uneventful and Mr. Keck even limited himself to two cocktails. Once in New York they took a taxi to the offices of White and Case on Wall Street. The office physically was no more accommodating than the Chadwell Keck office. After certain pleasantries, Dick and Mr. Keck began working with seven New York lawyers on a brief that was due in one week. The only interruption was the consuming of a chicken sandwich (on white) for lunch. It was not until 8:30 p.m. that anyone suggested that their efforts for the day be adjourned for a new day beginning at 7:30 a.m.

Dick and Mr. Keck and two of the client's lawyers left immediately and headed for Pietros, a favorite eating place of Mr. Keck. During the course of an elaborate dinner, cocktails were consumed rather briskly with a matter of fact air. By ten o'clock only the Chicago lawyers remained and Dick only in body, for his spirit had gone to bed. At Mr. Keck's insistence they headed for the Stork Club, El Morocco, the Latin Quarters and several other of the lesser known clubs. At each, Dick had a coke or 7-up until he was almost ill. Mr. Keck consumed twice as much liquid only of a type that knows no satiation. His speech became slurred and the more the evening progressed the more he insisted that Dick was not with it - he was not aggressive enough - he was not one of the boys. By the El Morocco he kept repeating himself only each time the words had more difficulty in leaving his mouth.

At 1:30 a.m., Mr. Keck insisted on going to Greenwich Village, and Dick felt compelled to go with him for fear that he would never find his way back to the hotel. With great effort he got him into a cab. However, in Greenwich Village they were refused admittance because of Mr. Keck's condition, which sent him orbiting in a blast of profanity which made their departure an immediate necessity.

At 6:30 the next morning Dick staggered into the breakfast shop, his head heavy from the lack of sleep and his disposition dampened by the compulsory festivities of the prior evening. After five minutes

Mr. Keck walked briskly into the restaurant, and with a pleasant smile, sat down and ordered a heavy breakfast of eggs, sausages, toast, orange juice, and coffee. His blue eyes were clear and his head already attuned to the days' work.

For three days this was the schedule that Dick kept. His arrival home Friday night was not without welcome. He was not discouraged by the work of day nor the abuse of night. He only asked himself more and more, "why"?

On Monday Dick arrived at his office earlier than usual. The prior week had left an indelible mark on his thinking, and he seriously contemplated leaving the firm. Two years had slipped by since graduation and he found it increasingly difficult to define, much less comprehend, the goals he sought. He knew he could not be a Chadwell, number one man in the firm whose yearly income exceeded $300,000 per year (1960s salary). The sacrifices demanded to achieve this degree of "success" are merciless. Year after year must be spent in excessively long hours, without a real respite, during which time children mature into adulthood. The Woodley Road, Winnetka, Illinois address of the Chadwells demands great sacrifice, but then that is the way the system works.

Dick stopped short, for he wondered whether his criticism of the system was born of an inward jealousy because he could not be a Chadwell. After all he had deep seated respect for Mr. Chadwell. He was a true gentleman, handsome with silver grey hair, a razor sharp sense of humor, and a flare for work - an unbeatable combination. His personality was like a magnet attracting some of the top legal minds in the city to his firm.

But the very charisma of Mr. Chadwell seemed to be changing Dick's basic character. The intense competition among the younger lawyers to work directly for Mr. Chadwell had left Dick short of temper with everyone, from his secretary to his bride. Dick began to sense that he could not stand this competition.

Perhaps the Harden case was merely an objectification of his inward need to succeed in the eyes of the firm; to establish an identity. As Dick thought about it he concluded that this was in fact his motivation. So be it.

Chapter 6

Continuing the Investigation

By 9:30, the mail was delivered and in examining it he found a letter from Harden. Remembering his inquiry about Norman Woodward's story, Dick anxiously opened the letter. Quickly, he perused the first two paragraphs and then read:

"I have also discussed the possibility of us appearing before a Judge on October the 10th with Sherrod, Wise and Brown, and none of them can remember any such incident. They are positive that the first judge we seen was on October 14th.

"I am sorry I must disagree with the statements of Norman Woodward, but I am sure he is mistaken about being in boys court with me on October 10th, because I would have remembered such occurrence. I am sorry that I couldn't verify Norman's statement, and I sorry that I regret that I erred so in my statement to have put your investigation on such a futile trail."

Dick too was sorry, but then it occurred to him that Harden's refusal to accept a perjured defense was a positive factor in the case because this increased his credibility.

The next day Dick received his first of a long string of letters from James O'Neil. His scratchy handwriting and poor grammar indicated a certain lack of formal education, but as Dick was to learn later, this unusual young man read widely and had educated himself along narrow lines. Yet it was the lack of formal education - the disciplinary process which is the foundation of knowledge - that labeled O'Neil incorrigible.

His letter began with a most casual greeting:

"Hi Richard"

In response to your most welcome letter I

took the first opportunity I had to reply. James Harden was very happy I know to uptain a lawyer such as you I only wish I could has as lucky as he. Richard any information that you have pertaining to my appeal which may result in my regaining my freedom would be very grateful. Could you see my brother and my sister. My sister name is Mrs. Betty Hargrave. I hope the Information has been very helpful and I am hoping to hear from you soon.

    James O'Neil #47757
    Box 1112 Joliet, Ill.

"P.S. I would appreciate it very much if you would go by my mother's house at 4500 State, apt. 1107. Mrs. Annetta Oliver and give her some confidence that my freedom is possible she's very worried. You see I've had Mr. Hansen for a year and eight months and I haven't received one letter from him. In the whole time so you can see why I is worried. I was trying to brief and abstract my own case but I don't know how so if you could help me I would appreciate it very much. Tell James I said Hello and to take it easy respectfully

    James #47787

  This letter hardly added any information to the case. Dick felt he had reached another blind alley and he had to find a new "blind alley" he could pursue. Finally he decided to call Gilbert, the ex-publisher of the West Side Booster hoping to get the address of John Dutton, the cub reporter who attended the line-up at 10th and State Street.
  Having obtained his home address, he drove there later in the afternoon but found he was not in. Leaving his telephone number with Dutton's mother, Dick then drove to James O'Neil's sister's apartment on South State Street. This was in another housing project which seemed to be crumbling from within. Although rats were not apparent, and roofs were not collapsing, it still gave the usual jungle

appearance that only mental poverty can create.

By the time Dick reached Betty Hargrave's apartment he was ready for almost anything. Instead, he was pleasantly surprised to see a very neat apartment, modestly but attractively furnished. Betty carried herself as though she cared, which gave her an air of dignity normally seen in more educated and economically secure persons. She talked pleasantly and with a vocabulary which demonstrated some degree of education.

Betty Hargrave and her husband Wilbur both worked, saving all they could for the house they one day hoped to purchase on the south side. Betty explained a simple story concerning James O'Neil's life, which began in want and went down from there. At seven he had been sent to a correctional home for young boys, and for the next ten years had seen more time within the confines of penal institutions than without. As Betty explained it, it is difficult enough to raise a child when both parents are concerned, but when there is only one parent, who in drunken rages repeatedly beat her illegitimate son, it is hard to call it a family.

Betty reflected a moment and then added, in a concerned voice: "Mr. Calkins, do you realize that in this project which covers many acres there are over 30,000 mothers and children and only 600, more or less, husbands and fathers - plenty of boyfriends," she added with a smile, "But this . . ." Betty hesitated for she was trying to choose her words. "This is our poverty, the only surroundings James has ever known."

Betty stood up. "I am not going to beg for you to help James. He is bad and probably always will be, but he does deserve another chance."

Dick was impressed, probably because for several months he was grasping at anything in this environment, which would justify the time he was giving to the case. Dick talked to Betty about the trial which she attended, when her mother refused to take an interest in her "rotten" son. After some discussion she did recall what Annetta Wise, Fess Wise's sister, had overheard that Birdia Jackson admitted she could not identify all the boys. Beyond this Betty could really add little to what Dick already knew. In taking his leave, Dick left a card in case anything further developed.

Dick returned to his office. He had decided that he would contact the families of the boys if for no other reason than to tell them that he was working for them and believed in the innocence of their sons. Towards the middle of the afternoon he had a telephone call from John Dutton, the reporter, and made an appointment to see him the next noon.

At the appointed hour Dick met Dutton at the Bamboo Inn, next to the Clark Street movie theatre. Dutton was small in stature, well dressed, and wearing a suit and tie. After only a few words were spoken, Dick knew he was well educated, which made Dick's job far easier.

After exchanging a few pleasantries, Dick explained what he was trying to do. Dutton sat pensively for a moment and then responded: "I can help you. I know for a fact this woman could not identify these boys, particularly Harden and Sherrod."

Dick could hardly hold back his enthusiasm. He still was not professional enough to mask his emotions, when he received good or bad news. "Look here, Mr. Calkins," Dutton continued, "I saw her when she came out of the line-up room and she said she could not identify all the boys, and ..."

"Wait a minute," Dick interrupted, "please start from the beginning and tell me everything that happened."

"Well, Mr. Gilbert, the editor-in-chief of the West Side Booster, told me to go to 11th and State Street and cover the line-up on October ... October ..."

"October 8," interjected Calkins.

"Yes, October 8, 1960. It was in the evening. When I got there Jud Hollis, a photographer, and Gilbert were already there. We were on the fifth floor and I saw Hollis and Gilbert go into the line-up room. I just waited outside. About ten minutes later Birdia Jackson came out first. She appeared to be upset, and as she walked out she was talking to someone immediately behind her. I distinctly heard her say that she was not sure about all the boys, and as she said this she turned and saw me. Moses Walker, the precinct captain, who was directly behind her, told her to 'shut up' and he grabbed her by the arm and yanked her towards the side in order to keep her from coming near me."

Dick sat there rather stunned. This was the first real concrete evidence he had found - evidence which came from an entirely disinterested source. Why would Dutton have any interest in this case? Dick asked Dutton a few questions, including where he could find the photographer Hollis. In parting Dick felt that Dutton would make a good witness because of his appearance, and also his evident educational background.

Dick returned to the office only to find that James O'Neil's brother, Willie O'Neil had been waiting for him. He was a teenager about sixteen years of age, with bushy hair and a leather jacket. Dick immediately noticed that his eyes were lighted up like Christmas tree ornaments.

"Mr. Calkins, James didn't rape that whore," his eyes flashed when he said the word "whore." You see, my brother has had a most unfortunate life and we is very close. He could not have done it because he would have told me. Beside I knows for a fact that he had spent the night with another woman. You see, me, James and my friend Bill were at my house until 11:00. At about this time Bill went out and got some gin and brought it back. We had several drinks and then my mother came home. My mother was very upset at our drinking in the house, but she smelled of liquor herself, so we ignored her and kept drinking. She kept screaming at us so we left the house and went to a nightclub around the corner. There James saw Saddie Collins, and he went over to talk to her. About ten minutes later he came back and asked Bill if he knew where he and Saddie could spend the night. Bill said they could stay at his house.

Willie stopped talking and seemed to be examining Dick to see whether he was interested in the events he was relating. Finally, he continued, "On the way to Bill's house we stopped at another nightclub for a night cap and continued to Bill's house. I asked if I could stay for a while, but James made me leave. This was about 2:30 in the morning. The next morning I went over to Bill's house and James and Saddie were still there."

Willie looked again at Calkins as though

searching for some sign of a response.

"What's Bill's last name?" asked Dick.

"I don't know, but I think I can find him."

"Where's Saddie Collins now?" asked Dick in a rather sharp voice which indicated some degree of disbelief in the story.

"I don't know, but I think she is in a girls' reformatory or something down at Pontiac."

"Find out for me, please. Now I have to get busy on some other work."

"Mr. Calkins," interrupted Willie, "it would be most appreciated if you could loan me $5.00 so I could get some food. You see, I spent all my money on my lady friend last night and I am a bit hungry today."

"How old are you, Willie?"

O'Neil hesitated a moment and then with some pride said, "Sixteen year old, and my lady friend is twenty-five."

"Aren't you in school?"

"Not anymore because I am sixteen now. I am going to make me some money and lead a life of style, you understand, Mr. Calkins.

"Willie, find Bill and Saddie and call me. Now I have got to work."

"Five dollars, Mr. Calkins. You know you can trust me."

Dick reached in his pocket and gave him two."

"Thank you Mr. Calkins. I am going to let you handle all my legal affairs." Willie turned and left.

Chapter 7

Meeting Harden's Family

The rain eased slightly and Dick got out of his car and ran for one of the houses across the street. The soft summer rain, which leaves the suburbs smelling sweet and fresh, somehow only stirs the stench of the near west side. Even though Dick ran up to a well maintained house in a conservative looking area, the odor of an oppressed class was only too discernible.

Finding 1926 South Christiana, Dick went to the door and pressed the buzzer. A moment later an attractive young black woman opened the door and with an air of expectancy gestured for Dick to enter.

"Mr. Calkins," she asked in a soft well-trained voice, "please come in. Reverend Wade will be here in a minute."

Dick thanked Rosie Harden Wade, James Harden's sister, and entered the modestly furnished home. Two throw rugs were on the living room floor with a couch along one wall and an arm chair near the front windows. A television set was in another corner, which was all the furniture there was. The room, however, was immaculately clean, and it was evident that the owners prided their possessions.

It reminded Dick of his days in Hawaii with the Counter Intelligence Corps. So many times he interviewed families of Japanese or Chinese ancestry in the so-called slums of Honolulu. Before entering an apartment he had to take his shoes off because the floors sparkled with cleanliness and floor wax. In these homes there might be only one couch or chair, but it was beautifully preserved, and the word "preserve" is the only proper way to describe the care the Orientals gave their personal belongings. Even the alleys in the "slums" were clean enough for children to play in.

A moment later Reverend Wade entered and in a confident manner approached Dick and shook his hand. He then turned to Rosie and in a firm voice, "two soft drinks for Mr. Calkins and myself, please." Without a moment's hesitation Rosie left the room.

Dick and Reverend Wade talked very easily with

one another. Wade was a man of about thirty-five years of age of medium height and nice looking features. He carried himself with the dignity and confidence one acquires when others depend on him for advice and comfort. In addition to being an ordained minister, which means conducting services in a store front church on Sundays, and trying to comfort and help people every night of the week, Reverend Wade was employed at General Electric's Hotpoint plant as a maintenance man.

It took only a few minutes of conversation until Dick inquired as to whether Reverend Wade knew anything that might help his brother-in-law. Wade hesitated a moment, then said, in a thoughtful manner: "Yes, my father, who is also a minister, and I visited Birdia Jackson shortly after the rape took place. I recall very explicitly that her mother met us at the door, and because we were wearing our collars she invited us in. We tried to establish some rapport with her until Birdia Jackson entered the room from the kitchen. We talked for about forty-five minutes mostly about Mrs. Jackson's mother's problems.

"We finally asked if she, Birdia, could identify James Harden as one of the boys who assaulted her. She responded that she could not."

Dick's face lit up as it had on other occasions. He still had no control of his facial expressions nor had he learned to temper great expectations with a certain dash of cooling pessimism. With great intensity he asked: "Did she explicitly say she could not identify James?"

"Yes, she did. There was no qualification to what she said."

"Well, did you in any way give the appearance you were threatening her, or were forcing her to respond in this way?"

"No," said Wade, looking somewhat askance.

"Will your father testify to the same thing?"

"Yes, he will."

Dick made a couple of notes and then inquired, "Where and when can I reach him?"

"He's at home right now. If you see him in the next half hour you can talk to him before he goes to bed. He's on the late shift at the Ambassador East Hotel."

Dick got up ready to leave when Rosie brought in two 7-Up drinks. Feeling obliged to stay a moment longer, Dick sat down again. There was a moment of silence with Rosie present, which Dick broke by asking: "Did you tell this to Jim Doherty?"

"Yes, we did," was the curt reply.

After a few more amenities, Dick left the house and drove several blocks to West Roosevelt Avenue where Reverend Wade, Senior was waiting.

The senior Wade was a God-fearing man whose only education came from the printed word of the Bible. He was a good man, who gave every penny he made as a janitor to maintain his store front church. Every free hour he had he gave to his flock. How can you fairly describe such a man except to call him the "salt of the earth" in its literal sense.

In a halting, barely audible voice he substantiated the statement made by his son. Dick was overwhelmed with this stroke of good fortune. As he parted, the kind old man said, "Please, Mista Calkins, share the gospel with us some Sunday at church." I will, Dick thought, I will.

Dick stopped at a drugstore and called the office and was informed that a Mrs. Rose Dillard had called and would be at her apartment until 5:00 in the afternoon if he wanted to see her. After some hesitation he decided to visit her as long as he was only five blocks away.

Dick once again stopped at a run-down apartment building and proceeded up the stairs to the second floor. He noted that this had once been a very exclusive area running along Douglas Boulevard. Even today the boulevard and parkway were attractive.

As Dick reached the second floor a heavy wine smell again hit his nostrils, which made him shake his head. Knocking on the door he waited, but there was no stir on the other side. He knocked again and finally it opened slowly. In front stood a very heavy-set woman who looked white. Dick looked again and quickly observed that the woman was so light skinned she could have passed for a white person. She had a few Negro features, but they were masked by the fat which covered her.

Dick quickly introduced himself and Mrs.

Dillard invited him in. As they walked to the dining room, which was shabbily furnished, Mrs. Dillard moved slowly with difficulty.

"Please sit down, Mr. Calkins. Now why do you wish to talk to me?" Dick explained what he was trying to do and told her that he had been referred to her as possibly possessing evidence that might help Harden.

At that moment a tall thin young man about 21 years old entered the apartment and started to walk to the bedroom without looking at the stranger in the living room.

"Sammy! You come here! This man wants to talk to you."

Sammy backed up and entered the living room.

"My name is Mr. Calkins, Sammy, and I am James Harden's attorney. I was trying to find out whether either you or your mother could help me."

Sammy remained quiet for a moment, and then he responded "I want to help Jimmy and the other boys but I can't because I wasn't there."

Mrs. Dillard then broke in, "Mr. Calkins, I should tell you that when they arrested Sammy along with the other boys, I went to the Criminal Building on South California Avenue to see the State's Attorney about Sammy. While we was sitting there a group of boys were brought in and I saw Fess Wise, a close friend of Sammy's. Fess waved at me and said that he had been to the Audy Home and Sammy was there. Harold, that's my other son, who was with me, went into the hall while I remained seated. Two Negro detectives, one I remember was Officer Lill, were talking to an assistant state's attorney. One of the detectives said 'What are you going to do about this woman, she can't identify these boys?' Then the state's attorney said 'We are going to railroad them because they belong to a gang.'"

Dick listened intently wondering whether he could possibly use this testimony. "Does Harold live here, Mrs. Dillard?"

"No, he lives at 128 South Homan."

"Would he be home if I dropped by right now?"

"I think he would be. He's not working now and probably won't be going out until after dinner."

Dick asked a few more questions and then left thanking both Sammy and his mother. He immediately went to South Homan.

As he parked his car he found himself in one of the worst areas of the city. The buildings were not only dilapidated but appeared to be collapsing. Garbage was everywhere. It was criminal that people lived in this environment, an environment of their own making. Slum landlords are normally blamed, but how can a building be maintained when it is being destroyed from within. It is not uncommon in the housing project for a family moving out of an apartment to rip all the plumbing and fixtures out, and sell them to a junk yard.

Dick entered 128 and climbed to the third floor. The hallway was dark and several of the stairs broken. When he reached the door of Harold's apartment, the door was open and seven children were racing around the living room. There was one couch, in shreds, a straightback chair, two orange crates and a new Zenith television set. Newspapers were spread over the floor.

Dick knocked and introduced himself. Harold got up from the couch with only his pants and undershirt on, and invited Dick in. Harold was a little taller and heavier than his brother. He too was light skinned and looked very much like Sammy.

Harold pushed some papers off the couch and invited Dick to sit down. Dick then explained the reason for his visit and what Mrs. Dillard had said. Harold listened intently and then said: "When I returned from the men's room I saw three men standing near the doorway leading into the Sex Bureau where my mother was waiting."

Dick interrupted "Did you hear the three say anything?"

"Yes, the white man, the other two were Negro detectives, looked over his shoulder at me and said 'Isn't that one of my boys?' I answered: 'You don't mean me.' One of the detectives said, 'This isn't Sammy - that's his brother.' The three went into an office and I remained in the hallway a minute longer. When I entered my mother said she had overheard the assistant state's attorney talking. He had said something about railroading the boys, I believe."

Dick made some notes. During the entire conversation several children sat listening intently

172

and staring at Dick. They may not have seen a white man before. By the time Dick got to the office it was 2:00 p.m., just in time to do some work.

Chapter 8

Meeting Mothers of the Defendants

There was little doubt in Dick's mind that James Harden was innocent. The question remained, how many of the other defendants were also innocent? He felt that perhaps Errol Meeks and even Johnny Sherrod might also be innocent - Errol Meeks because he had taken a polygraph test which was inconclusive, and Johnny Sherrod because in several statements taken from the boys, as well as the newspaper article in the West Side Booster, he had not been named.

Dick had his secretary locate the mothers of Sherrod and Meeks and arrange for a visit over the following weekend. On Saturday morning at about 10:00, he pointed his car to the near west side of the city, and it took off with little direction from him. He first visited Mrs. Sherrod, who had an apartment in the northeast corner of West Roosevelt and Central Avenue. On the street level of the building there was a pool hall and a corner saloon.

As Dick parked his car he received numerous glances from people loitering along the street. He quickly disappeared into the entrance way and went up to the second floor. After a moment's wait the door opened and a plump round faced middle-aged woman welcomed him in.

Mrs. Sherrod, who was a handsome woman, was dressed neatly, and spoke very clear and precise English. From Mississippi, she had spent much time reading and trying to educate herself.

"Mr. Calkins, thank you so very much for coming. We have heard so much about you from Johnny. All the mothers want to meet you for we feel you are the only one who really wants to help our boys."

"Thank you, Mrs. Sherrod," responded Dick, obviously pleased with the compliment. Essentially, a lawyer must feel needed, and perhaps that's the reason it is so easy for a young lawyer, stuck in a law library researching and writing briefs, to get discouraged. Talking to people, giving advice, and being successful is the name of the game, and you don't do that when you are fourth man down on the litigation team and expected to handle all the research assignments.

"Mrs. Sherrod, I wanted to meet you and the other mothers to learn a little more about the boys and their backgrounds."

As Dick spoke, he noticed that the apartment was nicely furnished with modestly priced furniture. There were several rugs on the floors. Everything looked immaculately clean. After five minutes a very attractive young teenager, Johnny's sister, passed through the living room to the kitchen.

"Gloria," said Mrs. Sherrod, "Say hello to Mr. Calkins." Gloria smiled and kept right on walking as though embarrassed by her mother's command.

Mrs. Sherrod spoke in glowing terms about her son and his many accomplishments at school, before he dropped out. He had never been in any real trouble before, but in the last year or so had been associating with the wrong boys. James Harden and Errol Meeks, had for many years been Johnny's best friends. She showed Dick a picture of Johnny, and he too, like his mother and sister was quite nice looking.

Dick inquired about Mr. Sherrod and was immediately informed that he had a physical problem -- down at the tavern one block south of Roosevelt on Central.

After about thirty minutes, Dick left, having enjoyed the conversation very much. He returned to his car and drove west along Roosevelt Avenue and then north until he came to Garfield Park. He then proceeded east along Washington looking for 315 North Grenshaw. As he drove along it was difficult to see the addresses. Finally, Dick reached the 300 block, parked his car and walked up to the nearest building to find the address. The address had been torn down so he went to the next one, and found it to be 315. He looked at the names above the mailbox but Meeks was not listed. He rang the first bell and there was no response. He rang the other bell and shortly a boy came running down the steps.

"Yes," said the boy looking rather shy. The lad was about eight years old.

"Does Mrs. Meeks live in this building?"

"In the basement."

"Thank you," said Dick, as the boy disappeared.

Dick walked outside looking for the entrance to the basement, but he couldn't find it. As he was walking down the alley adjoining the building, a young girl rode by on her bicycle and he inquired again of the residence of the Meeks. Without a word the girl pointed to a rear entrance that led to the basement. Dick walked down the steps and a woman came to the door.

"Mrs. Meeks?"

"Yes," said the woman looking puzzled and very suspicious. She was thin and appeared to be easily excitable.

"My name is Mr. Calkins..."

Mrs. Meeks interrupted and invited him in immediately.

"Mr. Calkins, I am glad to meet you. We all appreciate what you are doing. It's terrible what the police did to our boys. That lying bitch should be the one in jail, not my Errol."

Dick looked around the basement apartment. It had a few pieces of furniture with several clotheslines hung in several places. A bed was in one corner. As they talked Dick learned that Mrs. Meeks was a widow and had purchased this building on installment contract only a short time before. In order to meet the payments, she had to rent out the two upper apartments and live in the basement. She also worked to make ends meet.

"One of the problems I have is that I buy a building and take years paying for it and in five years the area is run down. My own tenants tear my building apart and I feel as though I am just going down, down."

Mrs. Meeks seemed to be quite despondent. Dick changed the subject to her son and life returned to her face. She quite emphatically declared that Errol was not involved with "that woman." In his own mind, Dick was becoming further convinced that Errol and Johnny, as well as James, were innocent.

That evening Dick thought long and hard about how he should proceed. He finally concluded that he would expand his efforts and help Sherrod and Meeks in any way he could.

The next day Dick began working on a Petition to file before the judge who tried the boys, Judge Brussell. In the petition he was going to include all the evidence he had uncovered. However, before filing it he decided he had better talk to some of the detectives who participated in the arrest.

Several days were spent in arranging a meeting place and time, but finally Dick met Detectives Lill and Manker.

Both were blacks, but their similarities stopped there. Lill was heavy set, almost squat in build, had a mustache, but was well dressed and groomed. He spoke authoritatively, with a cocky sureness, and was quite clearly the brains of the operation. Manker spoke haltingly and kept looking at Lill each time he spoke, as if he were seeking a clearance on what he was saying. He was tall and dressed neatly. He was now a detective and therefore wore a suit.

Certain amenities were attempted, but the two detectives knew that Calkins sought information, and they were not about to divulge any evidence that might be helpful. How many times a Chicago officer ran into a do-gooder who threatened their work if he found out too much. After all they were fighting to survive in their elite position. Their struggle was a real one and any outside challenge that could demean their work in any way was to be feared. Their only interest in speaking to Calkins was to neutralize his efforts, which they had heard about.

"Look at it this way, Calkins," said Lill in a professional voice, "these boys are guilty, guilty as sin. They belonged to a gang and believe me, they are better off where they are."

"But what about Harden?" I explained his medical history "and ... "

"Look it, my friend, he was there. Whether he had intercourse with the bitch, I don't know, but I know he was there. He is better off where he is - off the street. You don't understand about these boys, they are vicious. They'll kill you if they can get away with it. Leave the detective work to us, alright?"

Lill's words were not a plea, for he spoke almost patronizingly.

"But what about the lie test that Meeks passed?"

"Mr. Calkins, he did not pass that test ... it proved inconclusive, and there is a difference.

These boys are so conditioned to lying that it is sometimes impossible to test them. But I can tell when they are lying. I used to be one of them. Just look at the top of their heads and the seat of their pants, for they will sweat profusely when you've got them and they know it. Believe me, Meeks is guilty, just as guilty as Harden."

Dick decided not to raise the perjury issue. This would be taken as a threat, not only to their detective status, but to their very survival on the force. Three days later, he made an appointment to see Detective, now Officer, Primous, one of the first officers to investigate the rape. It never occurred to Calkins that Primous was no longer a "Detective", but had been demoted to "Officer" status.

Dick met Primous walking a beat, in uniform, near Marshall High School. He had a quiet non-aggressive appearance unlike so many of the black detectives and "cops" he had met in the past. He spoke clearly and commanded his choice of words.

"Officer, my name is Dick Calkins, and as I mentioned on the phone I am working on the Birdia Jackson rape. I was hoping that you might help me." Primous did not respond, his only reaction seemed to be his anticipation of Calkins' request.

"How soon after the rape did you talk to Birdia Jackson, you and Officer Johnson?"

Primous hesitated a moment and then responded, "If I am not mistaken we saw her the following Monday and Tuesday. On Monday we talked with her only a couple of minutes because she stated she was not feeling well, but on Tuesday we spoke with her for thirty minutes or so."

"Do you recall now what essentially she said?"

Primous looked down for a moment as though in deep thought. Dick was encouraged because Primous was evidently trying to help. After a moment, he said, in a halting voice, "It's been sometime now, but as I recall .." and he broke off.

"Wait a minute," Primous continued, "as I recall, we went to her apartment the day after the rape at about 8:00 in the evening . . . that was a Sunday and my day off, but I was ordered to work around the clock if necessary to find the boys who committed the rape. Evidently, a number of complaints had been received about the speed at which we were investigating the case."

Primous hesitated and then continued, "and if I am not wrong, she refused to see us because, we were told, she was not feeling well. On the next day, we visited her at her place of employment, but again she refused to talk to us. It wasn't until Tuesday, in the evening, at her apartment, that she talked to us."

"What did she say?" inquired Dick.

"Well, she stated that a group of boys, she couldn't say how many, approached both sides of the car she was sitting in and pulled her out. After taking her down the alley she said they raped her countless times."

"Could she describe the boys to you?"

"She seemed to have some difficulty describing her assailants. First she said she could only describe one or two of the boys, but I don't recall the description she gave. However, you can get my report."

Dick tried to hide his elation, which was not easy. He blurted, "Did she say why she couldn't identify any more boys?"

"Yes, as a matter of fact, she indicated that she could only identify two of the boys because so many were around the car and when she was taken down the alley it was too dark to see them. Furthermore, she said she was just too frightened through the whole thing."

"Officer Primous, if I wrote up an affidavit covering what you have just said, will you sign it?"

"I will, if my sergeant will permit me."

"Will you testify at a hearing?" Dick continued.

"I will if you subpoena me."

Dick departed overjoyed with what Officer Primous had disclosed. Even though no more than a layman himself in such criminal matters, he knew that Primous' testimony would be devastating to the prosecution's case. He understood why Detective, now Officer Primous, never testified at the trial nor was ever mentioned.

Dick now had enough evidence to prepare his petition under the Illinois Post-Conviction Hearing Act.

Chapter 9

Calkins' First Argument in Court

Snowflakes whipped past Dick Calkins in a horizontal swirl with such speed and intensity that it seemed they would never reach the ground. Dick leaned heavily into the wind which forced itself upon each unsuspecting pedestrian that tried to reach public transportation. This cold windy November day was the real Chicago which gave the city the name "Windy City."

Dick reached the office with his uncovered ears almost frozen and his nose and face drunken red. On his desk was the usual third class mail solicitations which he pushed aside, and picked up the first draft of his petition. For the remainder of the morning he worked over the petition, which he was certain would entitle Harden to a new trial. Completing the draft, he gave it to Margaret for final typing. He was satisfied with it and would liked to have shown it to Mr. Keck, but did not because of the growing criticism in the office of his work on the case.

Increased crime in the city, and growing gang violence created a new antagonism towards Dick's efforts. How many times he explained that his sole motivation was to free an innocent man. Dick was convinced that Birdia Jackson could not identify the defendants, including Harden, but that the police had gotten her to perjure herself. The innocence of Harden was too well established now, and every effort had to be made to vindicate the now three and one-half year wrong done to him with no more delay.

By the end of the week Dick filed his petition with Judge Brussell, whose courtroom was now downtown. Having served his two-year novitiate on the criminal bench, he had been transferred to the more desirable civil bench.

After two weeks, Dick received the State's response to his fifteen page petition, a one and one-half page form motion to dismiss which in effect denied the charges made by Dick and called his petition frivolous. Dick was taken aback by this the perfunctory response because it indicated the State thought little of his petition. Dick began to wonder whether his petition did have merit, not realizing that the State treated his petition in exactly the same manner it treated the thousands of others received each year.

The following Tuesday was set for argument. This meant that Dick had to go before Judge Brussell and argue the reasons why his petition should not be dismissed as the State urged. Dick prepared for his oral argument by finding a number of cases he thought would assist him. But he was warned by other lawyers that petitions such as his were normally dismissed because of the volume of frivolous petitions that the court had to consider each year.

The date for oral argument finally arrived. To describe Dick as being nervous is perhaps a kindness. His stomach was turning violently and he wished only for the moment when the argument would be over. Dick arrived at the County Building with its vast pillars standing guard over the multitude of courtrooms within its bowels. Across the street the new brown rust-colored Daley Civic Center was rapidly reaching completion. This would eventually house, in physical splendor, the same dilapidated judicial system that creaked along in the County Building.

Dick noticed none of his surroundings as he walked down the long corridor on the fifth floor to the courtroom. His anxieties were such that he was conscious only of the cases he had read and his argument which was swirling around in his mind. As he walked into the courtroom he was met by a big smile from his wife, and knowing smiles from his mother and father, who were probably as nervous as he was with his first argument.

Suddenly, without warning the bailiff's gavel fell with a thud. "Here ye, here ye, here ye. This court is now in session, the Honorable Abraham W. Brussell, presiding. Be seated and please come to order." The clerk helped Judge Brussell sit and then said, "People of the State of Illinois vs. Harden, petition under the Illinois Post Conviction Hearing Act."

Dick quickly rose and approached the bench. How do you describe your first argument in court. It is like entering a football game, or giving your first speech before your class, or performing on the stage or taking an important final examination ... you just wish it was over, win or lose.

"Counsel for the petitioner ready your Honor," Dick heard himself say.

A partially bald man in his fifties who represented the State in all its post-conviction matters, and had won 98 percent of them, answered, in a matter of fact voice, "The State is ready, your Honor."

Judge Brussell, who was a good looking man, very erudite, turned to Dick, who had pictured him quite differently, and said, "you may proceed counsel."

In order to get over his nervousness Dick read the first few paragraphs of his argument. Then as he became more accustomed to his surroundings, he relied less and less on his notes. Step by step he described the evidence he had uncovered and the way Harden had been denied a fair trial. He emphasized the fact that there was much evidence that could have been offered on Harden's behalf, but was not because it would have prejudiced the other defendants whom Doherty also represented. "To place a defendant, because of poverty, in such an untenable position, is, I submit, a lack of adequate representation of counsel, a denial of due process." As Dick heard himself speak, he thought, not bad, not bad.

Forty-five minutes later Dick completed his remarks and the assistant states' attorney began his comments. He spoke for only fifteen minutes and argued essentially that Harden had been convicted at a very fair trial, "conducted by your Honor, yourself", an obvious attempt to play on the judge's own prejudices.

At this point Judge Brussell cut off the assistant state's attorney and started asking questions about why the newspaper article was withheld at the trial, and why the police reports indicating that Birdia Jackson could only identify two of the boys, were withheld from the public defender, and why the attack on Harden which had left him, temporarily impotent had not been disclosed. The rapidity and force of the Judge's questions indicated he was concerned and was not going to be satisfied with the routine arguments he normally received from the assistant state's attorney. Dick was most impressed with Judge Brussell, not only because of his almost instant grasp of the legal questions, but the constant notes he was taking of the points made on both sides.

When oral argument was completed the judge stated: "I will take this case under advisement. Mr. Clerk, set a hearing for two weeks from today."

Dick turned to meet his family, but as he did, the assistant state's attorney came quickly over to him with his hand extended.

"Nice job, Dick. You may have a chance on this one."

"Thank you, Mr. Robbins. I enjoyed working on this case with you. Here, I would like you to meet my family."

Dick introduced the assistant state's attorney to his family. More amenities were exchanged as is always the case among lawyers no matter how bitter the battle has been in the courtroom. Outside the courtroom, Anita beamed and said little, her smile and eyes saying all that was necessary. Dick began to relax, feeling the let-down after the excitement of the past hour and one-half. Now it was just a matter of waiting two weeks.

Each time during the next two weeks when Dick thought about the case, a heavy lump came into his stomach and he had to catch his breath. He kept telling himself that it really didn't matter for few young lawyers ever won such a case and no one expected this to be an exception. Dick knew, however, that a loss here would be a serious blow to his ego. Certainly the freedom of a human being was important, but Dick knew that the battle he waged was just as much for himself and his standing in the office - a rather selfish attitude - but he was willing to be honest with himself.

The day before the decision was to be handed down, Dick arrived at the office at 9:15. As he walked into his office, Margaret handed him an envelope from the Illinois Supreme Court. When he opened it he found it was the opinion of People of the State of Illinois v. Cole, one of the boys convicted with Harden. Dick quickly remembered that Norm Rothenbaum had argued this in the Illinois Supreme Court some two months before. Without looking at a word of the opinion he fumbled through to the last page to find the outcome of the case, and there in boldfaced letters were the words: "Reversed and Remanded for further proceedings not inconsistent with this opinion."

Dick was at first elated with joy. He sat down and quickly read the opinion to see if the reasoning of the opinion covered Harden as well. After reading only five paragraphs it was clear that all seven defendants were entitled to new trials because the reversal was based on the fact that the State had failed to produce the police reports which contained favorable evidence for all the defendants. Then for the first time a heavy sober feeling or let down came over Dick for this was the work of another lawyer. However, Dick picked up the phone and called his brother lawyer; "Norm, congratulations, how did you ever do it?"

After finishing his conversation with Rothenbaum, he slowly went through the Chadwell, Keck office telling some of his colleagues the good word. Most of the younger lawyers were quite profuse in their congratulations, which Dick did not try to discourage out of any false modesty. Dick was fully cognizant of the fact that he had little to do with the Supreme Court case. The partners he spoke to showed little interest.

The same day Dick sent a telegram to James and prepared a petition, based on the Supreme Court's opinion, requesting a new trial. The lawyers representing the other defendants did the same, and within two weeks all seven boys had their convictions reversed and they were returned to the Cook County jail for new trials.

Upon reflection, Dick began to feel some disappointment in not receiving the outcome of his hearing before Judge Brussell. However, one week after the Cole decision came down Judge Brussell called him into his office. Dick arrived feeling some excitement over the judge's invitation. Judge Brussell was extremely cordial and poised. He looked and acted every inch the judge he was. "Mr. Calkins, thank you for coming," the judge began. "First, I wanted to compliment you on your argument. I was inclined to rule with you on it and would have done so if the Illinois Supreme Court had not ruled the way it did. But enough of that. The reason I called you is because I want you to write a law review article. I did a considerable amount of research on the legal questions you raised and would like to see this research put to good use."

Dick was taken aback. He was most pleased at the judge's comments concerning the case, but his remarks about a law review article caught him off guard. Without thinking he responded: "That's a wonderful idea, judge. Perhaps we could write it together."

"No, Mr. Calkins, I would like you to write it - I'll edit it for you if you wish. But let's talk about that later. Care for some lunch?"

"That I would enjoy," Dick responded, and the two left the judge's office for LaSalle Street.

Judge Brussell was a strong man, intellectually keen, a true student of the law. He was endorsed by the Democratic party for the bench, being Jewish and a registered Democrat. But he exercised great independence, which not infrequently raised the ire of the Daley machine, when he handed down an opinion adverse to the city's interests. More than once he had been shown the errors of his ways with a threat of being shuffled into judicial obscurity if his intellectual sense of right interfered with his good sense. Not infrequently problem judges are assigned insignificant functions, such as motion judge in divorce court, or trial judge in traffic court. To a man of Judge Brussell's intellect this was banishment from the profession he loved.

Dick learned at lunch that Judge Brussell's true forte was the appellate bench, for he spent much of his time writing opinions, some as long as eighty or ninety pages. This was unheard of in the Cook County Circuit Court, for trial judges were expected to do nothing more than orally rule, "Motion Granted," or "Motion Denied". This gave far more time for leisure, particularly during the inviting summer months.

The friendship that began with this first lunch became warm and lasting and of great meaning to Dick, for he was mature enough to realize the benefits to be gained from observing the thought processes of a man of such intellect and experience.

Chapter 10

Giving Sherrod, Meeks, Brown Polygraph Tests

This cold December day was an important day. Dick quickly examined the few pieces of mail left on his desk by Margaret and then picked up a law book as though he was going to read it. But his eagerness for the next half hour to arrive was too great. When you are young, a new member of the profession and you are winning, it is difficult to think of mundane matters like working for billable clients. "They're here," exclaimed Margaret in a hurried voice.

"Send them in," Dick responded.

A moment later, three black youths sauntered into Dick's office - Johnny Sherrod, Errol Meeks, and Eugene Brown. Dick was genuinely happy to see them and the smile on his face showed his feelings. "It's great to meet you boys at last. Margaret, could you get us another chair please?" Dick motioned for the three to sit down. "When did you get out of Cook County Jail?"

Johnny spoke first, "My mother brought my bond money yesterday afternoon, and I got out about an hour later."

"I got out this morning first thing, Mr. Calkins," said Errol. Eugene nodded indicating that he too had been released early in the morning.

"Have things changed much since you went away over three years ago?" asked Dick.

Johnny spoke again for the group because he had always been the leader. "Man, there's a lot of construction going on - I hardly recognize some places." As Johnny spoke his eyes flashed with enthusiasm. He was a fine looking young man whom one could not help liking. As Dick looked at the three boys before him he was convinced more than ever that they were innocent, the victims of poverty and a judicial system that was insensitive to the indigent. So convinced was he that most of the boys, including Harden, were innocent that he volunteered to represent them all in preparation for their new trial set for February 4th. The other lawyers on the case were more than happy to acquiesce, being busy with more pressing office matters. It was understood, however, that at the time of trial they might have to participate if separate trials were not granted.

"The reason I asked the three of you to come down here, and I would have included James Harden if his sister had raised enough money to get him out on bond, is because I want you to tell me precisely what happened on October 1."

The boys looked at each other not certain who should go first. Finally, Johnny spoke: "Errol and me had gone to this party that evening on Roosevelt and Hoyne. After the party we brought some records over to my house and listened to them until about 1:30. I was tired and decided to go to bed, and Errol stayed over as he often did. My mother can verify that we was there.

"Did you hear any commotion at all outside at the gasoline station, which I believe was near your apartment building?"

Errol then spoke, "Well. I heard some commotion but I didn't pay no heed to it."

Dick then turned to Eugene, "What about you, Eugene, what were you doing?"

"Mr. Calkins, I was at my Auntie's all evening. She will speak for me." Eugene was small and spoke with a weak voice that was barely audible.

At this point Dick looked at the boys squarely in the eyes. "I have good news. John Reid and Associates has agreed to give you polygraph tests to help us prove your innocence. I think if you pass the State's Attorney will release you outright."

The boys said nothing at first. Then Johnny said, "That's fine, Mr. Calkins."

"I want you to take the tests this afternoon," Dick added, "unless you don't think you can pass them."

The boys said nothing.

In the afternoon Dick took the three to John Reid and Associates, reputed to be the finest polygraph test center in the nation. Dick carefully explained to the technician, who was going to give the tests, the circumstances of the crime and the purported involvement of each person to be tested. From this the technician made up a series of questions. His first half hour of questions would be innocuous, asked simply to relax the person being tested. Then each of the prepared questions involving the crime would be asked one at a time until the questioning was completed.

Dick walked out of the technician's office to the waiting room where the boys were looking at magazines. As he walked into the room the three stood up looking rather anxiously at him. Dick noticed that each of them was sweating profusely, their eyes seemed inordinately bright, and they were definitely nervous. Dick became concerned that maybe he had made them nervous by stressing the importance of these tests.

"Look here," he said, "you might as well relax because no one will hear about these tests unless they turn out favorably. So, slow down now." The three boys forced a smile and sat down. "I am going back to my office. They will call me with the results as soon as they have completed their reports. Just relax now. I believe in you and I know that the tests will prove your innocence."

Dick walked out the door to the elevators. He was concerned because the boys seemed very nervous. Back at the office he could think of nothing but the tests: he was hoping so much that they would prove the innocence of his clients. He was not quite sure how he would handle an adverse report.

Five o'clock went by and there was no call from John Reid. Dick picked up the phone and then put it back down. I just have to be patient, he thought. Six o'clock passed and he knew he would not hear anything until the next day. It was not until 11:05 a.m. the next morning that Mr. Christiansen, a supervisor of John Reid, called.

"Mr. Calkins, I have some bad news for you. I have the reports before me and they did not turn out well at all."

"Which one failed," interrupted Dick, hoping that it was only one.

"I am afraid all three failed. As a matter of fact, each failed so badly that they gave us classic patterns of guilt. I will send the reports over right away."

Dick was stunned and just sat there saying nothing. All the work he had done over so many months, motivated by the thought that he was freeing innocent boys from years of imprisonment was for naught. This cast a shadow over James Harden. To think he had believed each of the boys when they proclaimed their innocence. He knew he had been naive because he had been warned that this could happen - oh, how he had been warned.

Christiansen broke the silence saying, "I am sorry about the results."

"Thank you, Mr. Christiansen. Please send the reports and the bill," said Dick recovering from the shock. Dick hung up the receiver; his enthusiasm which had so long sustained him was suddenly drained as he sat there staring at the wall. That afternoon Johnny Sherrod called asking about the tests. Dick instructed him to come down to the office as soon as he could with Meeks and Brown.

When the three arrived he made them wait twenty minutes. He then told Margaret to let them come into his office. He let them stand in front of his desk while he looked at a document. Without looking up he said, "Well boys, you failed the tests. You are guilty of the rape. What is worse, you have been lying to me." For a moment there was an awkward silence. The three shifted their weight from one foot to the other.

Dick continued, "I can do one of two things - either get off the case and let the Public Defender handle the retrial, or sit down with you and listen to you tell me the truth." At this point Dick looked directly in each boy's eyes to emphasize what he was saying.

Of course, Dick knew that a professional criminal lawyer does not ask his client whether he is innocent or guilty, nor does he insist that his client take a lie detector test. But Dick was not a criminal lawyer and had no intention of becoming one. He was giving his time, over 1000 hours worth, free of charge, and therefore he felt he had the right to expect more of his clients than is normally the case.

"Please tell me one thing. Was Harden there?"

Johnny spoke first. "Please, Mr. Calkins, I know we lied to you, but believe me, Harden was not there. He knew nothing about what happened."

"Wait a minute," interrupted Dick, "are you saying that Harden was not even with you that night?"

"No, we saw him earlier in the evening when we

went to the party we told you about. But he left early in the evening because his stomach hurt him and we never saw him again. He said he was going home and I am sure he did. He was sick, Mr. Calkins."

"Please, boys, don't lie to me because I don't want to waste money on another lie detector test."

Errol broke in, "Mr. Calkins give Jimmy the test. I swear that he will pass it because he wasn't there at any time. I ought to know because I was there the whole time."

There was silence, for Dick was deep in thought, and the boys hesitated to say anything more. "Tell me exactly what happened that night."

Johnny immediately responded, "Well, everything we told you about returning to my folks' apartment with the records is true. However, later that night we heard a commotion by the gasoline station and went down to watch what was going on. When we got there we saw Eugene here kicking this man on the ground. When he passed out we went to the woman and Fess Wise was pulling at her bra. He said, "Let's take her." So we did. And that's it."

"Well, who carried her down the alley?"

"I did," said Meeks. "Me and Fess and Johnny."

"Were Cole and O'Neil involved?"

"Oh, yes, they came down the alley later on when we had her under the porch. So did some three or four other boys who were never caught."

"Did you then carry her across the street to the second place she was raped?"

"No," said Johnny. "We left. I think that was O'Neil and Cole and several others."

Dick asked many other questions and the three seemed to answer them candidly, but Dick would never be certain again. Once he had pieced the entire story of the rape together he was uncertain as to what he could do at the retrial. One thing he knew he would not do, and that was to let the boys get on the stand and perjure themselves as to what occurred that night.

As Dick's thoughts turned back to Harden, he felt it was imperative to raise the bail bond money to get Harden out and allow him to take a polygraph test. After contacting Harden's sister and several others over the next few days, sufficient funds were raised to cover the $5,000 bond.

When Harden was released, Dick was there waiting for him as he walked out of the lockup. "James, it is good to see you again. I have made arrangements to take you directly to John Reid and Associates for you to take a polygraph test. I hope you don't mind the rush."

Harden stood silent for a moment and then said, "Mr. Calkins, whatever you want me to do is fine with me. I guess I want to get home as soon as I can to see my girlfriend, but that can wait."

"James, we are not out of the woods yet. You heard that the others failed the test didn't you? Do you think you can pass?"

"Mr. Calkins, I promise you that I was home in bed that night. I am certain I can pass the test."

That is exactly what Dick wanted to hear. While driving over to Michigan Avenue where John Reid was located, Harden said little and Dick was deep in thought. Arriving at the office, Mr. Christiansen welcomed them and called the same operator to administer the test. After a few words, wishing Harden luck, Dick left and went back to his office to await the results.

Two hours later, Christiansen called. "I have the results."

"That was fast," responded Dick. "How did it come out this time?" Dick's voice was tense but subdued. A lot was riding on what Christiansen was about to say.

"Let me read the results to you," said Christiansen, purposefully putting the young attorney more on edge with the delay in the ultimate answer.

> "On December 15, 1963, James L. Harden voluntarily came into the laboratory for a polygraph examination to investigate his involvement in the forceable rape of Birdia Jackson in an alley near Grenshaw Avenue and again in an alley near Fillmore on or about September 30, 1960 or October 1, 1960.
>
> "There was no significant emotional disturbances indicative of deception on

this subject's polygraph records on the following questions:

(1) On September 30 - October 1, 1960 did you force Birdia Jackson to have sexual intercourse with you in an alley near Grenshaw?
Answer: No

(2) On September 30 - October 1, 1960 did you force Birdia Jackson to have sexual intercourse with you?
Answer: No

(3) Did you force Birdia Jackson to have sexual intercourse with you in an alley near Fillmore Avenue? Answer: No

(4) Did you have sexual intercourse with Birdia Jackson on the night of September 30 - October 1, 1960?
Answer: No

(5) Were you in that alley stairwell near Grenshaw on September 30 - October 1, 1960?
Answer: No

"It is the opinion of the examiner, based on this subject's polygraph records, that he is telling the truth in the above listed questions."

Respectfully submitted,

Robert J. Abson

There was a long pause. Finally, Christiansen said "That's it." Another pause ensued.
Then Dick, with a sigh of relief said: "Well, that's the best news I have had in some time. After the prior results, I was really concerned." Dick started talking faster and faster, a nervous reaction to the news just received. He finally ended by thanking Christiansen and asking him to send the

bill.

"That's alright," said Christiansen. "We like to help out in indigent cases like this, particularly when we can help establish the innocence of an accused -- it so rarely happens, as you know. It's on the house."

"Thank you very much," said Dick. "We do have a limited budget. In fact we have no budget at all."

Dick sat heavily back in his chair as he hung up the receiver. Finally, he had been vindicated and the long hours he had spent justified. An innocent person was going to be saved, at least he hoped the State's Attorney would now release Harden.

Later that afternoon he reached Harden who was at his sister's home and relayed the good news - news Harden had known since he was picked up and thrown in jail over three years before.

Chapter 11

Harden Is Freed

Dick sat in the chambers of the very courtroom in which the defendants had been convicted several years before. This February day was dark with the threat of snow in the air.

Dick felt an inner excitement as he waited for Judge Plusdrak to call his case. The seven defendants were all present with many of their family members sitting beside them in the back of the courtroom. Each was out on bail and anxiously waited to learn whether he would have to go back. They knew that Calkins was inexperienced, but his energy and enthusiasm for their cause gave them great hope.

The assistant state's attorneys, Atkins and Nelson, were handling numerous motions before the judge. As each case was called one or the other would speak and the judge ruled, normally in their favor. Dick noticed how professionally they handled each case and wondered if he would eventually become as skilled. His thoughts were suddenly interrupted when the clerk called out "People of the State of Illinois v. Errol Meeks, et.al."

Dick jumped to his feet and moved before the judge's bench. Judge Plusdrak looked down at Dick as assistant state's attorney Henry Nelson walked over to the front of the bench. "Are the attorneys in this case ready to proceed with trial." Dick immediately answered in the affirmative. Nelson stated that the State was ready. The judge hesitated a moment and then asked:

"Would there be any benefit in having the attorneys meet with me in chambers to discuss a possible disposition of the case?"

"Yes, it would," answered Dick looking at Nelson.

"Your Honor, Mr. Calkins and myself have discussed this case and a possible plea by the defendants. At this time the State feels that the input of the court might be quite helpful in resolving the matter." What Nelson was saying was that he and defense counsel had met and agreed on a plea of guilty for each of the defendants, but

Harden, with a sentence of one year and one day. This meant that with the time already served, the defendants would be released as quickly as their papers could be processed, not more than two or three months.

Dick had discussed the plea of guilty with each of the defendants and the proposed sentence. He told them that at a trial the chances were good that there might be a "not guilty" for most of the boys; however, two possibly three, who had been positively identified by both Head and Jackson, would be convicted. His evaluation was based on the fact that the police reports and witness statements indicated that Jackson could not identify most of the boys because, as she said, she was frightened and it was dark. The confessions taken could be kept out because they were coerced in violation of the new Supreme Court Escabedo rule. However, Head's testimony collaborated by Jackson would convict Wise and Sherrod without question.

All the defendants but O'Neil agreed to the terms laid down if Dick could get the court to agree. Dick then met with Atkins and Nelson. They took the position that there would be no deal unless all the defendants agreed. As for Harden they were willing to recommend to their boss, State's Attorney Stamos, that the charges be dropped.

Dick met again with O'Neil, who refused to give in taking the position that he was innocent and entitled to a trial. Dick became quite exasperated with him knowing full well that O'Neil had been a prime mover during the rape. He finally told O'Neil that if he persisted in demanding a trial he would have to get his own attorney or have the public defender represent him. O'Neil finally capitulated, which cleared the way to a plea bargain.

Dick knew that what he had done in pressuring O'Neil was unprofessional. He had a right to a fair trial. But Dick also knew that he could not be part of the perjured defense O'Neil anticipated putting on -- he would have to have another attorney. Dick knew he was getting a good deal for the boys if the judge agreed and therefore the pressure he put on O'Neil was for everyone's benefit.

"Gentlemen, please come to my office so that we may discuss this in private." The attorneys followed the judge into his office to the right of the bench.

Nelson spoke first. "Judge, the defendants are willing to plead guilty if they are sentenced to no more than one year and one day. For the record, your Honor, the State is recommending three years except for Harden. We are meeting with Mr. Stamos later today about him and will report back to the court."

When Dick heard three years he almost jumped and was about to speak when Nelson put his hand on his arm. Holding back he waited for the judge to react to the plea bargain. Finally, Judge Plusdrak said: "I will accept the pleas of guilty and will sentence each defendant to one year and one day. You will, of course, report back on Harden as soon as possible."

Dick gave a sigh of relief for he had never witnessed a plea bargaining session before. Many jurisdictions will not entertain them at all, but in Cook County, where so many criminal cases must be disposed of each day, it becomes an essential tool of justice, if the court is to continue operating at all. The three year sentence recommendation of the State was, Dick quickly realized, for the record only.

Dick left the judge's private chambers with a big smile across his face. He signaled for the boys to meet him in the hall where he explained the terms of their plea of guilty and sentence. Several of the boys, including O'Neil were disgruntled, but this was more for show than an honest response. Each was grateful that at last the nightmare would come to an end.

Later that afternoon, Dick went to the State's Attorney's office. He sat down on one of the couches and picked up a Newsweek magazine. Within minutes Atkins and Nelson walked in and spoke to the receptionist.

"Mr. Stamos will see you now."

"Thank you Alice," said Atkins as he, Nelson and Calkins entered the States Attorney's inner office. Stamos, who was slender and of medium height, sat behind a large mahogany desk. An American flag was standing to his left behind him.

"Gentlemen, what can I do for you?"

"Sir, this is attorney Dick Calkins who was

appointed by the Illinois Supreme Court to represent a defendant charged in a rape case."

"Glad to meet you Calkins. What do you have for me?"

"Mr. Stamos, I represent a young Negro named James Harden. He was charged and convicted of a gangland rape on the near West Side."

"Who was the complaining witness in the case?" asked Stamos.

"There were two. The rape victim was Birdia Jackson and her boyfriend was Arthur Head."

"Ah, I remember that case. Quite a conviction as I recall. All the defendants got fifteen years I believe."

"Twenty years, Mr. Stamos, and one of the eight received a directed verdict."

"What's the story on Harden?" Dick began to tell about his investigation, which he had done many times to anyone who would listen. But before he got very far Stamos interrupted.

"I don't have time to hear about your investigation. What is the bottom line?"

"Mr. Stamos, I want the State to drop all charges against Harden. Here is a polygraph test he took at John Reids. The results speak for themselves." Stamos looked at the report, and, putting it down, said: "Atkins, what do you think?"

Atkins hesitated a second and then said, "We have reviewed all the evidence and feel we have no case against Harden, therefore ..."

Stamos interrupted and said, "Done; tell the judge the charges have been dropped. Thank you gentlemen, have a nice day." Stamos picked up another document and began reading as the three attorneys exited his office. They immediately went to the judge's chambers where the final papers were signed by the judge. A new date was then set to dispose of the pleas of guilty and sentencing for the other boys.

After completing this business Dick took his leave. As he walked to the elevator he felt light headed and elated. It was a feeling he had never experienced before. It was the professional joy of winning. It was the feeling a skier enjoys when he glides down a mountain slope, or a surfer feels when riding the curl of a large wave, or an investor has when he sees his stock rise ten points in a single day. He had won - Harden was now free with all charges dropped, and the remaining six boys would be freed within three months.

As Dick exited the criminal court building he suddenly realized that the elation he was experiencing was because he won, not because an innocent person had been freed. Only now did he realize the game he had been playing.

Dick did take great pride in summarizing the case in his own mind. He did it many times over the next few months.

As Doherty surmised, the trial of Harden and his seven co-defendants was a frame up. Birdia Jackson at most could identify only one, Fess Wise, and Arthur Head, only two Fess Wise and Johnny Sherrod. The rest she could not identify because it was dark and she was scared. She said this in police reports, in the preliminary hearing before Judge Epstein and in her grand jury testimony. Her testimony about Harden carrying her down the alley and putting his coat down and attributing to him such remarks as, "let her go," "I have a sister too," "she's had enough," were fabrications. The identification of Meeks and his beard was made up when the police got a photo of him.

There is no question that the rapes took place and Head was severely beaten. However, for some reason the police would not take a statement from Jackson at the 25th District police station. Birdia did complain and it got in the newspapers, including the West Side Boosters. Pressure was placed on the police department to solve the crime and the Sex Unit was brought in on the case. They were determined to get a conviction. Detective Lill was the mastermind in helping Jackson make up her story. He had her memorize the names of the eight defendants so she could identify them in court.

The police worked on the weakest of the defendants, Brown and Wise, to get them to confess. And Detective Lill perjured himself in saying Brown and Wise identified O'Neil and Cole for neither would ever have admitted to the crime. But there was no way to contradict the police - the defendants' word against the police. The police had Jackson lie that she identified Harden and the others in a police lineup. The West Side Booster reporter, who took a photo of the lineup, said she did not identify Harden.

The clincher in the entire case for the defendants was police officer Primous, who was not permitted to testify because he would have destroyed the State's entire case. He verified that Jackson could not identify any of the boys but Fess Wise because it was dark and she was frightened. This would have totally undermined Birdia Jackson's testimony and would have raised a reasonable doubt. But Officer Lill kept him away from the trial.

As the case turned out, the seven, including Meeks and Sammy Dillard, who was never identified, did commit the rape. The moral question is were the tactics of the police justified when they netted seven out of eight. Perhaps the answer is self-evident. The laws we now have, requiring the police to give a suspect his Miranda warnings - he has a right to an attorney and the right to remain silent - and requiring them to turn over all admissions of the defendants as well as exculpatory evidence, is intended to protect that one innocent person, and not the seven guilty ones. Had those laws been in place in January 1961, two of the seven would have been convicted, and six, including Harden, would have gone free. The question then is, is this too great a price to protect just one innocent person, who had no criminal record, not even an arrest, from spending three and one-half years of a twenty-year sentence in the penitentiary? I leave that to the reader to decide.

BOOK III
A GOOD FAITH EFFORT

Chapter 1

Helping His Boys Find Jobs

"Pass the tea, please. Frankly, I don't know why I drink hot tea on a warm day like this. It's like eating hot cereal on a summer morning; it must raise my body temperature five degrees. I guess we really are creatures of habit." Dick Calkins slowly poured hot team into his small Chinese cup.

"Alright, Calkins, this was your idea not mine. You issued the invite. I really didn't want Chinese food. Say, did you see where a fourteen year old girl was shot in a riot last night on the West side? Her mother was ranting and raving that the police shot her, when the autopsy proved it had to be one of those snipers firing from the tenement house off Hoyne Street. As far as I am concerned if they gunned down about ten or twenty of them they would stop those disturbances in two minutes flat. Think of it! They shot a police captain in the back and wounded five others. It's utter anarchy. The only way to deal with this Negro and Puerto Rican problem is to let them know you mean business. You notice how quickly the riots stopped when the National Guard moved in? You know why, don't you? It's because General Gardner told his men to shoot to kill and these Negros knew it. This is the only way to teach them right from wrong. To think that those young teenage punks that were looting had the gall, when interviewed on TV last night, to demand swimming pools and recreational facilities. They have to learn to live like human beings first, before they deserve such advantages. As far as I am concerned, they're nothing but animals, and that is the way they should be treated."

"David, calm down!" said Dick. "Why get so worked up over this thing. Of course this rioting is wrong, and I confess that I agree with much of what you say." Dick in actuality agreed with few things that Dave Power said. They were on opposite sides of the fence on so many issues: religion, politics, social concerns. But Dick did not want those differences to affect their friendship. "Say, this fried rice is good. I am glad you recommended it," said Dick trying to change the subject.

Dave Power, a junior partner in the firm of which Calkins was now a senior associate, was an intelligent, astute and capable lawyer of about thirty-six years of age. He was the son of a Chicago policeman of Irish descent, who had made that added sacrifice which enabled Dave to emerge from the working class of the big city to suburbia in Park Ridge. At moments like these he showed all the determination, obstinacy, bigotry, and righteousness that were inborn characteristics of an otherwise happy and wise-cracking individual. It was only on certain subjects that his keen sense of humor failed him, and this was one. On religion there was only one church -- the Catholic Church; on politics, one party -- the party of Mayor Richard Daley; and on politicians, only one type -- the Irish alderman.

To Dave the great issues of the day were so easily defined. As he described it, there were basically two evil forces in the country: the Negro movement of Martin Luther King, Jr. and the Protestant South which created the crisis, giving rise to all civil rights problems in the North and South. In his mind one was as bad as the other, and his classic solution was to create a large reservation in the West to which all Negros would be sent and kept until one by one they proved themselves worthy of returning to the white man's society. In the South he would create a large national park covering several states where all southerners would be let loose to run around unrestrained and barefoot. The rest of the country could then come and watch them - like the bears in Yellowstone Park. It goes without saying that Anita had some reservations about Dave's sense of humor for he was touching matters which southerners do not find amusing.

"Dave, I can't believe you are really serious about your 'solution'. In the first place it is hardly turning the other cheek, and in the second it is --"

"Don't kid yourself -- I am dead serious," said David, gritting his teeth. "The only way to teach them a lesson is to kill a few." By this point his agitation was showing in the higher pitch of his voice and the flush of his round face.

Dave took a sip of tea and then continued: "For a society to survive much less exist it must destroy those elements which seek to undermine it. And when those elements turn to anarchy and rebellion the rules of war must be invoked. So when I say kill them, that's just what I mean. The sting of death makes its impact even in the depths of the jungle."

Dick was taken aback by the intensity of Dave's feelings which he knew were unhealthy, but shared by many in Chicago and other northern cities with large Irish, German and Italian populations. Dick also felt his temperature begin to rise, but he checked himself for he felt that Dave might be baiting him just a bit to see if he could get a reaction. Finally, in a calm voice Dick said, "But do you think killing people, whether under the color of law or not, cures the basic evil? If the only question was teaching them the difference between right and wrong, as you say, I would agree that the community-imposed discipline of the police might be a partial answer. But I wonder if it is as simple as teaching a segment of our society the virtues of right and the evils of wrong. Remember those Negro boys I helped --."

"Stop! Don't get started on those indigents again. That's all you have talked about at lunch for three years and to be honest I am tired hearing about their trials and tribulations."

"Well, now, hold on just a minute. Muster together all the Irish patience you can and hear me out." Dick was beginning to feel some irritation of Dave's outright rudeness.

"Make it short for the hour is more ephemeral than your discussions of the Harden case."

By this time, Power's sense of perspective was returning and along with it the normal twinkle in his Irish eyes. Dick, seeing this, also relaxed somewhat and said   "First, you recall that the boy I originally was appointed to represent was nolle prossed by the State, and Errol Meeks, one of the other six I helped at the retrial, was released immediately on a plea of guilty. The other five pleaded and were sentenced to one year and one day which made them eligible for immediate parole because of time served. It took about four more months to get them released for good.

"Getting them out of prison however, was just the first step," continued Dick, "keeping them out and helping them become useful members of society was the real challenge. I decided I would help them get jobs and counsel them if they would listen to me. I must confess that the last year and a half has been an education in itself and perhaps sheds some light on what we have been talking about."

Dick hesitated, took a sip of tea and then looked at Dave for some encouragement to continue. Seeing none, he continued anyway. "James Harden was the first one I helped primarily because he was the one I was appointed to assist and because he had been sent to prison an innocent man serving three and one-half years before we could get him out. You would have thought he would have been angry and bitter because of the prime years he had lost. Before he went to jail he was planning to get married, which had to be delayed all those years. But his girlfriend faithfully waited for him."

Dick looked intently at Dave to be certain he was listening. He seemed to be, or else he was just being polite. "If that had been me," continued Dick, "I would have been so angry that I would have been a wild man. He just remained complacent and never once complained. And to think those police officers had induced Birdia Jackson, the complaining witness, to perjure herself and identify the defendants when she could not. At most she was able to identify one of the defendants, but the police had her memorize the names and faces of the others to get the convictions."

"So he was innocent," said Dave, "but don't think for a moment that he had not committed some other crime and therefore deserved to be in jail."

"Dave, I don't believe what I am hearing. You're supposed to be a lawyer. How could you suggest such a thing?" Before Dave could answer Dick continued: "You don't know this, but Harden had no police record, not even an arrest before this case. And he has a very caring family that were most supportive through the whole thing." Dick did not dare mention that Harden's sister's husband and father-in-law were ordained Baptist ministers with store front churches. This would have brought a new avalanche of words condemning those "children of Satan."

"Dave, I think you are baiting me, but just in case you are serious, you know what would happen to our judicial system if we became lax in our protection of the rights of the accused. There are too many innocent people in our penitentiaries today as it is, and there is no way to help them."

There was a momentary pause, and then Dave said, "Well, if you feel so strongly about what happened to Harden, put your efforts where your mouth is and file an action against the state for wrongful imprisonment, and get him some money."

Dick reflected a moment, weighing what David had said and then answered: "I am not certain filing a lawsuit is in the best interest of Harden for they drag on for so many years, raising so many expectations, and then they often fail creating even more disappointment. I wanted him to get on with his life and not plan for the future thinking he was going to receive a big windfall."

Dick took another sip of tea, which was getting cool, looked at his watch, and realized that he had only a minute or two to tell his story. "The day after Harden was nolle prossed by the State, he came to my office and we talked about his future. The night before I talked to my father who agreed to hire him as a laborer on a construction job. I asked Harden if he was interested in the job and he stated he was. I tried to impress upon him the importance of not missing work and working hard.

"We also talked about his coming marriage and how happy he was. He really seemed to be determined to make a good life for himself and his wife. But you know, Dave," - Dick hesitated, looked down, and then continued, "neither Harden nor any of the other boys really thanked me for all the work I did to gain their freedom. In Harden's case it was almost as though he expected it. Even getting him the job, he never thanked me or my father."

Dick got up. "It's getting late. We had better get back to the office." As they walked to the cashier and stood in line, Dick continued: "Harden began working at the Illinois Bell Telephone

Building at Franklin and Randolph, as a construction laborer, at $3.30 per hour or $120.00 a week, which was more money than Harden had ever seen in his life. And this was the beginning of his problem. In a few weeks he had saved over one hundred dollars and rather than saving it for the wedding, he spent it all drinking one weekend."

Dick and Dave paid their bills and left Jimmy Wings restaurant, walking east on Monroe. Dave noticed that Dick was limping, and said, "I don't mean to interrupt, but what did you do to your leg?"

Dick smiled, appreciating the interest, and said, "I hurt it sliding into third base in the lawyers' sixteen-inch baseball league in Grant Park. I play for our firm's team."

After a moment's hesitation Dick continued his story. "Needless to say, Harden missed the next three days of work without telling the foreman. He didn't call me either. Finally, he went back to work and they gave him another chance. But six weeks later the same thing happened and he lost his job. I was so disappointed, because he had so much to look forward to."

"Well, what happened to him? Did he get married?" asked Dave.

"Yes, he did get married and now he has a son. When he was fired I decided to wait for him to get in touch with me, which he did a month later. He apologized for what had happened explaining that he started drinking and gambling and was just too tired to work. But now that he was married he wanted to settle down."

The two entered the Field Building, recently renamed the LaSalle Bank Building. As they got on the elevator, Dick continued: "I helped him get another job, only $80.00 gross per week, but he likes it and has held it for over a year now.   I rarely see him, but he seems quite happy with his life, enjoying his little family. His wife is such a nice and stable person. She has kept her full-time position at the city's service department even though she has a baby."

Dave had been patient listening to Dick. As they entered the waiting room of the Chadwell office he asked if Dick had similar success with the others. But before Dick could answer Dave took off down the hallway to his office. As he walked away, he raised his right hand and without looking back said, "See you later, bigot."

Chapter 2

Al Larson of Inland Steel Helps

It was 6:15 p.m. and time for Dick to leave the office if he was to catch his 6:35 train to Wilmette. He left the office, took the elevator down, and walked out into the summer heat onto LaSalle Street. As always, he looked across the street at the sign hanging from the building at 208 South LaSalle Street, which showed the stock market advances and losses. A red arrow showed that on this day the market lost seven points. That's the third day in a row that it has been down, thought Dick. The Dow Jones is down to 820 from a high of 1000 just months before.

Not infrequently, Dick would step into the waiting room of one of the investment houses during the lunch break to watch the big board tick away. All his savings, which were not considerable, were invested in stocks, but he was not making any money. In fact, after five years, if he was even, including paying the brokers fees, he was doing pretty good.

After looking at the sign he turned to hurry to the train station, for he only had twelve minutes to make the 6:35 train. He walked down LaSalle Street to Madison, then west on Madison, over the bridge to the Northwestern station. At the entrance way to the station he bought a Daily Newspaper, to read on the train during the thirty-five minute train ride.

Dick reached the train just as the doors were closing, found a seat, and settled down. Glancing at the headlines he shook his head: "KING DEFIES COURT ORDER" "We'll march anyway because the court's injunction is unconstitu-tional," says Martin Luther King. Dick began to read the story, but stopped and pulled out the White Sox's box score -- behind by three in the seventh. I wonder if they won, thought Dick. They just have not been the same team since the championship year of '59; and always such hope each budding spring.

There were other articles on the front page concerning Vietnam and the Dominican Republic, but somehow they seemed so remote, so far away. After all, we have to trust President Johnson, for he knows what he is doing, thought Dick. Dick put the paper down and began thinking about the force being used by the police to quell the riots in Chicago sparked by Martin Luther King. Maybe Dave is right, he thought, for force has succeeded as history shows. It saved Korea, it ousted the communists from Indonesia and Malaysia, and it's winning the battle in Vietnam. In fact, the whole course of history has been molded by force, not by turning the other cheek.

In thirty-five minutes exactly the train reached Wilmette and Dick got off and began his fifteen minute walk to 1725 Central Avenue. How he enjoyed walking through Wilmette to his home. He had so much for which to be grateful, a beautiful wife, two lovely children, a fine home in Wilmette, a good job at a respected LaSalle Street law firm. It was certainly easy being a good Republican for that was the surest way to maintain the status quo.

At 7:25 p.m. Dick walked into his house, and shouted "I'm home!" Anita and two-year old Chrissie came running, welcoming Dick who barely got beyond the door, one with a kiss and the other with a hug around the leg; two persuasive reasons for keeping things as they were. The third, Tad, was asleep in his rocker in the front room.

"Your mother just called and wants you to call her right away. You'll never believe what happened so I'll let her explain it." Dick went into the kitchen and dialed his parent's number.

"Hello, Mom, Dick." Dick listened for five minutes as his excited mother explained what had happened. "Now wait a minute. Tell me that again, slowly, and calm down, please ...."

"I am sorry, Mom. I did not mean to suggest you were not calm." Dick listened for another two minutes and then finally hung up the phone when their conversation was completed, and looked at Anita with a stunned expression. Then he started to laugh, and said, "I can't believe it. I just can't believe it! And to think my own parents. Anyone in the world, but not my own parents."

So much had happened since the summer of 1964 when the boys were finally released from prison and Dick met with them to help them plan their futures. Dick's expectations had been so high, but one by

one, failure and disappointment had set in, and now
this.

Chapter 3

Meeting His Boys For the First Time

How well Dick remembered that Tuesday morning in early July, 1964, when he met with the boys, except Harden, to discuss their future plans. Harden, because of his earlier release, was already working and had just gotten married. Dick was extremely excited for his boys, for they were proof that he was a good lawyer, and now he wanted to prove he was a caring lawyer. In his own way, he envisioned establishing a program to help disadvantaged Negroes released from prison establish new and meaningful lives.

On the day the meeting was set, Dick got to the office at 7:30 a.m. to get his other work started so he would not be criticized for spending more time on the Harden case during office hours. Needless to say, his cause was not a popular one with the partners at the Chadwell office.

At 10:20 a.m. the boys arrived for the 10:00 a.m. meeting. Margaret brought them into Dick's crowded office. Johnny Sherrod entered first, followed by Errol Meeks, then Fess Wise, and Edward Cole. Extra chairs were brought in and the boys sat down.

"Where is Eugene Brown and James O'Neil," asked Dick. Johnny answered: "Eugene moved to Milwaukee to live with his auntie, and I have not seen O'Neil."

Dick hesitated a moment and just looked at his boys feeling a great sense of pride and hope for the future of these young men. Smiling, he said: "Boys," and that was the wrong thing to call them, for they were now adult men, and a Negro male finds it extremely offensive to be called "boy", but Dick was speaking with affection and pride, for these were his "boys" for whom he had worked so long and so hard.

"I have good news for you," Dick continued. "I am going to help each one of you get a job. And if you will let me I will work hard to help you keep your jobs. You deserve a few breaks in this world after such a bad start."

The boys shook their heads agreeing with Dick.

"Thank you, Mr. Calkins," said Sherrod, in a very polite voice. "I knows that I speak for the others when I say we appreciate all that you have done. We only hope we can justify the trust you have placed in us."

"That's right," said the other boys, almost in unison.

Oh, how Dick loved to hear those words of gratitude and determination to succeed. It had been a long time since Dick had felt so elated with so much hope for the future. After a slight pause, Dick continued: "I have a challenge to make to you. I have talked to several friends, and we are prepared to help any of you to purchase a small house in Evanston, where you can move with your families and begin a new life. Evanston has a very nice Negro section with access to excellent schools for your brothers and sisters. What do you think of the idea?"

The boys sat in stunned silence. Dick looked at each hoping to get a positive reaction. Fess Wise and Edward Cole looked down while the others simply avoided his look. Finally, Johnny Sherrod began to speak, "Mr. Calkins, I do appreciate this offer," he hesitated. Finally, he continued: "Speaking for myself, I think it would be very hard for my family and me to live so far away from our home on West Roosevelt. That's where all our friends and relatives are."

Errol Meeks then picked up the conversation, "I agree with Johnny. We just would not feel comfortable moving to a strange neighborhood."

"Well, just think about it and if you are interested, let me know. Remember, it's not as though you were moving down under to Australia, or someplace like that." The subject never again came up.

Dick explained that over the next two weeks he would contact each boy and line him up with a job. Dick had been calling his friends, and anyone else who was interested, soliciting jobs for his boys.

The first two jobs he was able to line up were with the Torcum Carpeting Company, located on South Michigan Avenue, not too far from Dick's office. Mr. Torcum had offered to take on two boys and teach them the trade. After careful thought Dick decided to send Fess Wise and Edward Cole. Based on Dick's recommendation the two were hired and started working the following Monday morning.

Dick next got Errol Meeks a job with the Schwitzer Construction Company at a salary of $120.00 per week, the union wage. Like James Harden, receiving this much money so quickly sowed the seeds for future problems. Actually, Dick had bigger plans for Errol, for he was quite intelligent and had great potential.

About a week and one-half later, Dick met with Al Larson of Inland Steel Company. He was one of the many industrialists making a concerted effort to hire Negroes, not just those most qualified, but young men who have had serious difficulties with the authorities. His practice was to talk to a young man, learn about his background, his present motivation and desires, and then offer him a job if he thought he would fit into Inland's scheme of things.

Al Larson was a great human being for he deeply cared about the young men he was helping. He worked with them, not only during office hours, but at night and on weekends, constantly giving of his time and efforts. On evenings and weekends he would visit with these young men at their pool halls or bars just to understand better their interests and problems. He was a dedicated servant who felt that a difference can be made if people in industry will get involved personally.

Mr. Larson agreed to work with Johnny Sherrod and James O'Neil. Dick contacted Johnny and an interview was arranged. However, he tried for several weeks to reach O'Neil, but he was unsuccessful. He finally gave up and did not hear again from O'Neil until several months later.

By the end of the second week, Dick felt quite satisfied with his efforts. Each of the boys, except for O'Neil had a job or would shortly. Harden had recently been married and settled down in his second job which he liked and was regular in his attendance. There was not too much more Dick could do, at least he so thought.

Chapter 4

Johnny Sherrod Gets A Job

"Mr. Calkins, Johnny Sherrod is on the phone. Have you time to talk to him?"

Dick put down the Corpus Juris Secundum he was reading and picked up the phone. "Thank you Margaret." Speaking into the phone he said, "Johnny, did you get the job at Inland?"

Johnny was quite excited, although he tried to mask this by lowering his voice. "Yes, Mr. Calkins, Mr. Larson gave me a job in the plant. He said that if I make the progress he thinks I will make, he is going to work me into a supervisor's position."

"Tell me what you had to do to get the job."

Johnny hesitated a moment, and then said, "I had to take a number of examinations, which Mr. Larson said I did fine on and he interviewed me three or four times. Now he says I am exactly the kind of person he wants."

Dick knew that Larson interviewed these young men several times and gave them tests in order to raise their expectations. He felt that by doing this and then offering them a job, rather than simply giving them a job at the outset, they would consider their new jobs important, giving them a sense of success. "When do you start?"

"I have already started and I think I am going to enjoy the work. But that is not why I called. I am going to get married next month to Renee and we want you and Mrs. Calkins to come to the reception to be the guests of honor."

Dick hesitated a moment, and then responded, "Johnny, that's wonderful. Congratulations! Let me talk to Anita and get back to you. I know she would love to come if we are free. What is the date?"

Dick was not quite sure how Anita was going to accept this one. She was a great person and willing to do most anything Dick asked, but there were limits.

That evening, when Dick arrived home, Anita informed him that they would be able to move into their new home in Wilmette on August 19th. The bank had called and had set the date for the closing. The smile on her face showed how pleased she was with the move. Dick immediately went into the living room to hug his baby daughter who was three months old. With a bigger smile, Anita said, "Guess what, your little girl has a present for you." Without hesitating Dick took the baby into the bathroom to change her.

From the bathroom Dick said, "And I have a surprise for you. We have been invited to a wedding reception."

"Who is getting married?" asked Anita with anticipation, for she so enjoyed weddings. Dick hesitated and said "Guess."

Anita came to the doorway and said, "I can't. Please tell me."

"Johnny Sherrod is getting married and wants us to be the guests of honor." There was a long lull. Then Dick added, "I told him I would check with you to see if the calendar was clear. It's the second Saturday in August." Again, there was a lull in the conversation.

"We do not have to go, of course, so let's just think about it," said Dick. Anita said nothing but went back into the kitchen while Dick completed his assigned task.

Nothing more was said about the wedding for a week, when Anita announced they would go. Dick hugged her for he very much wanted to accept the invitation as a show of support for Johnny and the boys.

The following Sunday afternoon Dick got a call from Mr. Torcum explaining that Edward Cole had been arrested for auto theft. He asked Dick to help Cole for he felt he was making excellent progress in learning the trade.

First thing Monday morning, Dick went to 11th and State Street to Boys Court and posted a bond with funds provided by Mr. Torcum. Dick and Cole then went to Dick's office.

"Alright, Edward, I didn't want to discuss the matter until we could be in private. What happened?"

"Mr. Calkins, I had no idea the car had been stolen. I purchased it from a car dealer, Mercury Auto Sales, and I received a bill. I paid $200 down and a second payment of $100.

"Do you have the receipts, Edward, because if you do we will have a good defense." As Dick spoke he made notes on a yellow legal size pad sitting on his desk.

"Yes, I do," assured Cole. "I don't have them with me, but I can get them at home."

"Do you recall the name of the car salesman?"

"Yes, I do. His name was Arthur. You can call him and he will verify what I said."

"Arthur who? What is his last name?"

"I don't remember, but I am sure I can find out. By the way I also paid $40 extra to Mercury Auto Sales for auto plates and a city sticker."

"This is helpful, Edward. Is there anything else that happened? Was anyone else with you?"

Cole hesitated a moment, and then he answered. "Yes, there is one more thing. There were two friends with me when I was arrested, only they were released because they paid the cop some money. I am sure they would speak on my behalf."

Dick became immediately upset. How could police officers do such a thing. This was not the first time he had seen police officers shake down a victim; maybe this time Dick could make an example of these officers. "Edward, bring in the bill of sale on the car, your receipts for the payments you made, the name of the salesman and his telephone number, and the names and telephone numbers of your two friends. I will need this by Wednesday. Can you do this by then?"

"I sure can, Mr. Calkins." Edward left the office and Dick got back to work on the General Electric case.

Dick felt a certain satisfaction in working with his boys which was lacking when he worked on these massive antitrust price fixing cases. This probably was because a corporation is so impersonal, and when you have so many partners ahead of you on the case you rarely do anything more than research and carry the bags. But Dick enjoyed the work, for he got to talk to top General Electric officers and drive around in chauffeur driven limousine cars when he and Mr. Keck visited the corporate offices.

Dick was still amazed at how blatantly officials at General Electric, Westinghouse, and Allis Chalmers had fixed the prices on turban generators for a thirty year period. In the 1930s, the three manufacturers had developed a "phase of the moon" scheme to fix prices on the sale of generators to public utility companies. When it was the phase of the full moon, General Electric got the bid; when it was the phase when there was no moon, Westinghouse got the bid. And Allis Chalmers got the bid in between the two phases. On those bids falling to General Electric, the other two companies bid high and etc.

Dick found it interesting that because the equipment was so complex, it was very difficult to establish a proper price. Any mistake could cost the company a fortune. It turned out that there was one General Electric employee, who was a pricing genius, who worked out the prices for all of the jobs being bid. The price he established, which was always accurate and, of course, according to General Electric and their counsel, not excessive, was then forwarded to the other two competitors, and the bidding worked off this price.

Dick still remembers when Senator Keefauver of Tennessee announced on television that the three companies and several of their officers had been indicted under the Sherman Antitrust Act. As the criminal case turned out, three executives actually went to jail, the first time this had happened up until 1960. The Chadwell office now represented General Electric nationwide in private treble damage lawsuits brought by the public utilities for alleged excessive charges for the equipment in question.

Wednesday came and Edward called to say he could not make it for the meeting because he had to go to the south side on a delivery. Another date was set for Friday, only this time Cole did not even call. On Monday morning Dick called Mr. Torcum and asked to have Cole call him. That afternoon Cole called and agreed to bring the papers over in an hour. Again, he failed to show up. On Tuesday, the receptionist, Nancy, gave Dick a note which Cole had dropped off earlier.

"Dear Mr. Calkins:

"I think I had better come in and talk to you. You and Mr. Torcum have been fair with me and it is only right that I square with you.

Thanks, Edward"

There could be no doubt as to the meaning of this note.

At 5:10 p.m. the next day Edward Cole arrived at Dick's office. With a voice laced with humility and sincerity he began talking as though he wanted to get this painful incident over with.

"Mr. Calkins," said Edward, sitting down in the chair in front of Dick's desk, "You and Mr. Torcum have trusted me and I want to be worthy of that trust." Edward was looking down, his face was drawn and he kept wringing his fingers. "All my life I have been in trouble and you are the first people who have had any confidence in me. If I am given a chance on this thing I know I can make good; I have to for myself, my wife, and my two little girls."

Dick silently listened. When Edward stopped, Dick said: "I didn't know you had a family."

"Yes, Mr. Calkins. Several months ago I moved in with my girlfriend and her two little girls. I have a lot of responsibilities now, and I have to make good."

Edward hesitated a moment. Sweat appeared on his forehead. "I did take the car. It was parked a short distance from my apartment building and the keys were in it. So I decided to drive it to the barber shop where I work evenings. When I finished my job cleaning the shop, I drove it home and parked it a block from the apartment building. The next day when I came home from my regular job it was still there so I drove it again to the barber shop. That is when I was stopped."

Dick just sat there and listened. He was amazed at how Cole had lied so glibly making up a story that he knew he could not begin to substantiate, and with such sincerity. Now he was pleading for understanding which Dick wanted to give but was not sure he could.

"One thing I noticed about the key," continued Cole, "was that it was a master key that would fit any Chevrolet. The police officer who stopped me said that the car had been stolen a month before."

"Edward, what about the bribe?"

"Oh, Mr. Calkins, that was true, believe me."

"Will the two boys testify on your behalf?"

Cole hesitated a moment, and then looking out the window, said: "One of them is in California and won't be back until the fall, and the other said he is afraid to testify because he is on probation and does not want to get in trouble."

Dick said nothing. He didn't even try to decide whether he believed this story or not, for it did not matter. He finally decided he would help Cole in spite of everything. If Cole was going to make it in the real world, it was now or never. Perhaps with a plea of guilty the court would allow him probation in view of the fact that his employer wanted him to continue working.

On Friday, Dick appeared in Court with Edward, and talked to the assistant state's attorney about the case. He did not seem impressed, but when the arresting police officer failed to appear in time for the hearing he agreed to drop the charges.

Afterward, Edward was quite relieved. "Mr. Calkins, you will never regret that you helped me, I promise you."

"We shall see, Edward." And Dick did not have any more problems with Edward until two years later, when Dick got the surprise telephone call from his own mother.

Chapter 5

Johnny Sherrod's Wedding

August came and the date of Johnny's wedding was quickly approaching. Dick and Anita never spoke of it but it was marked on the calendar in the kitchen where Anita listed their social engagements.

On the day of the wedding Dick gave Anita every excuse to back out but now she was determined to go. She was not going to let Dick go to the reception alone.

Dick was proud of Johnny Sherrod, for he was making excellent progress at Inland Steel. Al Larson had called Dick to tell him that Johnny had received a nice raise and promotion. So there were added reasons for Dick to want to go to the reception.

Anita got a baby sitter for Chrissy and they left the apartment around 8:30 p.m. to arrive at the reception at 9:00 p.m. Driving down West Madison Street, just as it was getting quite dark, made both wonder if they were doing the right thing. They easily found the address and parked the car in the street in a lighted area. Dick locked the car hoping that it would be in the same condition when they left the reception. The hall was on the second floor of a two-story brick building which had an empty store on the first floor. Opening the door, they started walking up the stairs to the reception hall. They could hear singing and shouting and exceptionally loud rock music. They walked into the hall which was packed full of happy people all dressed in tuxedos and formal evening gowns – and Dick only had a business suit on and Anita an evening dress.

Standing in the doorway, Errol Meeks spotted them first and came running over to welcome them. "Dick, Anita, what an honor to have you here," he shouted over the music and noise. "Come, let me introduce you to the bride." Looking around, he said, "Now where is Sherrod? There he is, and there is Renee. Follow me through this crowd. Johnny is really going to be happy to see you. I told him you would come."

Errol was dressed in a black tuxedo with a white tuxedo shirt with frills down the front.

"Errol, you really look handsome," said Dick. Errol said nothing; just smiled.

At that moment Johnny spotted them making their way across the floor, and he rushed over "Mr. Calkins, Mrs. Calkins, what an honor it is to have you at our wedding reception. I want you to meet my bride."

Johnny took Dick by the arm and led him to a group of several people talking to the bride. "Renee, Renee, look who is here. I told you they would come. It's Mr. and Mrs. Calkins."

Renee was a beautiful young woman with light tan skin. She had the appearance and stature of a model. Dick took Renee's hand in his and said, "Renee, this is my wife Anita, and we want to wish you and Johnny all the happiness in the world. Johnny is a fine young man and has a chance to really make something of himself. He is so fortunate to have such a beautiful bride as you."

"Thank you, Mr. Calkins. Johnny has told me so much about you that I feel I already know you."

At that point Johnny shouted to the band leader and asked him to stop playing for a moment. When he did not respond, Johnny worked his way over to him and shouted in his ear. He signaled the band to stop. With the sudden cessation of the music, everyone turned to see what was happening. Finding his moment to speak, Johnny shouted: "Ladies and gentlemen, our dear friends. I am pleased to introduce to you our guests of honor for our wedding reception, my lawyer and his wife. We are so proud they came."

With that everyone clapped and started talking again. The band immediately started playing and Johnny led Dick and Anita to a lone table on one side of the hall, which was covered with food. "Please sit here in the middle -- the place of honor," said Johnny.

Dick and Anita sat down. By now the noise level was so loud that it was difficult to hear anything. At that moment Errol appeared again with Mrs. Sherrod, whom Dick immediately recognized. Dick stood up and gave her a big hug. "Mrs. Sherrod, this is my wife, Anita."

Mrs. Sherrod, who looked quite attractive in her pink evening gown, shook Anita's hand, and said,

"I am so glad you came. I hope you will not be overwhelmed by all this noise and the crowd of people. But we are all so happy for Johnny and Renee. I know your husband was partially responsible for this happy occasion."

Up to now Anita had hardly said a word. She just looked around in wonderment. Everyone was dressed so beautifully and she wondered how they could afford such clothes. She was at the same time very conscious of the fact that they were the only white people at the reception.

As the evening progressed, the noise level increased and the cigarette and cigar smoke became more penetrating. The bride and groom cut the cake and everyone sat down at tables to enjoy the cake and food that had been provided, as well as their drinks. Finally, Errol, the best man, got up, raising his glass.

"Ladies and gentlemen, I want to toast the bride and groom. I have known Johnny all my life and he has been a great friend. I know that he and Renee will be happy all their lives together and they will have many Johnnies and Renees to fill their home." Everyone clapped.

"I also want to toast our guests of honor, our lawyer and his wife, Anita. He is a great man and never lost faith in our innocence." More applause.

When Errol finished, James Harden, looking very embarrassed got up and said a few words. Johnny then rose and toasted his bride and then gave her a big kiss. Following this, everyone wanted to make a toast to get into the act.

Dick looked around and recognized some of the mothers. Mrs. Meeks came to the table and said hello as did Mrs. Harden. Reverend Wade senior was there wearing his collar, for effect, which made him stand out. He seemed genuinely pleased to see Dick and Anita.

Dick saw Fess Wise, and waved to him. Fess waved back, but made no attempt to go over to the table to speak with Dick. Dick learned later that Cole and O'Neil had not been invited. Before leaving Dick drew Errol Meeks aside and asked him to call him at work on Monday.

About 11:30 p.m., Dick and Anita excused themselves, thanking Johnny and Renee and Mrs.

Sherrod for inviting them to the reception. By this time the party was in full swing with alcohol beginning to take effect. As they walked down the steps to Madison Street, Anita said, "I don't know if I enjoyed that very much, but I am glad we went. Everyone was so proud that you were there."

Dick opened the car door for Anita. "I am glad we went too, even if it was so loud. Johnny certainly has everything going for him. He has a real chance to make good." Dick and Anita drove home in silence.

Dick wondered what Anita really thought about the affair. He knew she would never tell her mother and father, true southerners, who would never understand. He certainly was proud of her to take such a step in understanding those less fortunate.

Chapter 6

Errol Meeks Goes to College

"Mr. Calkins, Errol Meeks is on the phone."

"Thank you Margaret, I will take the call."

Dick picked up the phone and hesitated before speaking, composing in his mind precisely how he would broach the subject with Errol. Finally he said, "Errol, I have a project for you which could change your whole life."

Dick realized that sounded a bit dramatic, but he went on. "You are the only one of the eight boys who has completed your credits for high school. What would you think of the idea of going to the night division of the YMCA Junior College here in the Loop?"

There was a long pause, and then a very faint voice said, "Would you repeat that please?"

Dick realized he was not going to get anywhere on the phone so he asked Errol to come to the office after he finished work. At 5:30 p.m. Errol went directly to Dick's office and knocked on the door. Because Margaret had already left, Dick went and opened it and the two went to Dick's inner office.

"Sit down, Errol."

Errol smiled and said "I guess I had better sit down."

Dick rearranged some papers on his desk and then looked at Errol, who by now was comfortable and waiting for Dick to speak. "Errol, I have checked with the YMCA Junior College just a block from here. I found out that they have a special program which will help you get a start in college. They concentrate on English, math, and composition and they give you credit towards your degree."

Dick looked at Errol intently to detect any reaction. What he observed did not look encouraging for the project. He was sure Errol could complete such a curriculum with tutoring, which he would provide, for Errol was highly intelligent and only needed encouragement.

"Mr. Calkins, I don't think I could make it in college. I barely got through high school."

"But Errol, you didn't work. This time I am going to help you with your studies, and I know that you can make it. You have what it takes, and think what you could do with a college degree."

"May I think about it first. This comes as quite a shock. I want to talk to my mother because I am not certain we would have enough money to do this."

"Don't worry about the money. I will get several friends to help us pay for the tuition and books."

"That's very generous of you, Mr. Calkins, and I do appreciate your kindness. When would I start?"

"The fall semester begins next Monday, so you would need to register by this Friday."

Errol hesitated a moment obviously becoming excited about the prospects of going to college. "Well, maybe I could make it. What do I do?"

"Take this catalogue, which lists all the courses available at the school. On page 19 I have marked in red the courses you might take which are held in the evening. Friday at 6:00 I will meet you at my office and we will go over and register."

Errol took a deep breath. Then he smiled slightly. "O.K., Mr. Calkins. If you think I can do it I will be at your office at 6:00 on Friday."

Errol got up slowly to leave. Dick walked around his desk and patted him on the shoulder, "Errol, you can do it."

On Friday evening the two walked over to the YMCA Junior College on LaSalle Street, just a block from Dick's office. It was hard to tell who was more excited, Errol or Dick. Errol was registered and started classes the next Monday.

In two weeks the noble experiment ended. Nothing was said.

Chapter 7

Errol Meeks and James Harden Go to Church

In the middle of September, Dick called Errol Meeks and James Harden into his office late one afternoon. When the two were seated, Dick said to them: "Errol, James, I was wondering if you would be willing to help me out?" He hesitated to see if there was any reaction. There was none so he continued, "I am working on Chuck Percy's campaign for the Governor of Illinois. He is running against Governor Otto Kerner and he needs our help with Negro voters."

"What would you like us to do?" asked Errol.

"I was hoping you would be willing to distribute some Percy literature around your area." Errol looked at Harden, and the two shook their heads in consent. "Do you have the pamphlets?" asked Errol.

Dick got up from the desk, and went into the outer office where his Republican literature was stacked in several boxes under a table. Grabbing one of the boxes he handed it to Errol. "This should be enough. If you need any more just let me know. What I would like you to do is place the literature in doorways, and give it to people on the street."

"No problem, Mr. Calkins," said Errol. "We will do the best we can."

"Thank you for helping. I know Mr. Percy will be pleased when I tell him what you are doing." The two smiled and left the office.

Errol and James returned home to West Roosevelt and began distributing literature in apartment buildings. They went to each apartment building along Roosevelt. They continued on the weekend until they were approached by several black members of Mayor Daley's political machine. They said very little except that they thought the boys should stop distributing such literature. They did not have to say anything further. That was the end of that project, and the literature was dumped in a vacant lot.

Later in October, Dick had another brilliant idea. He asked Errol and James to go to Reverend Wade's store front church with him. The two were

226

reluctant to do this, but they did not want to turn down such a request, especially after failing in their prior endeavor. Dick called Reverend Wade and explained that they were coming the next Sunday and that he hoped the Reverend would mention Mr. Percy's name to the congregation. Reverend Wade was delighted to have visitors to his church and he was more than happy to tell his flock to vote for Mr. Percy. Dick was elated and looked forward to Sunday.

Sunday came and Anita decided, reluctantly, to go also. "Honey, are you certain we will be welcomed at Reverend Wade's church?"

"Of course, I talked to him earlier in the week." Anita knew this was another outing that she would be unable to talk about with her family in Shreveport, Louisiana. They would not understand.

As a matter of fact she did not understand what her husband was trying to prove. But he was so enthusiastic with these projects that she just went along for support.

With Chrissy dressed in her Sunday best, they got into the car and drove from their new home in Wilmette, down to West Roosevelt to pick up the boys. After a rather long wait they finally got James and Errol into the car and headed for "The Church of the Living God," a store-front "cathedral" whose "shepherd" was Reverend Wade.

When they arrived at the store the service was already in progress. Inside, the air was damp and there was the dingy smell of a building falling apart. Plaster was falling from the ceiling and walls, but the floor was clean. Thirty chairs were lined up with an aisle going down the middle. On the left side of the aisle, seven children, ranging from four to twelve, were wiggling in their seats. A woman sitting with them was making an earnest effort to make them pay attention.

On the right side of the aisle an elderly man sat alone, leaning far back in his chair. The potential voters were rather sparse, at least at this service, thought Dick. In front there was a platform with an old lectern standing in the middle with three chairs behind it. To the left of the platform there was an old piano with Mrs. Wade seated at it.

"Come in friends," said Reverend Wade with a

broad smile and an exaggerated wave of his right hand. "We have been waiting for you. Please sit up here in front." At this time James Harden's sister came in with one other adult, and the service continued.

"May I say to all of you here how happy we are to have our friends visit us, and have two of our own boys return to the flock, James Harden and Errol Meeks." With these words Errol and James lowered their heads in obvious embarrassment as everyone looked at them. They knew what was to come.

"These two boys have been gone for a long time and they have now been led to return to the Lord with gratitude in their hearts. This man here," looking at Dick, but not recalling his name, "worked hard and, with the help of our prayers, got these boys out of jail."

Errol and James sank even lower in their chairs. They wanted to get out of that room. "Now these boys have returned to us and they plan to be with us regularly on Sunday. Isn't that right, James?"

"Yes, sir."

"Isn't that right, Errol?"

"Yes sir, Reverend Wade."

The boys looked around but there was nowhere to escape. The Reverend went on at some length speaking of the importance of church and regular attendance. Finally he stated: "And now I am going to ask James to get up and say a few words."

James Harden started turning red and his face became flush. Perspiration broke out on his forehead and he panicked. The only thing that kept Errol from snickering was the knowledge that he was next.

James rose slowly and shuffled his feet a few times. His words were obviously going to be extemporaneous, if he could speak at all. "I . . . I would like to say that it is . . . it is wonderful to be home . . . and thank you for your prayers." Harden sat down so hard that his wooden chair lurched backwards, almost into the row behind him.

Reverend Wade then turned to Errol, who refused to look at him. "Errol."

Errol rose, looking at James who started to smile. "I . . . I would . . . I would like to say the same thing Jimmie did. Thank you." He sat down quickly, which was not too difficult as he had barely raised himself off the chair in the first place.

Reverend Wade, with deep dedication and commitment to his flock, asked that the collection be taken. "James and Errol will you please pass the collection plate for us." The boys got up and received the plates from Reverend Wade and handed them to the members of the congregation. Then they took the plates back to the Reverend and returned to their seats.

"And now we will have a few words from our distinguished guests, Mr. and Mrs. ... Mr. and Mrs. ..."

"Calkins," whispered James' sister.
.. Yes, Calkins."

Dick nudged Anita to get up, but she just ignored him looking straight forward. Dick then rose and Anita smiled. "Reverend Wade, it is certainly a great pleasure for us to be here on this lovely Sunday morning. We, of course, share in your joy at having our boys back. If it had not been for your constant prayers, their release could not have been accomplished. I know Mrs. Calkins shares with me in giving our best wishes to the success of your church and the fine work you are doing."

Anita then handed Chrissy, who was asleep, to Dick, and rose. "As Mr. Calkins said, we are pleased to be here and to have the boys join us in coming to your church. We do wish you the very best."

By now it was 12:15 and Reverend Wade was ready to launch into a new matter, when he said "Oh, yes, I almost forgot. I want all of you to vote for ... for ... what's his name?"

"Mr. Percy," whispered Dick.
"Yes, Mr. Percy."
"Who is he?" asked the man sitting in the rear on the right side.
"He is running for Governor," said Dick.
"Governor," repeated Reverend Wade. "Don't forget to vote for him. He is a good Christian and Mr. ... our friend here knows him personally."

All the adults in the congregation, and several of the children shook their heads agreeing that they would vote for Mr. ..."

"Percy."

At 12:50 church concluded and James and Errol were the first to reach the sidewalk. Dick and Anita stood around shaking hands and talking with the others. James' sister held Chrissy, who had been quiet and as good as always throughout the whole ordeal. After ten minutes they left, drove the boys home and headed north.

"You know," Dick broke the silence, "I don't suppose that church service meant anything to James and Errol and they probably won't go back. But I got something out of it."

"So did I," said Anita. "You can't help admiring Reverend Wade and his family for their devotion to their little church."

Dick hesitated a second and then said: "It is a real inspiration to see someone like Reverend Wade devote all his free time to his church. He probably puts all his money into it just to pay the rent and other expenses. James told me that he works forty-eight hours a week as a doorman at the Ambassador East Hotel."

Dick reflected for a moment, and then said "You know, in the simplicity of his words today, you could feel true Christian devotion and honesty."

"Yes, I know what you mean." said Anita. "Reverend Wade certainly has a unique dignity and a sense of tranquility that one must admire. He is a happy man in the service of others."

Chapter 8

Fess Wise Accused of Stealing $400

November and December passed uneventfully, other than the fact that Percy lost his bid to become Governor of the great State of Illinois. Each of the boys, except O'Neil, was holding on to his job and seemed to be staying out of trouble. Then in January things began to unravel.

Mr. Torcum called one morning. "Dick, I have some bad news. Mr. Brown, a long-time employee of mine put $400 in his locker and it was stolen. The only one who had access to the area at the time was Fess Wise, so Brown thinks Fess took the money. And now Fess has not shown up for work this morning. What do you suggest we do?"

Dick sat back in his chair. Things had gone so well, now this. He knew he had no obligation, legal or otherwise, but he decided that if Fess had taken the money, Dick would pay Brown back himself. "Let me contact Fess' mother and find out where he is. I'll call you back."

Dick immediately dialed Fess Wise's mother and learned that Fess had gone to the hospital that morning. He asked her to have Fess call him as soon as he arrived home.

At 11:20 a.m. Fess called. "Fess, where have you been? You know the importance of always informing Mr. Torcum when you are not going to go to work.

"Mr. Calkins, I went to the hospital before the shop was open. So I couldn't call in."

"It doesn't matter. Somehow you have to get word to Mr. Torcum. Please don't let this happen again because it could cost you your job. The reason I am calling is to ask you whether you took some money belonging to Mr. Brown?"

There was a moment of silence, and then Fess responded: "Mr. Calkins, I didn't take no money. Why would I take money when my job is so important to me. As a matter of fact in the evenings I sometimes walk by the safe when it is open. I have never thought of taking money."

"Well, Fess, I believe you, but we will have to establish your innocence. Will you take a lie detector test?"

"Mr. Calkins, I will gladly take a test because I didn't take his money."

"Okay, Fess. I'll talk to you tomorrow."

Dick hung up the receiver and decided to go to Torcum's shop over the noon hour to do a little detective work. At 12:15 p.m., he walked out of the Field Building, east on Adams past the Federal Building to Michigan Avenue. The temperature was in the thirties and Chicago was enjoying a dirty wet thaw.

As he proceeded south on Michigan Avenue he looked up at the row of tall buildings lining Michigan Avenue. What a splendid skyline Chicago has, he thought to himself. Looking across the street at the Chicago Art Museum, with its two stately lions standing guard, he promised himself he would stop in there one of these days and gain a little culture. He felt like a tourist, but he never ceased to enjoy this man-created beauty of symmetry and balance, almost a poem of brick and mortar. No question about it he thought, Chicago is the finest city in the world.

Torcum's small shop was just one of many hundreds of quality stores lining Michigan Avenue. Walking into the shop Dick looked for Mr. Torcum. The walls of the shop were crowded with racks of carpeting of all colors and quality. Torcum saw Dick and quickly came forward to meet him. He looked very serious.

Torcum spoke: "What can I do? I give these boys a chance and they let me down. First, Brown has his money stolen and Fess fails to appear for work."

Torcum seemed to have a need to get this off his chest. "I can appreciate how you feel, Mr. Torcum. You have been very good to Fess and Edward Cole, and I want you to know that I deeply appreciate your efforts. May I see the locker where Brown put his money?"

"Certainly you can. Follow me." Torcum led Dick to the rear of the shop and then up some stairs to a rear room. Dick was introduced to Mr. Brown, who was on his way down to the display area of the store. He had grey hair, was about sixty years old, wore glasses, about 5'4" tall and fairly heavy.

"Mr. Brown, will you show Mr. Calkins your

locker where you put the money?"

"Certainly, Mr. Torcum." He led Dick to a floor locker with four vertical compartments, each of which required a separate key.

"Here is where I placed my money," motioning to one of the compartments. He took out his keys and proceeded to unlock the compartment. "I put the money in here last Thursday or Friday. When I returned, it was gone."

"Was the locker locked at all times?" asked Dick.

"Yes, it was, but I figured they must have had a key made or they jimmied it open."

Dick looked carefully at the lock and could see some scratch marks. He then tried the lock several times and it worked perfectly. "It does not appear as though the lock was forced in any way. Was the locker locked when you first opened it and noticed the money was missing?"

"Yes it was," answered Brown.

Dick moved his fingers over the surface of the lock. "It is clear that whoever took the money had to have a key for the locker, for it would be one thing to get it open with some kind of instrument, and quite another to get it closed again without leaving a mark. Does anyone besides yourself have a key?"

"No."

"Would it be possible for anyone to get your keys to make a copy?"

"I don't think so."

"Tell me, Mr. Brown, why do you suspect Fess Wise?"

"Well, I seen him standing back over there, watching me when I put the money into the locker. Furthermore, I don't trust them niggers because they have done this to me before. Three other times this has happened, only on those occasions the money was in my coat pocket. This was before Fess and Cole came. We got rid of them though, and I think we should get rid of Fess Wise."

"Tell me, Mr. Brown, what was Fess Wise doing when you saw him look at you?"

"He was cutting carpets."

Dick noted how poor the lighting was around the locker, and how bright it was across the room where Brown indicated Fess was cutting carpets.

"Mr. Brown, we want to get this cleared up immediately. Fess Wise says that he did not take your money, and Edward Cole was not here. Wise is willing to take a lie detector test on the condition that you pay for it if he passes it. I hope you will think that is a fair offer."

Dick stopped to see if Brown was reacting in any way. Because of the lighting, Dick could not detect any reaction. "I am going to ask you to think this whole thing over and search your own house for the money. If you want Fess to go ahead with the test call me tomorrow or the following day at the latest."

Dick turned and walked down the stairs to the main part of the store satisfied that Brown had misplaced the money or that this was all a ruse to get Fess fired. Torcum caught up to Dick as he was about to leave the store. He agreed with Dick's analysis of the situation, and was satisfied to await the outcome.

Brown never did call or ask for the test. A month later he "retired" and Fess was promoted to his job.

Chapter 9

James O'Neil Makes His Appearance

Many times, Dick wondered what happened to James O'Neil. He never contacted Dick after his release from prison, nor did the other boys know what had happened to him. It was in early December, 1964, that Dick got his answer just before closing. On a Tuesday afternoon, Dick received a frantic page from Nancy at the reception desk.

"Paging Mr. Calkins. Please come to the reception area immediately." Dick was in the library so he picked up the phone. Nancy came on immediately.

"Hon, you had better get to the reception area pronto. If one of the big bosses sees your client, or should I say dude, you are in big trouble." Nancy had to say no more.

In seconds Dick burst into the reception area. As he did he stopped in his tracks, for there was James O'Neil big as life. He had a black leather suit on with a red vest, a purple handkerchief in his lapel pocket, slicked back processed hair, sun glasses (in spite of the fact that it was a dark winter day), and a cigarette dangling from the side of his mouth.

"James, this way, quickly." Dick turned and walked out the door, down the stairs to his office. James O'Neil just sauntered slowly after him, taking deliberate steps. Once in his office Dick shut the door and sat down behind his desk in relief. O'Neil stood at the desk and just stared at Dick. Dick was about to speak, when O'Neil said: "Richard I need $200 right away. Can you help me?"

Dick hesitated a moment, and then said: "James, it has been a long time since I have seen you. How have you been, and what have you been doing?"

"Cut the crap. I just asked you a simple question. Can you help me?"

Dick was getting a little heated under the collar by this abrupt confrontation. "James, I don't have that kind of money to loan out."

"Richard, I thought you were my friend," said O'Neil with increasing intensity. I need $200 and I will pay you back at 100 percent interest."

"James, I can't do it. I just don't have that much money to loan anyone. Believe me."

"I know. You think you are too good for me, don't you? You didn't do a thing for me, and I don't need your kind of friendship."

Dick was struck dumb. It was not so much what James said that left him aghast, but the manner in which it was said. His face was angry, intense, and drawn. His eyes were as threatening as any Dick had seen on any man, white or black. Dick was not sure if James intended to become violent, but it was clear that he was in no mood to argue.

"Listen here, Richard, you didn't help me, in spite of what you think. I got myself out of jail while all you wanted to do was send me back for another twelve months and for a crime I did not commit. You made me plead, when I wanted to go to trial and prove my innocence. You owe me something."

There was a slight pause, for he was evidently running out of thoughts to express. But it was clear from his eyes that his anger was only increasing. Finally, Dick said: "James, I did the best I could."

"Look here, I didn't commit no rape. James Harden got off, why didn't I?"

Dick did not know whether he should respond or just try to end the conversation. He finally said, "James, I explained that to you when you were in jail. Harden was innocent, and the evidence against you was quite strong and you would have been convicted, in my opinion."

"I disagree with you. You just wanted to send me away. Tell the truth."

Dick did not respond, but just sat there. He knew that he was only making the situation worse. O'Neil finally turned and walked out of the office. "I don't need you or anyone else." As he slammed the door in the outer office, Dick breathed a sigh of relief. His only hope was that O'Neil would never return.

A week later, O'Neil called on the phone and asked to come over to talk. Dick hesitated and then consented. He knew he was taking a chance with such a volatile person, but he had to take a chance.

About an hour later, O'Neil knocked at Dick's outer door. Before Margaret could respond, Dick rushed to the door and opened it. The instant he saw O'Neil, he knew that he was a different person. Although he had the same clothes on, his facial expression was soft, almost humble. His eyes were downcast and slightly red.

The two walked into Dick's office, and O'Neil sat down. After a moment he looked up and said: "Mr. Calkins, I want to apologize for what I said to you a week ago. I know you did what you thought best at the trial, and that you are trying to be my friend. Please understand, that I want to make good, for I will die if I ever get sent back to Statesville." His voice trailed off. Dick did not respond.

O'Neil lowered his head again. Without looking up, he said "Mr. Calkins, can you tell me what love is? I want to love and I want someone to love me, but I don't know what it is. I can have a woman anytime I want, just look at these fine clothes. But I feel so empty. Nobody really cares about me for what I am. Is there something wrong with me?"

Dick did not respond for a moment. He wanted to digest the question before answering. Finally, he said, "Everyone is capable of loving and being loved, but let me ask you a few questions first. May I ask, where did you get those clothes?"

"Mr. Calkins, I can't tell you what I have been doing, so please don't ask. If I get caught I am going to be in real trouble for life. I have to make a decision. I thought getting a lot of quick money would make me happy. I have been living at Marina City, and I have money, but I am not happy, and I don't know why. I have reached the point where I either go all the way with them or I get out. They told me to decide this week."

"James, who are 'they' . . . are you talking about the syndicate?"

"Yes, but please ask me nothing more. The point is that I have to make a difficult decision. On the one hand I can live like royalty and really enjoy life for a year or so, until I get caught, or else I can go back to the nickel and dime jungle and try to survive. White people won't give a person like me much of a chance."

"James, stop a minute. The decision you have to make is your own. No one else can do it for you, but if you are not happy, that should tell you something. You at least owe it to yourself to give it a try. There are good jobs available and I will help you get one, if you want me to. I am sure you know that we helped the other boys."

James looked up at Dick. There was slight moisture in his eyes. "You mean you would help me after all I said?"

"Of course I will if you're willing to try. Don't decide now but think it over, and call me in a few days. If you want my help, we will get the ball rolling on a new job."

O'Neil rose, and without a word, extended his hand to shake hands, turned, and walked out.

It was most astounding to see one person be two such different people. This time he was quiet and humble, a complete contrast from his previous visit. His facial expression was different and he radiated a friendliness which Dick had never seen in O'Neil before.

A week later O'Neil called and said he wanted to get a job. Dick contacted Al Larson, who agreed to talk to O'Neil. Dick explained the situation and the fact that this was a really difficult case with little hope of success. This seemed to peak Al's interest rather than discourage him. Two days later, O'Neil met with Larson and the interview process began.

After a number of interviews, during which Al really tried to get to know O'Neil, he told him that he was under consideration and would be notified within one week. O'Neil called Dick and said that even if he didn't get the job, it was a worthwhile experience meeting with Mr. Larson.

In working with O'Neil, Larson immediately realized that he found a most difficult challenge. No longer a teenager, O'Neil was too old to associate with a gang, he had no family with whom he could identify, and he was too unprepared to take a responsible position in society. He had nowhere to turn for security or to anchor his emotions. He was vulnerable to everything that was bad in society and literally could not tell the difference from right and wrong. He was a living time-bomb, and his was the struggle of life itself.

O'Neil arrived at Dick's office at 8:00 a.m. and waited for him to arrive. When Dick walked down the hallway to his office, he saw O'Neil's beaming face. "I got the job. I passed all those tests, and Mr. Larson said I would be a good worker if I was faithful to my work. I want you to know, I am going to make good. I am not going to let you and Mr. Larson down. I am going to save my money and go to college and then law school. You wait and see."

"Congratulations, James. I can't tell you how proud I am of you. I know that you are going to do a good job. Do you want to come in for a moment?"

"No, Richard. I start tomorrow and I have lots of things to do." With this he walked off hurriedly down the hall.

Chapter 10

Fess Wise Buys A Car

As the months passed, Dick became more and more uneasy with his charges. It was as though he was sitting on a time bomb and he did not know when it was going to go off again. Hidden in the recesses of his mind was a fear that at any moment the phone would ring and it would be a call from the county jail. Dick tried to tell himself that he could not live their lives, and if they could not make it on the outside then they would simply have to pay for their actions on the inside.

Dick was more concerned with some of the boys than others. He was confident that Harden, Sherrod and Meeks would make it. He was certain that it would take a miracle for O'Neil to survive. He did not have any feeling for Fess Wise or Edward Cole that they would make it.

Fess concerned him because he was easily led and prone to get into difficulty. But for six months he seemed to be doing fine at Torcum's store. The last two times he saw him, Fess did complain about his low wages, almost the legal minimum, and his six-day work week. Dick had told him to be patient and learn the trade. And when Brown quit and Fess took his job, he did get a modest raise, but not enough to satisfy him.

At their last meeting in Dick's office, Fess had expressed a desire to get a car. Dick had promised to take him for a driver's test and help him make the purchase. However, Fess could not wait for this.

Early on March 3, 1965, the telephone rang at Dick's home. "Mr. Calkins, this is Fess." His voice was barely audible, and this could mean only one thing. "May I come to your office this afternoon after work? I am having a slight problem."

Dick gave a sigh of relief. He wasn't calling from jail. "Certainly, Fess. I will see you after 5:00 p.m."

Fess arrived at 5:10 and went directly to Dick's office on the twenty-second floor. Dick opened the door and they went into his office.

"Mr. Calkins," he drawled in a barely audible

voice, "you know that car I wanted to get? Well I got it. Only, as I was driving home from the used car lot I was stopped by a policeman. I tried to explain that I just bought the car and had not had a chance to get my license plates, city sticker, and driver's license, but he would not listen to me."

Dick sighed a sigh of relief. This was serious, but only paled to the kind of problems Dick knew Fess Wise was capable of getting involved in. Dick asked, "What kind of car did you get, and what did you pay?"

"It's a sleek '59 Pontiac, and I have to pay a little over $1,000 at $41 per month."

Dick made no comment, but it was clear that a car of this vintage could not be worth more than $500. Although $41 a month seemed insignificant, for Fess it could be the first step to financial trouble with one of the notorious Chicago collection agencies.

"Fess, the first thing the judge is going to ask for is evidence that you have a driver's license, your license plates, and the city sticker. You take care of the latter two right away, and next week I will take you for your driver's test."

Fess paid $30 for his city sticker, $18 for his plates, and Dick paid the $10 when he took his driver's test, which he proceeded to fail, but he did receive a temporary license, which permitted him to drive with any person having a license. His court date was the following week, and Dick felt confident that the judge would be fair with Fess.

One day before the court appearance, in the late evening when Dick and Anita were in bed reading, the phone rang. Anita answered it. "It's for you, dear. I think it is one of your boys."

Dick's heart jumped as he took the receiver. "Hello ..."

"Mr. Calkins, Mr. Calkins, what am I going to do?" said a panicked voice that sounded like Fess Wise. "I didn't mean to run."

"Just a minute; is that you Fess?"

"Yes it is, and you have got to help me."

"Well, what happened?"

There was a long pause, then Fess said, "This evening I wanted to show a group of my friends my new car, so we all went to look at it and sit in it.

I sat behind the wheel. All of a sudden the car started. One of my friends said he had a driver's license, so I pulled out to drive just once around the block. I no sooner got down to the corner when a policeman stopped me and asked to see my driver's license. I showed him my temporary license and he asked if anyone in the car had a driver's license. My friend said he did, but when he looked in his wallet, he couldn't find it. The policeman let him go to his house to get it, but he never came back. We stood there and waited and waited. Finally, the officer said I would have to go to the station, and as we turned, I pushed one of the other boys into the cop and ran. Now they're looking for me and I don't know what to do."

    If Dick had been sleepy, this had now passed. "Fess, where are you now?"

    "I snuck home."

    "Do you know what station the police officers are out of?"

    "No, I don't, but I know they towed my car to the car pound."

    "All right. Go to work tomorrow and call me around 11:00 a.m. I'll see if I can't get this straightened out. What is the registration number of your car?"

    Fess gave him the number and hung up. As he got back in bed he was certain that what had occurred would reward him with one of those sleepless nights. However, after explaining what had happened to Anita, he drifted off to sleep ... much to his relief in the morning.

    The next day at work, Dick called the city pound and through the registration number he was able to locate the car and the officers who had brought it in. He then called the district station they worked out of and left a message for either officer to call. Later in the afternoon one called and Dick explained the circumstances of what had happened. An appointment was made to meet at the police station at 6:00 p.m.

    Fess came to the Field Building at 5:15, and he and Dick waited at the LaSalle Street entrance for Anita and Chrissy to pick them up. Anita was not pleased with the arrangement for plans for the evening had to be rearranged because of this "business" diversion. The four drove to the station, and Dick and Fess waited for the police officer.

After ten minutes, Officer Czuk arrived and walked up to the two. "Are you Calkins?"

"Yes, I am, officer, and this is Fess Wise."

"I recognize him. Mr. Calkins, perhaps you and I should talk alone for a moment." Fess walked toward some seats and sat down, looking very sad and dejected.

Dick and Officer Czuk talked for fifteen minutes, and then Dick motioned for Fess to rejoin them.

"Fess, I can't over-emphasize the seriousness of what you did; resisting arrest is a felony. The officer is going to drop that and charge you only with driving without a license. If you can get your friend to come in and show his driver's license, I think they will drop that also."

Fess mumbled a few words which were inaudible, but his face, which lighted up perceptively, said it all. Dick thanked Officer Czuk, and said that he and Fess would be at court on the date set.

Fess and Dick got back into the car and Anita drove to the pound. With Dick's wallet $50 lighter, they retrieved Fess' car and Dick drove it to Fess' mother's apartment, where they parked it in an empty lot.

"Fess, please think. Don't drive the car again until we get your license."

"Yes, Mr. Calkins. You can be sure I won't do it again." Please give my best to your bride."

As Dick and Anita drove off, Dick explained that he had just learned from Fess that he recently had gotten married, but they were not living together except on occasion. Instead, each was staying with their respective mothers until they could save enough money to get their own apartment.

Dick hesitated a moment, and Anita said, "No, you don't. Don't even think what you are thinking." Anita's voice was so firm that Dick dismissed the idea of helping Fess and his bride, without further thought.

Fess now had two court appearances. After the first, he was fined $30, which Dick had to pay because Fess was broke. At the second hearing, Fess' friend appeared with his driver's license and the charges were dismissed. As they walked away, Officer Czuk came up to Dick, and said, "that wasn't the friend who was in the car with Fess, but I decided to give you a break. You owe me one."

"Thank you, officer," said Dick. "I appreciate this very much."

Two weeks later, Fess came to Dick's office unannounced, and explained that he owed creditors $41 on the car, $20 on a gift he bought for his wife, and $10 for some clothes he had to have. He asked Dick for a loan, but the latter apologized when he did not have the money.

"But Mr. Calkins, I need the money now or they will take my car. Can't you get it from one of your rich friends?" Fess did not hide his displeasure at being turned down, and kept on explaining why he had to have the money.

When Dick absolutely refused, he left somewhat upset. Dick learned later that he borrowed $60 from Mr. Torcum, and then, as a sign of his appreciation, did not show up for work for the next three days.

Torcum was outraged and called Dick several times. For one thing Fess had been given more responsibility and helped run the shop so that his absence created scheduling problems for the delivery boys. When Dick reached Fess, he claimed he had been sick, but his mother told Dick that he had been drinking again. Dick finally asked Fess to come to the office for a "man to man" talk.

"Mr. Calkins, I am just not making enough with Torcum. I do all that work six days a week and I'm tired." Fess looked thinner than usual and his long drawn face was sadder than it normally was. "That new man they hired comes with no experience and right away Mr. Torcum gives him exactly what I am making. And he orders me around, just because he is white, and he doesn't know half about the business that I do."

There was a moment of silence as Dick reflected on what Fess had just said. Fess looked at him waiting for a sympathetic response. Finally, Fess continued: "I just don't know what I am going to do because I keep falling farther behind in my payments on the car and the things I bought."

As Dick listened he realized there was a perceptible change taking place in Wise. It was not that he lacked justification for being unhappy with the income he was receiving. It was obvious to Dick that Torcum was using these young men to run his shop, but paying them minimal wages because they were black. And from what Torcum said they were doing a good job.

The change he saw was something he observed in several of the others as well. It was a lack of patience and a lack of basic discipline which are so needed to anchor a person to the mores of society required to survive the battle of life. And turning to the corner bar out of frustration was the tip of the iceberg. It was indeed, a slow surrender to failure in life. Dick finally asked, "Fess, are you and your wife getting along?"

"What has that got to do with it?" snapped back Fess. Then he caught himself and said, "Well ..." There was a pause and Fess' head dropped down. "We ain't getting along so well, I guess. She went to Tennessee with her mother and I don't know if she is coming back."

"Tell me, is the reason you're having so much trouble because you are drinking again?"

Fess looked up. "No, that is not true. I do have a drink now and then, but no more than Johnny or Errol." Fess was clearly on the defensive.

Dick hesitated again. How do you tell a "child-man" he should not drink during the week because of the effect it has on his work? Or how do you impress upon a young man that he must call his employer when he is going to miss work because of illness?

"Fess, I guess you know you have probably lost your job, and this means you will have no chance to pay your creditors. This could, of course, have been avoided by calling Mr. Torcum. The only way you can keep your job is to convince Torcum that you are responsible. This is the only way you are going to get a raise also. He has to feel that he can rely on you."

"Mr. Calkins, I will try harder, I promise. Do you suppose you could loan me $20 to pay my creditors?"

Dick was caught off guard by this request although it should have been expected. He took out his wallet and gave him $20. He knew he was doing the wrong thing, but he wanted so much for Fess and the others boys to make it that he made himself vulnerable. He realized that if this conversation was not heeded by Fess, the latter was not going to survive.

Fess got his job back, but three weeks later Torcum called Dick and told him that Wise had been fired for missing three days in a row. The next day, Fess came to Dick's office. He did not look contrite or apologetic. He stood in front of Dick's desk and said in an aggressive voice, "Will you please loan me $50 to pay for some new clothes that I need for my new job at Just Manufacturing Company?"

This time Dick was ready. "Fess, I don't have $50 to loan you. I am sorry."

Without saying a word, Fess Wise turned around and walked out. Dick did not hear from Fess again for several weeks. He finally called his mother and was informed he had been drinking heavily and she couldn't get him to come home to change his filthy clothes.

Dick hung up the phone. He felt very sad for he knew the battle was lost. There would be one more call.

Chapter 11

Errol Meeks Goes Back to Prison

Several months passed and Dick heard nothing from his charges. Then one day in June, at 3:00 p.m., there was a knock at the outer door to his office. Margaret was out, so Dick got up and went and opened the door. There was James O'Neil. Dick was surprised for O'Neil should have been at work.

"James, what are you doing here?"

O'Neil smiled. He looked quite different than before. His clothes were modest and his hair was cut short. "Ain't you glad to see me, Richard? You look so serious. I hate to see you looking this way: maybe I can cheer you up."

"James, the only thing that will cheer me up is a plausible explanation of why you are not at work. Have you lost your job already?"

"No, I haven't. I just decided I needed a day off so I could come and see you."

Dick hesitated before responding. There was no common denominator between the two that would help them in their communications. Dick was concerned that O'Neil was losing his job, and O'Neil was anything but concerned about it. Dick finally said "James, you know that taking off like this for no reason can cost you your job?"

"Richard, I told you not to worry. Al Larson likes me, and he is not going to fire me. Frankly, being in the plant on that machine is almost as bad as being in prison. I just had to get out to find freedom of movement and thought, understand what I mean?"

O'Neil hesitated and then continued, "You see, Richard, I want to use my brains rather than my hands and arms. I know I am intelligent and I shouldn't have to be tied down to a job like this."

Dick knew this was it with the Inland job. He just sat there and listened.

"I want to be a smart lawyer like you. And with a broad grin he added, "We could go into business together. Calkins and O'Neil, lawyers at law; or better yet, O'Neil and Calkins. I like the sound of that better. How does it sound to you?"

"James, there is nothing I would like more

than to have you become a lawyer; but it requires years of preparation."

"Well, maybe I could become your clerk then." O'Neil at this point was quite obviously jesting, but Dick was not in a laughing mood. Perhaps it was because he was fretting over O'Neil's job, or the lack thereof, or he was annoyed that he was wasting time with this conversation for he had so much to do.

O'Neil just kept on talking, lighting a cigarette as he did.

"You know, I think I am beginning to settle down a little now getting all that energy of youth out of my system. Last evening I was walking down the street and I saw a drunk lying in the alley. And you know I didn't even stop but just kept walking right on by."

He stopped, looking for a reaction. Dick thought a minute and realized that he wanted to be praised because he had not rolled the man and taken his wallet, if he had one. "Well, James that is real fine and I am pleased to hear this. You keep going like this and above all keep your job and you are going to make it."

"Of course I am going to make it, Richard, because I have brains and ambition."

After a few more amenities, O'Neil finally left. Dick sat there in amazement. I should praise him for not rolling someone? He shook his head and got back to work.

Later that day, Dick got a call from Errol Meek's mother explaining that Errol had quit his job shortly after getting married. Worse than that he was back in jail for burglary. Dick was stunned. Why hadn't Errol contacted him? What had happened?

Dick decided to write Errol and find out if he wanted him to visit. On June 26, 1966, Dick received a letter from Armster Meeks: Errol had assumed his brother's name for the latter had no police record. The letter said:

> "Hello, Dick!
> "I hope calling you by your first name does not catch you off balance, as your letter caught me.
> "How is life treating everyone? Fine

I hope. As for me I'm doing as well as can be expected of me.

"I know its been a long time since you heard from me, but after I messed up with you I thought the best thing for me to do was to just drop out of sight and leave everything. But as you can see it only added to it. One thing came after another but they were not in my favor or not the way I wanted them, so I tried to change everything but only ended up changing myself.

"I have a lot to say to you in the form of explanations but I would only be trying to find another way of asking you not to look upon me as what some people might call me an incompetent fool. I wouldn't blame you because I have been every bit of it, and I am only sorry it took some more time behind bars to make me realize it.

"If you want to come you can, it would be sort of a relief off my mind, you know.

"Well, I will let you go for now and anything you want to know when you come out I will be more than glad to answer then, being that you will be my first visitor, and I do owe you a lot. I only hope I will be able to pay you and not be dropping out on you!

"So take it slow and I will be expecting to see you.

       Sincerely yours,
       Armster Meek #18293

Dick put the letter down. He knew he wanted to help Errol, but a defensive mechanism told him he was getting into another Fess Wise or James O'Neil situation, and he could not win. He did not want to succumb again to "sweet talk"; however, Errol did sound sincere.

The next day, a Saturday, Dick drove to the Cook County House of Correction, just south of the Criminal Court Building on South California Avenue.

This is the facility where individuals committing misdemeanors are housed. The outer fence extends almost half a mile along California Avenue. Inmates take care of the lawn and grounds. There is minimal security along the fence and main entrance, certainly nothing compared to the penitentiaries.

Dick parked his car on the street on California Avenue, walked through the main entrance to the reception room. The guards were courteous and directed him to the hospital, a separate building, where Errol worked and lived. Once in the visitor's room he waited for Errol to appear. Finally, Errol walked into the room. He smiled and walked over to Dick. "How are you Errol?"

"Fine, Mr. Calkins. I did not think you would come."

"You are certainly looking good. When do you get out?"

"In January. I only have to serve nine months."

There was a slight pause and Errol looked down. Then he looked at Dick and smiled again, "Mr. Calkins, thank you for coming. I know I don't deserve having a friend like you, especially after the way I never called you. I hope I can make it up to you."

"Enough of that," said Dick. Has your mother or family been here?"

"No. I wrote them several times, but I haven't heard from them," said Errol.

"What about Johnny or James? Have any of them visited you?"

"Mr. Calkins, no one has come. I don't blame them for not coming – I am just no good."

"Well, what happened, Errol? How did you get sent here?"

"Mr. Calkins, you aren't going to understand this because I don't. In fact I just don't understand myself at all. After I quit the job you got me I had six other jobs -- some pretty good. In the last one I was making almost $4.00 per hour and I had some responsibility -- book work. But I was so restless that I just couldn't stay with them. One night I broke into an apartment while the people were out and took a typewriter. While I was walking down the sidewalk a police officer stopped me and asked where I got the typewriter, so I told him. I was arrested and pleaded guilty and was sentenced nine months here."

"Why did you take a typewriter? Did you need one?"

"No. I already have one. There was money I could have taken, but I didn't. I was just restless. I can't explain it. I wish I could find out what makes me tick. I have been reading lots of books, some on psychology to try and find out why I am so mixed up. I left my wife. I couldn't hold a job and now I am back in prison. In a way I think I wanted to come back so that I could have time to think and get away from all that confusion. Since I have been here I have slept a lot and just thought about the past. I am beginning to feel now that I can face it and make it when I get out in February. I know I have to make it this time or there may not be another chance. It was good to come back here for I had almost forgotten what it was like, although this is a country club compared to Statesville. Being here again convinces me that there won't be a next time."

"I am sure there won't be, but why do you feel that you are confused?"

"I don't feel so confused now, but before I found that I was just drifting with no purpose in mind. I was just waiting, having a lousy time, working all day, drinking at night with no goal or objective in mind."

"Have you thought about leaving the west Roosevelt area, coming to Evanston, or just getting away from the area?"

"Yes, I have, but for some reason it's hard to leave. I guess my friends are all here . . . " Errol faltered and fell into silence.

Dick picked up the conversation: "I'll send you some books if you would like. What are you interested in?"

"Mostly books on psychology and things like that. Books that will tell me what makes people think and act as they do. I have just got to find out what makes me no good."

"Errol, don't you have any faith in God and the fact that he cares about you?"

"I tried that once, too, but I didn't get very

good results. Actually I have had conversations with a minister here and he wants to help me. I guess we will see what happens."

There was a little more conversation and Dick promised to send some books. He then turned and left while Errol walked slowly to the big iron door, looking over his left shoulder in the direction Dick had just traversed.

It seemed strange, almost pitiful, that here was a young man that not one person in the world cared enough about to visit or even send a short note. No member of his family came to visit him although they lived only thirty minutes away by public transportation. No friend brought him food or fruit. Is it any wonder then that Errol found life confusing without any real support from his family or friends?

While driving back to the office Dick recalled what a Hawaiian guide once told him while he was in the military in Hawaii. She explained that there are no orphans in Hawaii, for a child left without parents will immediately be adopted into another family. It is the Hawaiian belief that each child has a soul which can only be nurtured through the love of a mother and father, brothers and sisters. For this reason, Hawaiian families are quite large with many nationalities represented -- Hawaiian, Japanese, Chinese, Korean, Haole (caucasian or mainlander).

Within a week Dick sent several books to Errol, including a Bible, which he thought Errol would enjoy reading. Several days later Dick received a letter from Errol. It said

"July 16, 1966
Armster Meeks #19293

I received the books you sent me yesterday and they sort of caught me like your letter did. (smile)

I hope everyone is doing well. As for me, my time is getting shorter as each day passes by you know!

How was your holiday? At least it didn't rain like the forecast said, so I imagine it was very nice.

To me, mine was just another day, but you can't expect this place to be the same as home. Although they were trying but it didn't turn out to well.

You know I was thinking about your little girl. She is two years old. It doesn't seem possible. That goes to show you how time flies by. Spelled fly wrong had to make up (Smile).

Mr. Calkins I don't know if I will like the books you sent to me but don't think I'm not pleased by the way you are thinking about me, but I guess it was my fault by not knowing how to explain to you the books that I read, but after I thought about it I decided upon the subjects that I like under my present conditions, poetry, psychology and medical books concerning the people. You know I like to know about people and try to find out things that make them act the way they do, and in reading the different books of that nature I will most likely find out what makes me think so contrary about the right things. Sometimes I think I have to prove something to some one when it's not necessary. Don't get me wrong about your books that you sent, but its kind of hard getting into those. I know you would rather have me tell you than to have you sending me books that I was not reading.

There is one thing else I want to know, and that is you will not have to worry about me abusing them. Will have them in the same shape as if they were my own.

Although you have told me once before about the kind of job you would like for me to have I would appreciate it if you would tell me some of the things I would have to overcome before I even thought about obtaining one. I know some but I would like to know some of yours. OK.

Well, I guess I will close for now. Tell everyone that I said hello. I'm running out of headings for you (smile). Hoping to hear from you soon.

>Sincerely yours,
>Armster Meeks
>#19293 Dorm 3 Kitchen
>2800 S. California
>Ave. City 60608"

In the next few months Dick received a number of additional letters from Errol. They were always frank, searching for answers as to who he was and about what he was doing. In one he stated that he had started writing about himself as Dick had requested. In reflecting on his life he stated:

> "Then I start to thinking I really haven't had much of a life mostly in jail, two years here, year here and there. You know! I can still remember most of it because I started when I was about eleven years old. How is that for a start would you like to know about the jail life first or would you like for me to start from the beginning? What would be best?"

In thinking where he had failed when released in 1964, he stated quite frankly:

> "You said you wanted me to do too many things when I first came home, well you were wrong about that because none of things you wanted me to do were going to hurt me, it was me. I wasn't ready! I just wasn't ready, not in my physical ability or mental ability, I just wanted to be free for a while and to have no worries or anything, just trying to make up for the time that couldn't be made up for. Now that I realize this for all that its worth, I see that there is only one way and that's by making it up by what you are doing in the present and what you will make of the future."

In trying to determine the cause of his past

failings he observed that he was really lacking in self-confidence.

"It's hard to admit to oneself but its time. I don't have enough confidence and it brings me nothing but hardship and you can't overcome that in one day. But I am working at it. If I put as much drive into obtaining it as to do other things it would be very simple."

Dick visited Errol's mother in an effort to find some way to help him. She still lived with a daughter in the basement of the apartment building she owned near Douglas Park. In the winter the basement apartment was damp and cold, and in the summer unbearably hot.

Mrs. Meeks was a hot-tempered woman who had struggled all her life. At times she held two jobs to support the family of Errol and his two sisters. Her husband had died an alcoholic ten years before when the children were young and she had little time to spend at home caring for them. Like so many in the area, Errol's gang, the New Braves, was his family.

In talking with Mrs. Meeks, Dick realized that it took all her strength and determination just to keep her own head above water, much less Errol's. As she said there was nothing she could do for him.

When Errol got out of prison the second time, he contacted Dick only once. Dick learned from Mrs. Sherrod that Errol and Johnny had started drinking heavily, with Johnny quitting his job, and leaving his wife and baby. The two got jobs occasionally, but they spent more and more time at bars on Roosevelt Avenue.

Dick never heard from Errol or Johnny again. Later he learned they ended up back in prison.

Chapter 12

James O'Neil Visits Again

After another month, O'Neil was back in Dick's office. Now it was official; he had quit his job at Inland.

As O'Neil walked into Dick's office it was clear that he was depressed; not angry, simply discouraged. He slumped in the chair in front of Dick's desk.

"I just don't understand myself. Today on my way down, I stopped at the Sears store on State Street and tried on some jackets. I found one I liked, $12.00, and put it on and started to walk out. Store detectives caught me at the door, and I pleaded with them not to turn me in. They finally let me go when I agreed to pay for the jacket. That was all the money I had. But why would I do that for only $12.00 and risk my whole future? What's wrong with me?"

Dick looked at James for a minute not sure what to say. Finally, he said "James, you will just have to try harder. The first year out is the hardest. If you will just hang in there you will make it."

"But why would I do this without thinking? I have just got to find out what makes me tick this way."

After a slight pause, O'Neil launched into what he thought was a philosophical discussion. It was obvious that his earlier depression was lifting and now he just wanted to talk, which was the last thing Dick could afford to do.

"Every man is a fortress to himself, don't you think? It don't matter if he is white or black; his primary struggle is within those walls. If you stop trying to break out you're dead. Sometimes I can mount those walls and peer into the distant fields and all seems calm and beautiful and orderly. I feel happy because I know that the day can't be far off when I will run free in those fields. But many times I feel chained in solitary confinement, in darkness; I just want to thrash out and destroy everything that comes across my path. Everything is black and in my anger I am alone. At moments like this I could be walking down the street and if a man accidently bumped me I could kill him on the spot."

Dick just sat there impatiently listening.

"Richard, do you understand what I am saying? I am intelligent. I know this. But by being smart I get depressed and I don't know how to control it."

Finally Dick said, "James, you just have to try." He knew that whatever he said, O'Neil would not listen. He wondered how much longer O'Neil would last.

Chapter 13

Fess Wise Arrested For Armed Robbery

On Sunday morning in September 1965, at 3:00 a.m. Fess Wise and two others were apprehended for the armed robbery of one Ames Jackson, in the parking lot just outside Fess' apartment building. At 7:30 a.m. Fess's mother called Dick at his home and informed him of what had happened. He immediately called the district police station and talked to Fess.

"Fess, did you commit the robbery?"

"No, Mr. Calkins, please believe me."

"Will you take a lie test?"

"I'd rather not they make me nervous." There was a long pause, and then Fess, in a pleading voice, said, "Mr. Calkins, will you help me?"

"I don't know Fess. I will have to think it over."

"But Mr. Calkins, they will send me back to jail if you don't help me."

"Fess, you should have thought of that this morning." When Dick hung up, Anita said "Is it serious?"

"Yes, it is," responded Dick.

"You try so hard with your boys, and it seems that one by one they are being pulled back under. I know it's discouraging for you but at least you are trying." Anita put her arms around her husband trying to show that he was appreciated.

The next morning, Dick showed up at the preliminary hearing, with the hope that there would be something he could do to help Fess. As he sat there in Boy's Court, he listened to the renowned Judge Saul Epton conduct court. The judge was a good looking man, tan from his recent vacation, who conducted his court with considerable enthusiasm. He was one of the great men who was dedicated to making Chicago a better place to live. He chose to remain on this court rather than seek a higher court with more prestige, for he felt he could better serve the public where he was.

As he handled case after case, it was clear he was able to see through the prevarications thrown at him time and time again. With first offenders he was lenient and released them after a short lecture. In some instances, when a defendant started acting "smart," he had him locked up for the day so he could see exactly what it was like in the lockup. In other instances, he required a defendant to give time to a charitable organization or his own church.

Judge Epton's court was run efficiently with a modicum of lost motion. As everywhere else, a large percentage of the boys were black with a few Puerto Ricans and Mexicans. Rarely did one see an Oriental. In one instance when this did occur, Judge Epton expressed shock and called him a disgrace to his family and people. He deserved a far more severe sentence, for as the judge stated, he clearly knew better and more was expected.

Lunch time came but Fess' case had not been called, primarily because one of the police officers had not appeared. Dick went to lunch with two of the police officers involved in the case. While seated at the table, Dick, after the usual amenities asked: "Officer Anderson, why were you able to rise above the environmental conditions that have claimed so many of the boys I saw in court today and become an officer? After all, you came from the same area as Fess Wise."

"I think the difference was in my home. Ninety percent of the boys come from broken families where there is neither parental love nor discipline. How can you expect them to turn out any differently than they do?"

It was clear from the way Anderson answered, that he liked to talk, and much of what he said made sense. For this reason Dick let him continue in the hope of gaining a new insight into the problem.

"It has gotten to the point now where these boys will swear at you and dare you to do anything to them. They spit in your face and tell you you can't touch them, and you know they're absolutely right. With the laws like they are today, no matter what you do everyone is shouting police brutality. It's gotten to the point where we have no public support. How can we do our job under such circumstances?"

Anderson took a big bite of his hamburger and then continued talking: "I had a father come in. His boy had been arrested on charges of theft. He asked his son if he had taken the goods from the store in question. His son said, no. So the father asked me for my belt and I gave it to him. He took his son into the next room and beat him. The door was closed but I could hear the blows falling. Some person in the waiting room heard the same blows and the boy crying, and although they saw nothing, called down to headquarters claiming police brutality. A city inspector was at our headquarters in thirty minutes to investigate. The father had to sign several forms and statements to show that he was inflicting the blows and not the police."

Officer Burford, sitting next to Anderson, had remained silent up to this time. He finally said: "It does no good if the police whip one of these boys even though that is what they need more than anything else. If we do it, they just go back and brag how they were beaten by the cops. It's only when the parents do it that it has any meaning. Unfortunately, there are few parents that will give these boys a good whipping and therein lies the problem."

Anderson continued, "Once these boys reach ten or eleven and have received no parental love or discipline they are lost. Their thinking is so conditioned to the ghetto that they cannot break themselves away from its temptations. The only hope is to reach the boys when they are young and this must be done through the family."

Anderson hesitated and took another bite, and with a full mouth said: "I'll tell you what should be done. Negroes love money more than anything else. They worship the almighty dollar. If the court required parents of every child under fifteen to come to court with their son and fined the parents rather than the boy, you would stop this problem overnight. Every time a boy is found breaking a curfew law, fine the parents $25 to $50, and I guarantee that boy won't be on the streets very long."

Officer Burford nodded his head in approval. "Hit the parents where it hurts. They're the ones who complain that the streets aren't safe, but when it's their son that's picked up in the middle of the night its always the same cry, 'police brutality'. One time I responded to a lady who reported a fight, and when I went to break it up she was the first one to complain that the boys were beaten by the police."

Dick looked at his watch and suggested they return to the courtroom for their case was first on the afternoon call. The case was called and Dick listened to the state's case in shocked silence.

The robbery victim testified that he and a lady friend were sitting in his car. The windows were down slightly and the doors locked. Three men pulled up in a car and jumped out surrounding the victim's car. One of them, whom he identified as Fess Wise, stuck a pistol through the open window demanding the man's wallet. He gave Fess his wallet and the three began to get back into their car. The victim then shouted for the police and Fess shot at him twice but missed.

Hearing the shots, a housing project police officer came running and ordered the three men to stop. He shot once over their heads and Fess dropped his gun and raised his hands above his head, while the other two ran away. The officer stated that Fess then identified the other two who were apprehended the following day. When asked why he shot at the victim, Fess had responded that he wanted to stop him from hollering.

Dick realized that this time there was nothing he could do to help Fess. Fess Wise was bound over to the grand Jury. Although his mother pleaded with Dick to handle the trial, Dick refused with a firmness and finality she knew would not change. As Dick left the courtroom, Fess' new girlfriend was in tears. His mother looked angry and his step-father shook his fist at Dick. By this time Dick was out of the door and could not hear their comments.

Fees Wise was sent to prison with a life sentence for armed robbery. Dick never saw Fess again.

Chapter 14

James O'Neil Sells Used Books

Later in the fall O'Neil visited Dick's office again, only Dick was out. Margaret allowed him to sit in her office until Dick got back. She felt that his waiting in the reception room might not be appreciated by the senior partners.

O'Neil waited several hours for Dick's return. He was depressed and said nothing to Margaret. Finally, Dick walked in and looked surprised at seeing O'Neil. Before he could say anything James blurted out "Richard you have got to help me. This morning I went to a pawn shop on Van Buren off of State Street with a gun. I wanted to rob the man."

O'Neil hesitated a second as though he had been relieved of a heavy burden. Then he continued: "When the owner asked me if he could help I just stared at him. I know he was frightened, but at the last moment before pulling the gun I walked out and came right over here."

"James, tell me. Do you still have the gun?"

O'Neil smiled for the first time and pulled out the gun.

"James, I am going to ask you to leave right now. I am not going to lecture to you but don't ever come to my office with a gun, do you hear me?"

"Richard, the only reason I was going to rob the pawn shop was because I needed some money to buy food. I am awfully hungry."

A moment later, O'Neil left with five dollars in his hand. Dick was becoming very uneasy about O'Neil. He was getting worse.

A week later he returned carrying a suitcase which he placed on Calkins' desk. "Mr. Calkins," he said in a businesslike voice, "you are now looking at a self-employed salesman of second-hand books." He then proceeded to open the suitcase to display a number of books.

"When did you begin this job, James?" Dick was a little skeptical about anything O'Neil did at this point.

"This morning, and you are my first real customer. Are there any books you want; I can get them at a substantial discount at the bookstore I work for."

Dick was in a hurry so with no further thought he said, "I want volumes seven, eight and nine of Toynbee's "Study of History." James carefully wrote down the order and left with a smile on his face.

Two days later he returned. Dick was working on a brief and when he looked up there was O'Neil standing in the doorway.

"Come in, James."

"Richard, I have only a moment. I have the books you ordered, and he placed three books on the desk. Dick looked at them quickly and noted that they were the Toynbee books, but volumes six, seven, and eight."

"James, you included volume six, rather than nine." He hesitated a moment and then said "but I will buy them anyway because I want to help you with your new business. How much do I owe you?"

Without hesitation, O'Neil said "Fifteen dollars. My boss said I could give you a special price."

Dick started to reach for his wallet, and then stopped and picked up one of the books. They were in good condition with a cellophane cover over each. Opening one of the books he let a few pages slip through his fingers and then he stopped and looked at one page again. Then he looked up at O'Neil.

"James, where did you get these books? Don't answer. I know where you got them. The Chicago Public Library, for the books are stamped."

"That's not true. I got them from the man. I gave him your order and he gave me these books."

"What man, James?"

"Look it here: if you don't believe me then I'll just take them back to the man."

"James, these books have to be taken back to the Chicago Public Library." By now Margaret was standing in the doorway listening to the exchange. She did all she could to suppress a smile.

"Richard, what are you asking me to do? I have to give the man his money. Look, I'll sell them to you for $14.00."

Dick gave a heavy sigh. He was not communicating. "Don't you understand that these books were stolen and must be returned?"

"Look here, Richard. I don't understand you.

You wanted these books, didn't you? Here they are at a special price, $13.00. Why do you care where the man got them? They're here and you can keep them."

"I don't want them and I am not going to pay for them. If you leave them, I am going to take them back to the library."

James took the books and put them in his suitcase and closed the lid. "If you don't want them I'll return them to the man. I need the money and you won't help me with my business." He started towards the door and then stopped. Slowly turning he put the suitcase on the desk and opened it and took the books out.

"Richard, if I leave them, will you read them first before you return them to the library?"

"James, just leave them and I will have them returned, please!"

James closed the suitcase, and then said: "By the way I need some new shoes, could you loan me $5.00?" He left with $3.00.

As soon as the outer door shut, Dick picked up the books and said, "Margaret, will you come here please? I have something I want you to do over the noon hour."

That was the last time Dick saw O'Neil.

Chapter 15

James O'Neil Jailed for Life

A letter from Statesville Prison sat on top of a pile of mail on Dick's desk. The return address indicated that it was from James O'Neil. When Dick arrived he put it on the bottom of the pile and opened his other mail first. It wasn't until later in the afternoon that he finally decided to read the O'Neil letter. He was deeply concerned about what the letter would say, because the last letters he had received from O'Neil since he was returned to the penitentiary six months before, made it clear that O'Neil's mind was seriously deteriorating.

As he unfolded the letter he noticed the writing looked like that of a seven year old with the words being printed, some in large letters and others small. As he wrote, O'Neil ignored the lines on the paper, he had no periods, and much of his spelling was phonetic.

Febr 10 1966

Dear Richard:

You muzt git Me ot of hir dey Tri to mak me du bad akts Lik an Anemal i tink am n goinnuts you hay to Hilp sav ur kids win the othr boys wre planig to kidnap thim

I wil pay You $100,000. cal 641-2121 and giv tem yir name - day wil giv yu $10,000 now if yu sa yu hilp. If yu du not hilp sumtin bad is hapin to yr kids.
James O'Neil #27360

This was the worst letter Dick had yet received from O'Neil. The last few had veiled threats but this was the most blatant. Just four months before O'Neil had called from prison. He was desperate and stated he had to get out because he was losing his mind. But O'Neil was never going to get out of prison this time for he received a life sentence for armed robbery.

Dick made an instant decision. He was severing

all further communications with O'Neil. There was nothing he could do for the poor fellow and to continue getting letters like this no longer appealed to him. Too much had happened.

This left Edward Cole. He was still working with Torcum and seemed to be making good progress. Then occurred the incident in the summer of 1966, when Dick arrived home and was told by Anita to call his mother.

After hanging up the phone, he jumped in his car and drove over to his parents' home just two blocks away. His mother and father were waiting for him in the living room. Walking in Dick said

"This new carpeting looks great, Mom. I like the blue very much."

Visibly upset, his mother said "The carpeting is fine, but can you believe what they did?"

"Mom, start from the beginning."

Dick's mother stood up and walked to a mirror and fixed her hair. Turning she said, "You know we used Mr. Torcum for the new carpeting because you asked us to, in an effort to pay him back for helping your boys? This afternoon they brought over the new carpeting. When they took up the old carpeting I had them haul it into the garage where it would be easier to put on the truck when they left."

At this point Dick's father broke in feeling that his wife was going too slowly. "They finished laying the new carpet at about 4:20 this afternoon. When they left they put the old carpet on the truck and drove off. About ten minutes later I went out to the garage and I immediately noticed that my tool chest was gone. I had used it this morning and I remembered specifically where I had set it. I looked around, but it was nowhere to be found."

He hesitated a second, and then continued. "I decided to call Mr. Torcum just to be certain, and explained what had happened. It turns out one of the boys who laid the carpet was your boy Edward Cole."

Dick's father hesitated again, and that was just long enough for his mother to pick up the story in an excited voice.

"Well, Mr. Torcum said he would check the matter out, and call us back. An hour later he called and explained that he had driven to the next stop the truck was making, and had the boys haul our old carpeting out of the back of the truck. When they unrolled it, guess what they found?"

"I can guess, Mom. You already told me on the phone."

"They found Dad's tool chest. I just knew those Negro boys could not be trusted. I warned you about doing all that work for them, that they would let you down."

"O.K. Mom, thanks for telling me about this. I will call Mr. Torcum first thing in the morning." Dick was quite discouraged, for he knew that Edward Cole was one of the two boys on the truck that had delivered the carpeting to his parents. He went home and washed for dinner, by now a rather late one at least for his little daughter, Chrissy.

Anita completed setting the table for dinner and rang a little bell summoning her family. After getting Chrissie settled in her high chair and comforting Tad, she rang again for the 'master' of the house who finally made his appearance, marching in like a soldier in an attempt to entertain his daughter, who delighted in his antics. Although he felt bad about what happened, he was becoming conditioned to almost anything now, and he certainly was not going to allow something like this ruin his evening with his family.

"What are you going to do with the two boys?" asked Anita. "They obviously committed a felony."

"I don't know; what would you do? This is obviously serious, but I need to find out if both of them were involved. If it was just one of them, I bet I know who did it." Anita did not respond.

Dick did nothing concerning the matter for the rest of the week, waiting for Cole to call him. He did not. On the following Monday Dick called Mr. Torcum who said that Cole had not come back to work.

At 10:00 the same morning, the receptionist at the firm called Dick to tell him that Edward Cole was there. Dick thanked Nancy and asked her to send Cole down to his office. Dick called to Margaret, "Make Cole wait in your office fifteen minutes before you bring him in."

Dick had not told Margaret or anyone else what had happened, for he knew he would be the laugh of the week in the Chadwell law firm and he was not prepared to handle that at this time. Dave Power would have a field day with this one, thought Dick.

After a while there was a knock on Dick's door. "Yes." There was a slight pause, then Margaret said "Edward Cole is waiting to see you."

"Please have him come in Margaret." The door opened and Edward Cole entered. He stood in front of the desk a few moments until Dick gestured for him to sit down. Dick had no idea how to begin this conversation, for how do you deal with someone you have spent many hours helping who has just robbed your parents? Perhaps Dave Power was right when he said that you can't trust these people, for when you do, they will either steal from you or take advantage of you.

Dick looked at Cole and realized that he looked pale as though he were ill. "Well, Edward, where do we begin? I can't tell you what a blow this is for me -- my own parents."

"Mr. Calkins, please believe me that I did not do it. I would never do such a thing after all you are doing for me. I would not let you or Mr. Torcom down like this. The job means too much to me."

Cole looked most intent. He looked straight at Dick, his eyes had an expression of almost tortured sincerity and he did not evade Dick's stare. "Look, Mr. Calkins. George took this here tool chest and he is trying to blame me, knowing that I am trying awfully hard to make good. He stole something once before and reported me to Mr. Torcom ..."

"Edward, I am not accusing anyone of this crime, but I can assure you I am going to find out who did it. The last thing I want from you is a lot of sweet talk. This is what I plan to do. I am going to ask each of you to come here. I want to know if you ... don't interrupt; just listen to me. I want to know if you did it. If both of you deny it, I am going to have you take a lie detector test and the one who fails has had it. I kid you not. I am going to throw the book at you and I'll make sure there is a felony conviction. Nothing will change my mind on that."

"On the other hand, if the one who did it will sit in that chair and admit it, I will work something else out. If you or George will have the guts to admit this then we have common ground from which to work. But, Edward, believe me, if I am forced to give you a polygraph test then there will be real trouble for you, if you did it. This is an important decision so think it over carefully."

For the first time Cole took his eyes off Calkins and looked down. There was a painful silence. Perspiration appeared on the top of Cole's bent head. Without looking up he said: "You don't have to call George in."

"What made you do it?"

"I don't know."

"And why my parents, Edward?"

"I didn't know the house we was working at was your parent's!"

"Was George involved in this?"

"No, he wasn't, but he knew I had taken it."

Dick got up and walked around to the front of his desk. He looked out his window and then turned to Cole. "Why would you risk so much for so little? At a minimum you would get a year to five years at Statesville, and what would happen to your children? You are fond of your family, aren't you?"

Still looking down, Cole answered in a barely audible voice, "Yes, very much." Then he slowly looked up. His face looked rather sickly. "I don't know why I did this, especially to you. I have done this sort of thing all my life. I don't want to, but it is so hard for me to resist. You don't have to believe me, but I am trying very hard to make a go of it this time. I have been in and out of prison so many times that I have just got to make it this time."

"Edward, don't make any promises to me or anyone else. I am telling you that this is going to be your last chance. You either make it this time or that's it. You simply have too much at stake to pull something like this again. I am not going to have my parents press charges. I'll also see if Torcom will keep you, only because you should be given a last chance."

Cole's expression did not change, but there was noticeable relaxing of his body. "I want you to leave this office, saying nothing; make no promises, but give some thought of what there is at stake if you make one more mistake. As for my parents, I will see if you can do some work around their house to make some form of restitution."

"One thing further, whenever you have this urge or desire or whatever it is, I want you to come to me first. Let's talk it over. If it is money we will work out something so that you can borrow it. Just remember what is at stake; the odds are stacked against you now ... you have everything to lose and absolutely nothing to gain. I think Torcom likes you and will give you another chance so you have job security at a place where you are welcomed."

Cole rose slowly.

"Mr. Calkins, I want to ..."

Dick's hand flew out in a gesture to stop Cole from saying anything further.

"Edward, call me in a week."

"I will, Mr. Calkins." Cole walked out the door. Dick stood there. David Power will never know about this, but what else could I do? To send him to jail would not change a thing and probably make things worse, certainly no better. His wife and children would go on relief. At least this way I might have some control over him if only he will come to me first. It's a gamble that has to be taken for there is no alternative.

Eight months later Dick was informed that Edward Cole, after an all-night drinking binge, was killed in a knife fight on West Roosevelt Street.

Chapter 16

A Discouraging Ending

Seven black young men released from the prison walls of Statesville and Pontiac into a world far worse than the confines of solid brick, steel bars, and armed guards. For the ghetto of Chicago is a world that slowly strangles all who dare challenge it. It is a world where hope and enthusiasm slowly dissipate into the hopeless stupor of despair. It is a quicksand that slowly pulls its victims under, first the feet and legs, then the torso, the arms and shoulders until all that remains is the face and head gasping for the last breath of life. Finally, it too is sucked under, till life is stamped out in a most agonizing suffocation.

This is a world that is without meaning -- where up is down and right is left. There is no such thing as a moral right and wrong here - the only "wrong" is getting caught and the only "right" is succeeding. Any youth or young man who has not spent time in jail is a conversation piece, an object of ridicule. Those who have actually spent time in the state "pen" emerge as heroes to the younger generation, an object of desire for the young maidens. Where are the families to protect these young people, to love them, and, oh yes, to discipline them? They do not exist.

Who wants to die such an agonizing death? Who would not grab at a branch thrown across that pit? Seven boys released from prison and where do they go? Back to the marshland. This is not a return to "home," for they have no home. Offer them a new home, a new chance in life, in an area where the air is fresh and is not contaminated with the smell of wine and urine, and what is their response? Nothing but a blank silence -- they just return.

Seven boys released from prison. One is dead, six are in jail for life and one, Harden, is still surviving. How can one describe the frustration and the pain at seeing these boys go under one by one. You shout, you lecture, you listen, you stand by them, you reason with them, you loan them money, but they will not make that simple effort to hang on. They are not necessarily blinded to the dangers;

simply conditioned to them. Their failure to respond to the warning, to the initial stages of sinking in the mire beneath them, arises not from a lack of alertness or awareness, but an absence of hope and confidence in what the future might hold.

    Dick turned from his window and sat down at his desk. Such thoughts do no good. So much had happened since that day over three years when he called his "boys" in after their release from prison. That was such a happy occasion, so filled with hope and promise. All but Harden, who was already working, and Eugene Brown, who had moved to Milwaukee, attended that meeting. Now none of the five that attended had survived. Dick wondered if James Harden would make it over the years. He certainly had the best chance because he came from a family that cared. But the others, Dick realized, never had any hope of surviving. He wondered if all that he did to try to help them was for naught. He will never know.

CONCLUSION

The tactics the police used in this gangland trial, which convicted seven of eight defendants, netted six guilty teenagers and one innocent. (Sammy Dillard, who was exonerated, did in fact participate in the rape of Birdia Jackson.) The moral question is, is it ever justified to convict one innocent to net six guilty.

Many complain about the safeguards that came into being after the Harden trial - the Miranda warnings before a confession may be taken, the production of exculpatory statements of complaining victims and witnesses, the production of grand jury testimony, etc. These protections, however, are not to protect the guilty, but the one in seven who is innocent.

There is another point to be made. Even with all the protection a defendant has in our courts, innocent men and women still burden our prisons. In recent years, numerous defendants on death row have been released based on DNA evidence, thereby demonstrating how imperfect our system still is. It is my belief that if the police wish to convict a minority person from the ghetto, they will still succeed.

EPILOGUE

Dick never heard from or saw the boys again. He heard that James Harden survived, raised a family, and was a productive member of society.

Dick wrote the law review article Judge Brussell asked him to write on grand jury secrecy, which was published in the Michigan Law Review in 1965 (63 MICH. L. REV. 455 (1965)). The United States Supreme Court cited it twice in changing the law on grand jury secrecy.

In 1966, Dick was again called to the office of Mr. Chadwell. He was deeply concerned and wondered what he had done this time, although he guessed it had to do with his indigent cases, which he was still handling. As he entered the office, he was greeted by Mr. Chadwell who asked him to sit at the conference table. The senior partners were also seated at the table.

Mr. Chadwell spoke: "We want to compliment you on your fine work here at the firm. The firm represents National Dairy, which is involved in a big antitrust case. One of the major issues is our motion for the government to produce the grand jury testimony of certain witnesses. We had lost in the lower courts, and we asked the United States Supreme Court to review the decision.

"The Supreme Court granted certiorari (agreed to review the lower court's decision), and they took the very unusual step of reversing the lower court without briefs or oral argument, citing another decision it had just handed down the day before. And that case cited your law review article as authority. We want to thank you for your hard work and recognize it was done in connection with your indigent cases." The partners applauded.

In 1968, Dick was made a partner, but on July 1, 1969, he left the Chadwell firm with George Burditt and Dick Wiley and formed the law firm of Burditt, Calkins and Wiley.

In 1970, Dick and Anita were blessed with their third child, Kathryn Alice, and now, after 50 years of marriage, have 11 grandchildren.

In 1980, Dick became dean of the Drake University Law School in Des Moines, Iowa. In 1988, he joined the firm of Zarley, McKee, Thomte,

Voorhees & Sease in Des Moines, and in 1993 left the firm and became a full-time mediator and arbitrator.

Richard Keck, Dick's boss, an alcoholic, was removed from all his major cases. The firm threatened that if he ever took another drink of alcohol at work or at home he would be fired from the firm. And to his credit he did not. He later retired to Arizona with his wife.

Dave Power became a senior partner in the Chadwell firm and one of its top litigators. He never did lose his Irish sense of humor, but did temper his bigotry.

Judge Brussell continued on the bench until age 70 when he joined Dick's firm. When Dick moved to Des Moines, Iowa the Judge joined another firm.

Assistant state's attorney Toler became a judge in the Circuit Court of Cook County, and assistant state's attorney Dillon became a partner in a Chicago law firm.

James Doherty continued in the Public Defender's office until he reached retirement age, at which time he became of counsel to a Chicago law firm.

State's Attorney Stamos became an Associate Justice on the Illinois Supreme Court and assistant state's attorney Egan became a judge on the Circuit Court of Cook County until he went back to private practice.

Made in the USA
Coppell, TX
10 April 2021